AMERICAN
CREDIT REPAIR

™

Everything U Need to Know...

about

RAISING YOUR CREDIT SCORE

TREVOR RHODES & NADINE SMITH, ESQ.

Mc
Graw
Hill

New York   Chicago   San Francisco   Lisbon
London   Madrid   Mexico City   Milan   New Delhi
San Juan   Seoul   Singapore   Sydney   Toronto

For Grammy and Gramps—
On behalf of Bennett, Brianna, Cameron, Jacob and Tyler

Acknowledgments

This *American Credit Repair* volume from **Everything U Need to Know...
(EUNTK)** would not be possible without the support and assistance from the
following companies and individuals: The National Association of Credit Counseling,
Federal Debt Consolidation Services, AmerUSA Corporation (AmerUSA.net),
Ronald and Mary Rhodes, Marc and Terry Banning.

Table of Contents

Introduction

STOP! **Before you do anything else regarding your personal credit, you should thoroughly read this entire book on *American Credit Repair*.** This volume is not a late-night infomercial made up of false promises from someone whose main goal is to take your money and run. **This book will cost you no more than its retail price and a modest amount of your time to empower you with *Everything U Need to Know...* about *Raising Your Credit Score*.**

It's a bold introduction – *but it's true*. **The American credit system is a game –** albeit a serious one – but this guide will show you **exactly how to play it without spending hundreds or thousands of hard-earned dollars** on some credit repair sales gimmick or **a so-called non-profit credit counseling organization that's really lining the pockets of its founders or executives**.

In the meantime, **set aside a portion of your time** to give *American Credit Repair* your undivided attention, because **you're about to see true story examples, copies of actual creditor correspondence, proven score-raising techniques and the whole enchilada**… No book before this has *ever* provided the general public such an *easily* digestible discussion of *what happens behind the scenes in the underworld of credit* and *how you can go about playing the game legally!*

Yes, *legally!* Welcome to America – **where you can't go to jail for being in debt** (fraud and tax evasion, maybe, but not for being broke). In fact (as you may know), being in debt is kind of "the American way." **Ironically, when done right, you can accumulate wealth with debt, but – unfortunately – consumers aren't taught that approach.** Instead, *each person is encouraged to spend compulsively.* Everywhere you look, **there's always an advertisement trying to manipulate you into buying something you can't afford** – and it's amazing how you'll always be able to **find a creditor to make sure you can stretch yourself thin enough to finance it.**

Helping curb the compulsive shopper, however, is a topic beyond the scope of this guide. What this book can do is show you how to play the credit game *so that you can achieve a higher credit score and be rewarded with lower interest rates and better financing terms!* So, sit back, relax and grab a highlighter – because *you're about to learn everything the credit reporting agencies and your creditors don't want you to know...*

And if you ever need further assistance with any of the EUNTK volumes, **check out the official website for this entire series** at **www.EUNTK.com** – for discussion groups, laws and statutes, as well as other subjects published in the series, plus a whole lot more… *for the absolute easiest way there is to learn* "**Everything U Need to Know…**"

Chapter 1

The Basics of Credit Reporting, Part I: The Agencies and the Laws

This Chapter Discusses:

- ★ Credit Reporting Agencies
- ★ The Fair Credit Reporting Act (FCRA)
- ★ The Fair and Accurate Credit Transactions Act (FACT Act)

America, the land of the free and the home of the brave – oh, and let's not forget, **a nation of debtors. That's right** – *you're not alone!* **Most people in the U.S. are waist-deep in debt,** *owing more than $10,000 just on credit cards.* **And most of them have made mistakes big enough to have damaged their credit rating at one time or another, resulting in penalties, fees and higher interest rates.**

So **if you're like the average American with a credit score in the 600s or lower**, it's time for you to **learn how to make your life a little easier and** *a lot less stressful* – by learning the rules of the game and how to improve your credit score. **Whether you're new to the game or simply have too much "experience" with a poor credit rating,** *you can "correct" many of your past mistakes and implement a better plan for the future.*

American Credit Repair is designed **to teach you to understand everything you need to know about credit reporting** *and how to play the game* **to achieve the highest score.** The goal of this book is **to prepare you for the times** *when you need to count on your credit report* – whether to earn a **credit card,** an **automobile, a home** or even a **job!**

Credit Reporting Agencies

Creditors who let you use their money in the form of credit cards and loans **want to be able to determine your creditworthiness ahead of time** and *they also want some way of disciplining if you don't pay them back.* So the idea of selling credit "report cards" on consumers came into play. Hence *thousands* of these credit reporting agencies *bloomed* like desert cacti in the olden days (actually, the 1960s) in response to the *wagonload* of **local and national lending companies feeding on the blossoming credit boom** and the **new computer technology of the decade.** Today, after years of mergers and buyouts, there are *three main credit reporting agencies* that compile your reports. You may have heard of **Experian** (formerly known as TRW), **Equifax** and **TransUnion.**

Credit reporting agencies are *profit-making companies that gather and sell information about consumers, especially their financial history.* Early on, these organizations somehow **gained their titles as "agencies" and "bureaus"** – and **their continuing self-promotion** as such only **perpetuates the unfounded (but common) view** that **these organizations are in cahoots with the federal government. The reality is** – *they're not!* They are *private companies* – and for that reason, they are loosely labeled in this volume as **credit reporting "agencies," or CRAs.**

The CRAs historically furnished information to just about anyone who would ask and who was willing to pay for it. Back in the heyday, needless to say, technology was not like it is today. **The unpopular reputations of all CRAs stemmed from their low concern for accuracy or completeness when dealing with the files of thousands of consumers,** *yet they continued to grow at an incredibly fast pace.* **Horrendous mistakes were plentiful** and most of the 50 state lawmakers didn't see any big concern until more recently. **The federal government got involved to correct a barrelful of problems by legislating requirements for these CRAs and drafting some laws.**

The Fair Credit Reporting Act (FCRA)

The law of the land was finally enacted by Congress in 1971 – the **Fair Credit Reporting Act (FCRA).** This law is rather lengthy, but in a nutshell, it *sets forth two main objectives*:

☆ The Two Main Objectives of the FCRA:

- The **FCRA enables consumers to obtain a report of their personal financial history from CRAs by simply requesting it.**

- The Act **requires both the CRAs,** and those who supply them with information, **to follow certain procedures and regulations regarding how consumer information is maintained.**

Incidentally, the FCRA applies to *consumer* credit transactions; it does not apply to *commercial* credit transactions such as certain business loans and large insurance transactions. You may have heard of commercial reporting agencies, such as **Dun & Bradstreet**.

The latest version of the **FCRA** is about **86 pages long** and **is included** for your review as **Appendix A** in the **back of this book**. Also, provided on the next page, is a direct excerpt from the **Federal Trade Commission** appropriately titled **"FCRA Summary of Rights."** It's *worth taking the time to read through it.* You may see this document again, more and more when you apply for mortgages and other credit.

FCRA Summary of Rights

AmerUSA Corporation
3665 East Bay Drive #204-183
Largo, Florida 33771
Ph 727.467.0908 Fx 727.467.0918

FCRA

FCRA Summary of Rights

A Summary of Your Rights - Under the Fair Credit Reporting Act

The federal Fair Credit Reporting Act (FCRA) is designed to promote accuracy, fairness, and privacy of information in the files of every "consumer reporting agency" (CRA). Most CRAs are credit bureaus that gather and sell information about you -- such as if you pay your bills on time or have filed bankruptcy -- to creditors, employers, landlords, and other businesses. You can find the complete text of the FCRA, 15 U.S.C. §§1681-1681u, by visiting www.ftc.gov. The FCRA gives you specific rights, as outlined below. You may have additional rights under state law. You may contact a state or local consumer protection agency or a state attorney general to learn those rights.

- **You must be told if information in your file has been used against you.** Anyone who uses information from a CRA to take action against you -- such as denying an application for credit, insurance, or employment -- must tell you, and give you the name, address, and phone number of the CRA that provided the consumer report.

- **You can find out what is in your file.** At your request, a CRA must give you the information in your file, and a list of everyone who has requested it recently. There is no charge for the report if a person has taken action against you because of information supplied by the CRA, if you request the report within 60 days of receiving notice of the action. You also are entitled to one free report every twelve months upon request if you certify that (1) you are unemployed and plan to seek employment within 60 days, (2) you are on welfare, or (3) your report is inaccurate due to fraud. Otherwise, a CRA may charge you up to eight dollars.

- **You can dispute inaccurate information with the CRA.** If you tell a CRA that your file contains inaccurate information, the CRA must investigate the items (usually within 30 days) by presenting to its information source all relevant evidence you submit, unless your dispute is frivolous. The source must review your evidence and report its findings to the CRA. (The source also must advise national CRAs -- to which it has provided the data -- of any error.) The CRA must give you a written report of the investigation, and a copy of your report if the investigation results in any change. If the CRA's investigation does not resolve the dispute, you may add a brief statement to your file. The CRA must normally include a summary of your statement in future reports. If an item is deleted or a dispute statement is filed, you may ask that anyone who has recently received your report be notified of the change.

- **Inaccurate information must be corrected or deleted.** A CRA must remove or correct inaccurate or unverified information from its files, usually within 30 days after you dispute it. However, the CRA is not required to remove accurate data from your file unless it is outdated (as described below) or cannot be verified. If your dispute results in any change to your report, the CRA cannot reinsert into your file a disputed item unless the information source verifies its accuracy and completeness. In addition, the CRA must give you a written notice telling you it has reinserted the item. The notice must include the name, address and phone number of the information source.

- **You can dispute inaccurate items with the source of the information.** If you tell anyone -- such as a creditor who reports to a CRA -- that you dispute an item, they may not then report the information to a CRA without including a notice of your dispute. In addition, once you've notified the source of the error in writing, it may not continue to report the information if it is, in fact, an error.

- **Outdated information may not be reported.** In most cases, a CRA may not report negative information that is more than seven years old; ten years for bankruptcies.

- **Access to your file is limited.** A CRA may provide information about you only to people with a need recognized by the FCRA -- usually to consider an application with a creditor, insurer, employer, landlord, or other business.

- **Your consent is required for reports that are provided to employers, or reports that contain medical information.** A CRA may not give out information about you to your employer, or prospective employer, without your written consent. A CRA may not report medical information about you to creditors, insurers, or employers without your permission.

- **You may choose to exclude your name from CRA lists for unsolicited credit and insurance offers.** Creditors and insurers may use file information as the basis for sending you unsolicited offers of credit or insurance. Such offers must include a toll-free phone number for you to call if you want your name and address removed from future lists. If you call, you must be kept off the lists for two years. If you request, complete, and return the CRA form provided for this purpose, you must be taken off the lists indefinitely.

- **You may seek damages from violators.** If a CRA, a user or (in some cases) a provider of CRA data, violates the FCRA, you may sue them in state or federal court.

FOR QUESTIONS OR CONCERNS PLEASE CONTACT

Federal Trade Commission
Consumer Response Center- FCRA
Washington, DC 20580 * 202-326-3761

In addition to affording you certain rights, **the FCRA provides the CRAs with a few rights as well.** For example, **they are allowed to show your report to anyone who has a legitimate business need.** This not only includes your *current and prospective creditors* – such as mortgage lenders, banks and credit card companies – **it may also include landlords, employers and insurance companies.** *Disturbingly, CRAs will even sell access to your credit file to strangers* (solicitors who can pull your credit report in a moments notice and without your permission or knowledge). Ever wonder where all that junk mail comes from?

If you want to stop most of the unsolicited financial offers (e.g., *credit cards* and *insurance products*) you receive in the mail, **you can choose to look on the solicitation itself for a toll-free number** (as required by law) **or better yet, you can preemptively stop these strangers from accessing your credit file and sending you junk mail by calling the following toll-free number serviced by all three credit reporting agencies: (888) 567-8688.** You can even submit your request online by visiting **www.OptOutPrescreen.com** and choose from one of two options: *1) You can opt-out of receiving firm offers for five years using their website* or *2) you can opt out permanently by using their mail-in form.*

Even today, **the CRAs are not held responsible for simply reporting inaccurate information as long as they follow certain basic procedures.** And *they are not required to inform you of any negative information that is being reported about you* (in fact, they found a way to make money from notifying consumers when negative information is being reported – by *selling them monitoring services*).

So, now you know **you are entitled to see your report** – and so are many others with whom you don't even do business! You also know **the CRAs are not responsible for the accuracy of the information in your file** and *they don't have to inform you if negative information is being reported about you.* It's no wonder that **millions of errors continue to hurt thousands of consumer credit files** *each year.*

The Fair and Accurate Credit Transactions Act (FACT Act)

In addition to genuine mistakes that may appear in your credit files, **many consumers suffer from intentional blights known as** *identity theft.* According to a 2003 U.S. Federal Trade Commission report, **consumers reported 9.9 million cases of identity theft between April 2002 and April 2003,** *with losses totaling approximately $5 billion.*

☆ The Three Main Objectives of the FACT Act:

- **Ensure that lenders make decisions on loans based on full and fair credit histories,** and not on discriminatory stereotypes.

- **Improve the quality of credit information,** and **protect consumers against identity theft.**

- **Give every consumer the right to request a free copy of his or her credit report once a year.**

The **FACT Act simplifies what has been a mounting mess of state laws and regulations on** *how consumers can and must report such frauds* **and** *how banks, credit card issuers and reporting agencies must respond.* **Chapter 4** discusses how to get a free copy of your credit report once a year and **Chapter 15** outlines two tactics for protecting yourself from identify theft.

Chapter 2

The Basics of Credit Reporting, Part II: The Data

This Chapter Discusses:

★ **Where Does Credit Report Information Come From?**

★ **What Is a Credit Score and Why Should U Care?**

It's safe to say that without the invention of the microchip, you wouldn't be concerned about that **three-digit number** known as your *credit score*. The mathematical calculations (algorithms) used to determine your credit score are **so complex,** *that it would take a statistician several hours by hand to calculate your mysterious number.* These calculations **rely on enormous amounts of data that are stored for 10 years.** Without that darn microchip, you might be able to dress or talk your way into a new home or car, instead of praying for a good score, which is based upon data that is literally updated monthly.

Where Does Credit Report Information Come From?

Basically, anytime you sneeze or cough, your credit file is updated. **Data about you is being collected at any given time.**

It begins when you first engage in a consumer-to-business financial transaction with a creditor and never stops until you have completely satisfied the terms of your agreement. It remains on your report for about seven more years.

Throughout the entire relationship, **information gathered by the creditor is reported to the credit reporting agency (CRA) and can include anything from your payment history to your home address and phone number.** And **if you thought you're protected because you avoid giving out your social security number** (or at least a correct one), *you're wrong!* **A creditor can easily report information using just your name and address.** This is *how many collection accounts, public records and bad checks appear on your credit report*.

Here is a sample list of *who may be reporting information about you*.

Common Business Types That Report Information to the CRAs:

★ **Credit Card Companies**

In addition to *major credit cards*, *gasoline companies* and *department stores* report your credit history.

★ **Banks and Lenders**

Anything offered by a bank or lender –including *auto loans, mortgages* and *lines of credit*.

★ Student Loans

Both *federally guaranteed and private student loan payment histories and delinquencies.*

★ Collection Agencies

These are *private organizations reporting on defaulted accounts assigned to them or purchased by them* – including loans, credit cards, medical bills and utilities.

★ Local, State and Federal Governments

These *include tax liens, child support* and *bankruptcy filings.*

★ Insurance Agencies

Information on your *application for insurance is often reported, as well as any deficiency balance you may owe to your insurer for overpayment of proceeds or underpayments of premiums, as well as obligations to third-party insurance companies* in the case of damage you caused while under- or non-insured.

★ Landlords

While *most landlords may not report your many years of good payment history*, rest assured they will likely report a *collection or judgment for uncollected rent or damage to the property*.

★ Utility Companies

Recently, some *utility services started reporting payment histories* although *the majority of remarks seen on your credit file will be for an unpaid bill that lapsed several months ago.*

As you'll learn, there is a legal distinction between a creditor and a collector. A creditor, as defined by the Fair Credit Reporting Act is: *Any person who offers or extends credit creating a debt or to whom a debt is owed.* This excludes collection agencies which are defined as "parties who receive an assignment or transfer of debt in a default stage solely for the purpose of facilitating collection of such debt for another."

In the spirit of Orwell's *1984* and his conspiracy theories, a lot of it *is* actually true after all. *Anything* you do – *even with the omission of your social security number – could be reported to the CRAs.* The latest craze is **when you are asked to verify information to establish a part of your identity** you thought was irrelevant and surely private. Try sending money using **Western Union** over the phone. They'll ask you to reveal all sorts of facts, such as a parent's date of birth. Or try opening an account with a cable company – if your service is based on **pay-as-you-go**, *why do they claim they need your social security number* (so they *now* have your address, social security number and telephone number all on one nice screen for thousands of their company reps to view at any time).

What Is a Credit Score and Why Should U Care?

A credit score is the result of a complex and highly proprietary algorithm (mathematical equations) *used to calculate your financial risk level* – and ranges from 350 to 850.

Many of those convoluted arithmetic problems you weren't able to grasp in junior high are being used to **determine if you are worth doing business with in the eyes of a creditor.** The most common of credit scores is the **FICO score**, which is named after the company that created it, the **Fair Isaac Company.**

The basic premise behind the **FICO score** is *to predict your likely rate of delinquency over the next two years.* In other words, what is the chance of you falling behind? **It's this risk assessment that ultimately sets the terms the creditor will extend to you,** such as your interest rate and down payment. *So what do the bulk of these fancy mathematical equations factor in when determining your credit score...?*

The Five Main Factors That Make Up Your Credit Score:

☆ Payment History (35%)

This means *exactly what it says*. **Late payments cause the worst damage to your credit report.** This *also includes collection accounts* (a *collection account* is a past due account that is assigned or sold to a collection agency for further collection attempts) *and charged-off accounts* (a *charged-off account* is also a past due account, however, it is written off as a loss on a creditor's tax return on the assumption that the account will remain unpaid). Conversely, timely payments, particularly **within the most recent 12 months, will help improve your credit score** – *especially if you continue to remain on time.*

☆ Balances (30%)

The outstanding *amounts you owe on your revolving accounts are the next biggest factor affecting your score* (e.g., *credit cards, gasoline cards, and department store cards*). The **FICO model equates the fact that if you don't pay your balances in full each month you have a poor ability to manage money.**

If all things were constant in your credit file and the only information to vary was a single credit card balance that kept increasing, your score would likewise decrease as the amount of available credit diminishes.

Let's say you have some money left over at the end of the month and you want to put some extra toward your bills. **Instead of spreading a little over every creditor, consider putting the bulk of your spare funds toward paying off the smaller balances first** – with the goal of zeroing them out as soon as possible. This will *begin to improve your score considerably* because **even one dollar remaining on your balance will indicate a balance not paid in full.** *Then, eventually get around to paying off the next smallest balance, and so on, until they are all paid off.* This might go against the grain of the mathematical notion to take care of your accounts with the higher interest rates first, but **this zero-out method is actually better for your bottom line score!**

FYI: *Installment balances* (e.g., **auto loans, boat loans, personal loans) also have an impact on your credit score,** *but not nearly as great as the proportion of revolving balances to their credit limits.* For example, a credit card with a $10,000 limit and $8,000 balance has *more of a negative impact* than a car loan that started at $10,000 and has since been reduced to $8,000.

☆ Length of Credit History (15%)

The longer you have been a customer with a particular creditor, the better. It's understandable – newer accounts have not stood the test of time, and so **the computer perceives you as a better risk the longer your accounts have been open.**

☆ New Credit (10%)

Believe it or not, *new accounts and new inquiries resulting from applications for credit actually reduce your score.* **New accounts will have a negative impact on your score for about six months** and you may experience as much as a **5-point drop** for every inquiry you initiate when you apply for credit.

⭐ Types of Credit (10%)

Surprisingly, *the types of accounts you have affect your score.* If you have *too many revolving accounts, your score will be impacted to a greater extent than having just as many secured loans.* **The FICO formula is top secret, but rumor has it that mortgages are given preference over finance companies and revolving accounts that are seen as more tenacious** – depending on how many you have and how well you've maintained them.

Now, these were just the main factors that make up your score. *But what does the score mean?* **The FICO score ranges from 350 to 850 (*the higher, the better*). This score is used to determine the likelihood of you fulfilling your commitment on a new or existing credit obligation over the next two years.** You are compared historically to other consumers whose score ranged within a few points of your own.

To better explain, **a chart below depicts the rate of delinquency for various score ranges broken down in 50-point increments.** As you'll see, *if your credit score is 599 or below, FICO says there is a greater than 50% chance you will fall behind on an existing or new obligation over the next two years* (or perhaps even file for bankruptcy). **This does not guarantee you will default**; it just means there's a greater chance that you won't pay your future bills on time.

The rate of future delinquency by FICO score over the next two years.

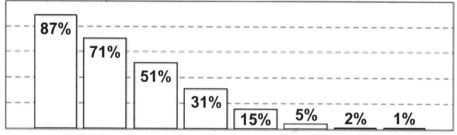

FICO score range							
350-499	500-549	550-599	600-649	650-699	700-749	750-799	800+
87%	71%	51%	31%	15%	5%	2%	1%

So now you know **the factors that make up the elusive *credit score.*** Just remember, ***the most important part is the current status of your accounts.*** So if you are behind with accounts that are not defaulted (usually no more than four months past due), contact the creditor to **find out if you can rehabilitate them and start bringing them current.** If they are already **charged off** or **in collections**, *you may want to consider another plan of action*, such as *negotiation.*

And, for goodness sake, **don't worry about a "settled for less" indication showing up on your credit report** if you were already past due with your accounts and your credit report score is already affected. **Once you pay off any negative account and you start paying your other original creditors on time,** *your score will keep climbing each month that goes by.*

Chapter 3

The Basics of Credit Reporting, Part III: Who Is Entitled to See Your Credit File

This Chapter Discusses:

★ **Permissible Purpose**

★ **Employers**

★ **Illegal Requests for Your Credit Report**

Who is entitled to receive your credit report? Now that's a good question. Sometimes it seems as if everyone has his or her hands on your private financial information. In fact, much of the mail you receive is driven by your credit report. You've seen *those pre-approved offers for credit cards, mortgages and auto loans. They come from prescreening services offered by the credit reporting agencies (CRAs).* So who is and who is not allowed to look at your report?

Permissible Purpose

This may come as a surprise, but *almost anyone can access your consumer credit file as long as their reason for the inquiry is justified* according to the broad language of the **Fair Credit Reporting Act (FCRA).** Common requests for your credit report include prospective creditors, current creditors, future employers and possibly current employers, as well as marketers who are trying to sell you more credit – anyone who has a "permissible purpose" to do so.

In addition, *more and more studies are showing correlations between a consumer's credit report and the risk that consumer will be to an insurance company.* As a result, **there is a growing trend among providers,** *specifically homeowners and automobile insurers,* **to review your report before they issue you coverage.** However, many state regulators have put the brakes on how and when an insurance company can use your report against you. So **if you feel your insurance coverage was increased or denied due to your credit report, contact your state's insurance commissioner.**

On the following 12 pages is **an actual copy of Section 604 of the FCRA which defines a permissible purpose.** This is worth reading to understand exactly can obtain access to your personal information.

FCRA Section 604 Permissible Purposes of Consumer Reports

Section 604 Permissible purposes of consumer reports [§ 1681b]

(a) In general.—Subject to subsection (c) of this section, any consumer reporting agency may furnish a consumer report under the following circumstances and no other:

(1) In response to the order of a court having jurisdiction to issue such an order, or a subpoena issued in connection with proceedings before a Federal grand jury.

(2) In accordance with the written instructions of the consumer to whom it relates.

(3) To a person which it has reason to believe—

(A) intends to use the information in connection with a credit transaction involving the consumer on whom the information is to be furnished and involving the extension of credit to, or review or collection of an account of, the consumer; or

(B) intends to use the information for employment purposes; or

(C) intends to use the information in connection with the underwriting of insurance involving the consumer; or

(D) intends to use the information in connection with a determination of the consumer's eligibility for a license or other benefit granted by a governmental instrumentality required by law to consider an applicant's financial responsibility or status; or

(E) intends to use the information, as a potential investor or servicer, or current insurer, in connection with a valuation of, or an assessment of the credit or prepayment risks associated with, an existing credit obligation; or

(F) otherwise has a legitimate business need for the information—

(i) in connection with a business transaction that is initiated by the consumer; or

(ii) to review an account to determine whether the consumer continues to meet the terms of the account.

(4) In response to a request by the head of a State or local child support enforcement agency (or a State or local government official authorized by the head of such an agency), if the person making the request certifies to the consumer reporting agency that—

FCRA Section 604 Permissible Purposes of Consumer Reports

(A) the consumer report is needed for the purpose of establishing an individual's capacity to make child support payments or determining the appropriate level of such payments;

(B) the paternity of the consumer for the child to which the obligation relates has been established or acknowledged by the consumer in accordance with State laws under which the obligation arises (if required by those laws);

(C) the person has provided at least 10 days' prior notice to the consumer whose report is requested, by certified or registered mail to the last known address of the consumer, that the report will be requested; and

(D) the consumer report will be kept confidential, will be used solely for a purpose described in subparagraph (A), and will not be used in connection with any other civil, administrative, or criminal proceeding, or for any other purpose.

(5) To an agency administering a State plan under section 654 of title 42 for use to set an initial or modified child support award.

(6) To the Federal Deposit Insurance Corporation or the National Credit Union Administration as part of its preparation for its appointment or as part of its exercise of powers, as conservator, receiver, or liquidating agent for an insured depository institution or insured credit union under the Federal Deposit Insurance Act or the Federal Credit Union Act, or other applicable Federal or State law, or in connection with the resolution or liquidation of a failed or failing insured depository institution or insured credit union, as applicable.

(b) Conditions for furnishing and using consumer reports for employment purposes.—

(1) Certification from user.—A consumer reporting agency may furnish a consumer report for employment purposes only if—

(A) the person who obtains such report from the agency certifies to the agency that—

(i) the person has complied with paragraph (2) with respect to the consumer report, and the person will comply with paragraph (3) with respect to the consumer report if paragraph (3) becomes applicable; and

(ii) information from the consumer report will not be used in violation of any applicable Federal or State equal employment opportunity law or regulation; and

FCRA Section 604 Permissible Purposes of Consumer Reports

(B) the consumer reporting agency provides with the report, or has previously provided, a summary of the consumer's rights under this subchapter, as prescribed by the Federal Trade Commission under section 609(c)(3) [§ 1681g(c)(3) of this title].

(2) Disclosure to consumer.—

(A) In general.—Except as provided in subparagraph (B), a person may not procure a consumer report, or cause a consumer report to be procured, for employment purposes with respect to any consumer, unless—

(i) a clear and conspicuous disclosure has been made in writing to the consumer at any time before the report is procured or caused to be procured, in a document that consists solely of the disclosure, that a consumer report may be obtained for employment purposes; and

(ii) the consumer has authorized in writing (which authorization may be made on the document referred to in clause (i)) the procurement of the report by that person.

(B) Application by mail, telephone, computer, or other similar means.—If a consumer described in subparagraph (C) applies for employment by mail, telephone, computer, or other similar means, at any time before a consumer report is procured or caused to be procured in connection with that application—

(i) the person who procures the consumer report on the consumer for employment purposes shall provide to the consumer, by oral, written, or electronic means, notice that a consumer report may be obtained for employment purposes, and a summary of the consumer's rights under section 615(a)(3) [§ 1681m(a)(3) of this title]; and

(ii) the consumer shall have consented, orally, in writing, or electronically to the procurement of the report by that person.

(C) Scope.—Subparagraph (B) shall apply to a person procuring a consumer report on a consumer in connection with the consumer's application for employment only if—

(i) the consumer is applying for a position over which the Secretary of Transportation has the power to establish qualifications and maximum hours of service pursuant to the

SAMPLE

FCRA Section 604 Permissible Purposes of Consumer Reports

provisions of section 31502 of title 49, or a position subject to safety regulation by a State transportation agency; and

(ii) as of the time at which the person procures the report or causes the report to be procured the only interaction between the consumer and the person in connection with that employment application has been by mail, telephone, computer, or other similar means.

(3) Conditions on use for adverse actions.—

(A) In general.—Except as provided in subparagraph (B), in using a consumer report for employment purposes, before taking any adverse action based in whole or in part on the report, the person intending to take such adverse action shall provide to the consumer to whom the report relates—

(i) a copy of the report; and

(ii) a description in writing of the rights of the consumer under this subchapter, as prescribed by the Federal Trade Commission under section 609(c)(3) [§ 1681g(c)(3) of this title].

(B) Application by mail, telephone, computer, or other similar means.—

(i) If a consumer described in subparagraph (C) applies for employment by mail, telephone, computer, or other similar means, and if a person who has procured a consumer report on the consumer for employment purposes takes adverse action on the employment application based in whole or in part on the report, then the person must provide to the consumer to whom the report relates, in lieu of the notices required under subparagraph (A) of this section and under section 615(a) [§ 1681m(a) of this title], within 3 business days of taking such action, an oral, written or electronic notification—

(I) that adverse action has been taken based in whole or in part on a consumer report received from a consumer reporting agency;

(II) of the name, address and telephone number of the consumer reporting agency that furnished the consumer report (including a toll-free telephone number established by the agency if the agency compiles and maintains files on consumers on a nationwide basis);

FCRA Section 604 Permissible Purposes of Consumer Reports

(III) that the consumer reporting agency did not make the decision to take the adverse action and is unable to provide to the consumer the specific reasons why the adverse action was taken; and

(IV) that the consumer may, upon providing proper identification, request a free copy of a report and may dispute with the consumer reporting agency the accuracy or completeness of any information in a report.

(ii) If, under clause (B)(i)(IV), the consumer requests a copy of a consumer report from the person who procured the report, then, within 3 business days of receiving the consumer's request, together with proper identification, the person must send or provide to the consumer a copy of a report and a copy of the consumer's rights as prescribed by the Federal Trade Commission under section 609(c)(3) [§ 1681g(c)(3) of this title].

(C) Scope.—Subparagraph (B) shall apply to a person procuring a consumer report on a consumer in connection with the consumer's application for employment only if—

(i) the consumer is applying for a position over which the Secretary of Transportation has the power to establish qualifications and maximum hours of service pursuant to the provisions of section 31502 of title 49, or a position subject to safety regulation by a State transportation agency; and

(ii) as of the time at which the person procures the report or causes the report to be procured the only interaction between the consumer and the person in connection with that employment application has been by mail, telephone, computer, or other similar means.

(4) Exception for national security investigations.—

(A) In general.—In the case of an agency or department of the United States Government which seeks to obtain and use a consumer report for employment purposes, paragraph (3) shall not apply to any adverse action by such agency or department which is based in part on such consumer report, if the head of such agency or department makes a written finding that—

(i) the consumer report is relevant to a national security investigation of such agency or department;

FCRA Section 604 Permissible Purposes of Consumer Reports

(ii) the investigation is within the jurisdiction of such agency or department;

(iii) there is reason to believe that compliance with paragraph (3) will—

(I) endanger the life or physical safety of any person;

(II) result in flight from prosecution;

(III) result in the destruction of, or tampering with, evidence relevant to the investigation;

(IV) result in the intimidation of a potential witness relevant to the investigation;

(V) result in the compromise of classified information; or

(VI) otherwise seriously jeopardize or unduly delay the investigation or another official proceeding.

(B) Notification of consumer upon conclusion of investigation.—Upon the conclusion of a national security investigation described in subparagraph (A), or upon the determination that the exception under subparagraph (A) is no longer required for the reasons set forth in such subparagraph, the official exercising the authority in such subparagraph shall provide to the consumer who is the subject of the consumer report with regard to which such finding was made—

(i) a copy of such consumer report with any classified information redacted as necessary;

(ii) notice of any adverse action which is based, in part, on the consumer report; and

(iii) the identification with reasonable specificity of the nature of the investigation for which the consumer report was sought.

(C) Delegation by head of agency or department.—For purposes of subparagraphs (A) and (B), the head of any agency or department of the United States Government may delegate his or her authorities under this paragraph to an official of such agency or department who has personnel security responsibilities and is a member of the Senior Executive Service or equivalent civilian or military rank.

(D) Report to the Congress.—Not later than January 31 of each year, the head of each agency and department of the United States Government that

FCRA Section 604 Permissible Purposes of Consumer Reports

exercised authority under this paragraph during the preceding year shall submit a report to the Congress on the number of times the department or agency exercised such authority during the year.

(E) Definitions.—For purposes of this paragraph, the following definitions shall apply:

(i) Classified information.—The term "classified information" means information that is protected from unauthorized disclosure under Executive Order No. 12958 or successor orders.

(ii) National security investigation.—The term "national security investigation" means any official inquiry by an agency or department of the United States Government to determine the eligibility of a consumer to receive access or continued access to classified information or to determine whether classified information has been lost or compromised.

(c) Furnishing reports in connection with credit or insurance transactions that are not initiated by consumer.—

(1) In general.—A consumer reporting agency may furnish a consumer report relating to any consumer pursuant to subparagraph (A) or (C) of subsection (a)(3) of this section in connection with any credit or insurance transaction that is not initiated by the consumer only if—

(A) the consumer authorizes the agency to provide such report to such person; or (B)(i) the transaction consists of a firm offer of credit or insurance;

(ii) the consumer reporting agency has complied with subsection (e) of this section; and

(iii) there is not in effect an election by the consumer, made in accordance with subsection (e) of this section, to have the consumer's name and address excluded from lists of names provided by the agency pursuant to this paragraph.

(2) Limits on information received under paragraph (1)(B).—A person may receive pursuant to paragraph (1)(B) only—

(A) the name and address of a consumer;

FCRA Section 604 Permissible Purposes of Consumer Reports

(B) an identifier that is not unique to the consumer and that is used by the person solely for the purpose of verifying the identity of the consumer; and

(C) other information pertaining to a consumer that does not identify the relationship or experience of the consumer with respect to a particular creditor or other entity.

(3) Information regarding inquiries.—Except as provided in section 609(a)(5) [§ 1681g(a)(5) of this title], a consumer reporting agency shall not furnish to any person a record of inquiries in connection with a credit or insurance transaction that is not initiated by a consumer.

(d) Reserved.—

(e) Election of consumer to be excluded from lists.—

(1) In general.—A consumer may elect to have the consumer's name and address excluded from any list provided by a consumer reporting agency under subsection (c)(1)(B) of this section in connection with a credit or insurance transaction that is not initiated by the consumer, by notifying the agency in accordance with paragraph (2) that the consumer does not consent to any use of a consumer report relating to the consumer in connection with any credit or insurance transaction that is not initiated by the consumer.

(2) Manner of notification.—A consumer shall notify a consumer reporting agency under paragraph (1)—

(A) through the notification system maintained by the agency under paragraph (5); or

(B) by submitting to the agency a signed notice of election form issued by the agency for purposes of this subparagraph.

(3) Response of agency after notification through system.—Upon receipt of notification of the election of a consumer under paragraph (1) through the notification system maintained by the agency under paragraph (5), a consumer reporting agency shall—

(A) inform the consumer that the election is effective only for the 5-year period following the election if the consumer does not submit to the agency a signed notice of election form issued by the agency for purposes of paragraph (2)(B); and

(B) provide to the consumer a notice of election form, if requested by the consumer, not later than 5 business days after receipt of the notification of

FCRA Section 604 Permissible Purposes of Consumer Reports

the election through the system established under paragraph (5), in the case of a request made at the time the consumer provides notification through the system.

(4) Effectiveness of election.—An election of a consumer under paragraph (1)—

(A) shall be effective with respect to a consumer reporting agency beginning 5 business days after the date on which the consumer notifies the agency in accordance with paragraph (2); (B) shall be effective with respect to a consumer reporting agency—

(i) subject to subparagraph (C), during the 5-year period beginning 5 business days after the date on which the consumer notifies the agency of the election, in the case of an election for which a consumer notifies the agency only in accordance with paragraph (2)(A); or

(ii) until the consumer notifies the agency under subparagraph (C), in the case of an election for which a consumer notifies the agency in accordance with paragraph (2)(B); (C) shall not be effective after the date on which the consumer notifies the agency, through the notification system established by the agency under paragraph (5), that the election is no longer effective; and (D) shall be effective with respect to each affiliate of the agency.

(5) Notification system.—

(A) In general.—Each consumer reporting agency that, under subsection (c)(1)(B) of this section, furnishes a consumer report in connection with a credit or insurance transaction that is not initiated by a consumer, shall—

(i) establish and maintain a notification system, including a toll-free telephone number, which permits any consumer whose consumer report is maintained by the agency to notify the agency, with appropriate identification, of the consumer's election to have the consumer's name and address excluded from any such list of names and addresses provided by the agency for such a transaction; and

(ii) publish by not later than 365 days after September 30, 1996, and not less than annually thereafter, in a publication of general circulation in the area served by the agency—

(I) a notification that information in consumer files maintained by the agency may be used in connection with such transactions; and

FCRA Section 604 Permissible Purposes of Consumer Reports

(II) the address and toll-free telephone number for consumers to use to notify the agency of the consumer's election under clause (i).

(B) Establishment and maintenance as compliance.—Establishment and maintenance of a notification system (including a toll-free telephone number) and publication by a consumer reporting agency on the agency's own behalf and on behalf of any of its affiliates in accordance with this paragraph is deemed to be compliance with this paragraph by each of those affiliates.

(6) Notification system by agencies that operate nationwide.—Each consumer reporting agency that compiles and maintains files on consumers on a nationwide basis shall establish and maintain a notification system for purposes of paragraph (5) jointly with other such consumer reporting agencies.

Public Awareness Campaign

[Sec. 213(d) of the Fair and Accurate Credit Transactions Act of 2003]

The Commission shall actively publicize and conspicuously post on its website any address and the toll-free telephone number established as part of a notification system for opting out of prescreening under section 604(e) of the Fair Credit Reporting Act (15 U.S.C. 1681b(e)), and otherwise take measures to increase public awareness regarding the availability of the right to opt out of prescreening.

(f) Certain use or obtaining of information prohibited.—A person shall not use or obtain a consumer report for any purpose unless—

(1) the consumer report is obtained for a purpose for which the consumer report is authorized to be furnished under this section; and

(2) the purpose is certified in accordance with section 607 [§ 1681e of this title] by a prospective user of the report through a general or specific certification.

(g) Protection of medical information.—

(1) Limitation on consumer reporting agencies.—A consumer reporting agency shall not furnish for employment purposes, or in connection with a credit or insurance transaction, a consumer report that contains medical information other than medical contact information treated in the manner required under section 605(a)(6) [§ 1681c(a)(6) of this title] about a consumer unless—

(A) if furnished in connection with an insurance transaction, the consumer affirmatively consents to the furnishing of the report;

 **31**

FCRA Section 604 Permissible Purposes of Consumer Reports

(B) if furnished for employment purposes or in connection with a credit transaction—

(i) the information to be furnished is relevant to process or effect the employment or credit transaction; and

(ii) the consumer provides specific written consent for the furnishing of the report that describes in clear and conspicuous language the use for which the information will be furnished; or

(C) the information to be furnished pertains solely to transactions, accounts, or balances relating to debts arising from the receipt of medical services, products, or devises, where such information, other than account status or amounts, is restricted or reported using codes that do not identify, or do not provide information sufficient to infer, the specific provider or the nature of such services, products, or devices, as provided in section 605(a)(6) [§ 1681c(a)(6) of this title].

(2) Limitation on creditors.—Except as permitted pursuant to paragraph (3)(C) or regulations prescribed under paragraph (5)(A), a creditor shall not obtain or use medical information other than medical information treated in the manner required under section 605(a)(6) [§ 1681c(a)(6) of this title] pertaining to a consumer in connection with any determination of the consumer's eligibility, or continued eligibility, for credit.

(3) Actions authorized by Federal law, insurance activities and regulatory determinations.—Section 603(d)(3) [§ 1681a(d)(3) of this title] shall not be construed so as to treat information or any communication of information as a consumer report if the information or communication is disclosed—

(A) in connection with the business of insurance or annuities, including the activities described in section 18B of the model Privacy of Consumer Financial and Health Information Regulation issued by the National Association of Insurance Commissioners (as in effect on January 1, 2003);

(B) for any purpose permitted without authorization under the Standards for Individually Identifiable Health Information promulgated by the Department of Health and Human Services pursuant to the Health Insurance Portability and Accountability Act of 1996, or referred to under section 1179 of such Act, or described in section 502(e) of Public Law 106-102; or

(C) as otherwise determined to be necessary and appropriate, by regulation or order and subject to paragraph (6), by the Commission, any Federal banking agency or the National Credit Union Administration (with respect to any financial institution subject to the jurisdiction of such agency or

FCRA Section 604 Permissible Purposes of Consumer Reports

Administration under paragraph (1), (2), or (3) of section 621(b) [§ 1681s(b) of this title], or the applicable State insurance authority (with respect to any person engaged in providing insurance or annuities).

(4) Limitation on redisclosure of medical information.—Any person that receives medical information pursuant to paragraph (1) or (3) shall not disclose such information to any other person, except as necessary to carry out the purpose for which the information was initially disclosed, or as otherwise permitted by statute, regulation, or order.

(5) Regulations and effective date for paragraph (2).—

(A) Regulations required.—Each Federal banking agency and the National Credit Union Administration shall, subject to paragraph (6) and after notice and opportunity for comment, prescribe regulations that permit transactions under paragraph (2) that are determined to be necessary and appropriate to protect legitimate operational, transactional, risk, consumer, and other needs (and which shall include permitting actions necessary for administrative verification purposes), consistent with the intent of paragraph (2) to restrict the use of medical information for inappropriate purposes.

(B) Final regulations required.—The Federal banking agencies and the National Credit Union Administration shall issue the regulations required under subparagraph (A) in final form before the end of the 6-month period beginning on the date of enactment of the Fair and Accurate Credit Transactions Act of 2003.

(6) Coordination with other laws.—No provision of this subsection shall be construed as altering, affecting, or superseding the applicability of any other provision of Federal law relating to medical confidentiality.

Effective Dates

[Sec. 411(d) of the Fair and Accurate Credit Transactions Act of 2003]

This section [604(g); § 1681b(g) of this title]shall take effect at the end of the 180-day period beginning on the date of enactment of this Act, except that paragraph (2) of section 604(g) [§ 1681b(g) of this title] of the Fair Credit Reporting Act (as amended by subsection (a) of this section) shall take effect on the later of—

(1) the end of the 90-day period beginning on the date on which the regulations required under paragraph (5)(B) of such section 604(g) [§ 1681b(g) of this title] are issued in final form; or

(2) the date specified in the regulations referred to in paragraph (1).

Employers

As most of us know, **employers cannot discriminate based on sex, age or race.** *But did you know they can refuse to hire you if they don't like what they see on your credit report* (bad credit is not a legally protected class!). It's important for you to **plan ahead if you are currently employed in or plan to work in certain fields, such as banking and securities.** *Even an application for a professional license or independent contractor position may hinge on the condition of your report,* such as for an attorney, insurance agent, loan officer and construction contractor.

What could your credit history possibly have to do with your job performance? **Tens of thousands of employers use extensive evaluation processes when considering offering a candidate a job, including reference verification, credit checks and criminal background checks.** Corporate theft (embezzlement as well as bribery) is the second oldest profession – it's understandable that businesses want to protect themselves to the extent the law allows. And employers should have an opportunity to use their own judgment regarding a potential employee's financial honesty and integrity.

In order to conduct a credit check, **a written authorization from an applicant must be obtained.** Your **criminal and driving records** are *not included in your standard credit file.* But beware that **your written authorization** to your would-be employer *may also allow the employer to obtain copies of those records as well.* Read everything you sign very carefully.

It's your right to refuse someone from requesting copies of your credit reports or other background checks. As a practical point, if you authorize an inquiry and your report comes back smelling like manure, you could be denied the job offer. *So it may be best to permit the investigation and then try to explain any negative marks.* After all, a good job opportunity is hard to pass up. By the way, **don't worry about the**

inquiry affecting your score. *The type of inquiry that employers make will not have any impact on your credit score* because you are applying for a job, not an extension of credit.

This is very important! When a potential employer asks for your written permission to obtain your credit report, *you must read what you are signing.* **Look to see if you would be giving permission to your employer to pull your credit report** *anytime in the future,* **as well.** Granted, a good job opportunity may be hard to come by, but use your own judgment as to *whether you feel comfortable knowing your boss wants to monitor your personal and financial activities on a regular basis.*

Illegal Requests for Your Credit Report

The **FCRA**'s language as to who has a permissible purpose to pull your credit file is broad-based. However, *there are specific prohibitions against pulling reports in certain situations.* **Here are two circumstances in which the use of your credit report are forbidden.**

Two Circumstances Which Prohibit the Use of Your Credit Report:

☆ Lawsuits

Your credit file cannot be requested or used by another party just because you are involved in a lawsuit. In other words, **a lousy credit rating cannot be used in an attempt to show a judge or jury that your intentions are fraudulent** or that they demonstrate

an act of desperation for money and that's the reason you are involved in the suit – whether you are the party who is suing or you are the party who is being sued.

★ Judgments

And even if you lose a case, **your credit report cannot be used by the party who wins the case to demonstrate that you are able to pay** or that you have assets that can be taken to pay the damages that were awarded. *There's simply no permissible purpose for someone to pull your report to see your address, types of accounts and other personal information in an attempt to collect on a judgment.*

If you are thinking about suing someone for fraudulently obtaining a copy of your credit report, *you must file the action within the two years allowed by law.* The only way bring a lawsuit after the two-year statute of limitations is to demonstrate to the court **you are legally entitled to a longer period of time because the person or business that pulled your report materially and willfully misrepresented what it was doing** (i.e., you knew the person or business pulled your report but lied to you regarding its purpose). *Needless to say, here's where you need to get a good lawyer.*

Your Credit Report:
Getting a Free Copy – For Real!

This Chapter Discusses:

★ **AnnualCreditReport.com**
★ **Annual Credit Report by Mail or Phone**
★ **FTC Facts for Consumers Brochure**

Now that you know who can and who cannot get a hold of your credit report, you need to learn how to get a copy of your own report. Even if there is no imminent concern for you to see your report today, if you haven't seen them in a while, or at all, do it now. Remember, *a credit reporting agency (CRA) is under no obligation to tell you when negative information is being reported about you.* **This should be one impetus for you to review your report, especially a month or two prior to making any big changes in your life, such as applying for a new job or a home mortgage –** *even before you get married,* as discussed in further detail in Chapter 13.

Fortunately, as mentioned in **Chapter 1**, the *FACT Act allows you a free copy of your credit files once every 12 months from the Big Three (Equifax, Experian and TransUnion)*. The question is, *"How do you get these reports?"*

AnnualCreditReport.com

The easiest and quickest way to get a copy of your report is to go online. Many infomercials and web advertisers encourage you to get your free credit report but they also try to sell you other products along the way. So go directly to **AnnualCreditReport.com**, *the official website created in response to the FACT Act.* **These interactive web pages are sponsored by all three major CRAs** in association with each other. **Once you're on this site, you'll be directed to each of the individual CRA's file on you –** *it is not a compilation of reports, so you need to make sure you request all three separate files.* And be sure to *order all three* because they don't share information with each other. And **if you have a spouse, get his or her reports as well.** And **the sooner you start – the better.**

Websites change frequently – so you may have to read the directions on the home page if it's been more than a few months since you were last there. At the time of this publication, the **first step at AnnualCreditReport.com is to choose from a pull-down menu to indicate the state where you live.** The **next step is to click on the name of one of three CRAs.** You'll then have to **answer some basic questions regarding your profile, including your name, address and social security number.**

Another question the CRAs usually ask is whether your address has changed in the past two years. *As long as the CRA has your latest address on file, you should only have to type in your current address and answer "no" to the question asking if your address is new.*

You'll then need to answer a few security questions to access each report. The individual CRA will then ask you **what kind of credit report service you want.** *This is where you need to be cautious!* If you don't want to sign up for a monthly monitoring service, then be careful to choose the option that indicates "report only."

You don't need to request your score or sign up for a monitoring service or a consumer comparative rating analysis. However, if you want to measure how well this book works for you – by all means, go ahead and pay a few extra dollars to have your scores included. *Just make sure you pay close attention to what you're selecting and that you are only paying for your scores.* While this website was originally intended to provide a free consumer-friendly service in response to the Fair and Accurate Credit Transactions Act (FACT Act), **the CRAs will try their best to charge you for some ancillary product or service.**

While Congress attempted to do a good thing by allowing your credit reports to be accessible to you online, **average consumers actually spend money when they go surfing for their report.** It's the typical American way: a law is passed allowing you a free copy of your credit report – but rest assured, the CRAs have capitalized on this as well by coaxing you into paying for other services. *The way this website is designed and worded, it's difficult for the average consumer to simply get a free report.* In fact, one of the CRAs requires you to submit an open, valid  credit card number before your order is completed with the explanation that **"in case"** you decide to place an order for an extra service, such as viewing your credit score, or signing up for their monitoring service, your credit card will be charged!

Annual Credit Report by Mail or Phone

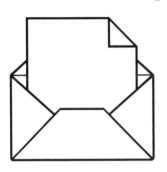

The three CRAs have not only set up a central website, but also provide a **toll-free phone number** and **a mailing address** through which you can order your free reports without being solicited with other services. However, it takes several days for you to receive your reports in this manner because they must be mailed to you as opposed to being delivered instantly online.

To order by phone, call **1-877-322-8228** and follow the automated menu for instructions on how to get your credit report mailed to you.

To initially request a copy of your credit report by mail, complete the Annual Credit Report Request Form contained in the FTC Facts for Consumers brochure in the following section (you may print a copy of this brochure by installing the enclosed CD-ROM which links directly to the Federal Trade Commission's website) and mail it to:

Annual Credit Report Request Service
P.O. Box 105281
Atlanta, GA 30348-5281

Note: The **FTC** *does not recommend contacting the three nationwide CRAs individually.* **Free annual credit reports** are safely provided *only* by the following: Online at **annualcreditreport.com**, Toll-Free at **1-877-322-8228**, and through the mail at the **Annual Credit Report Request Service address above.**

Even if you have received copies of your report within the last 12 months, you are entitled to another free copy if an adverse remark on your report affected the outcome of an application. These situations include being denied credit, employment, insurance or rental housing. You may also be entitled to a report if your creditor reduced your credit limit due to something that occurred on one or more reports, you were a victim of fraud, you receive public assistance, or you are currently unemployed and planning on applying for a job within 60 days. **A letter has been provided on the enclosed CD-ROM to help you obtain your reports in any of these situations**.

Now, be aware – **when you initially try to order your reports through the Annual Credit Report service, there's a chance one or more of the CRAs might claim they can't release your own file to you.** For example, they might claim you didn't correctly answer the barrage of multiple choice identity questions they asked you online or, in the case of mailing your request, the copy of your social security card was too faded for them to read. So they ask for more identification items, including your driver license.

Unfortunately, this presents a dilemma. The problem is that *whatever information you provide to the CRAs, they can put it on your credit file.* While this is true, **the CRAs do not have the right to pull up your driving record and there is certainly no law that compels them to put your driver license number on your credit file.** So if you must send them your license, disguise your number on the copy you send them by whiting- or blacking-out some or all of the digits. Your address and date of birth are adequate proof of who you are, as long as this information matches what is already reported on your credit file.

Don't use a copy of your telephone bill as proof of your identity if you don't want your phone number in your file, because it will be included on your report. On the other hand, **if you ever have any fraud issues with your credit, such as identity theft, then you may have to provide a number for lenders to call** in case someone tries to illegally use your identity. **See identity theft in Chapter 15.** And while we're on the subject, your phone number is only a small wall against fraud and identity theft.

CAUTION

FTC Facts for Consumers Brochure

The **Federal Trade Commission (FTC) which governs the Fair Credit Reporting Act and the Fair and Accurate Credit Transactions Act** produced a six-page brochure to help consumers understand how to access their credit reports for free once a year. Even though most of this information was already discussed on the previous four pages, it may interest you to see first hand how the federal government is protecting and educating the American public. To that end, a **copy of this brochure is provided on the next six pages, and a link has also been provided on the enclosed CD-ROM if you wish to visit the FTC website to access and print it.**

FTC Facts for Consumers Brochure: Your Access to Free Credit Reports

FTC Facts
For Consumers

focuson CREDIT

FEDERAL TRADE COMMISSION
FOR THE CONSUMER

www.ftc.gov ■ 1-877-ftc-help

February 2008

Your Access to Free Credit Reports

The Fair Credit Reporting Act (FCRA) requires each of the nationwide consumer reporting companies – Equifax, Experian, and TransUnion – to provide you with a free copy of your credit report, at your request, once every 12 months. The FCRA promotes the accuracy and privacy of information in the files of the nation's consumer reporting companies. The Federal Trade Commission (FTC), the nation's consumer protection agency, enforces the FCRA with respect to consumer reporting companies.

A credit report includes information on where you live, how you pay your bills, and whether you've been sued, arrested, or filed for bankruptcy. Nationwide consumer reporting companies sell the information in your report to creditors, insurers, employers, and other businesses that use it to evaluate your applications for credit, insurance, employment, or renting a home.

Here are the details about your rights under the FCRA and the Fair and Accurate Credit Transactions (FACT) Act, which established the free annual credit report program.

Q: How do I order my free report?
A: The three nationwide consumer reporting companies have set up a central website, a toll-free

telephone number, and a mailing address through which you can order your free annual report.

To order, visit **annualcreditreport.com**, call 1-877-322-8228, or complete the Annual Credit Report Request Form and mail it to: Annual Credit Report Request Service, P.O. Box 105281, Atlanta, GA 30348-5281. The form is on the back of this brochure; or you can print it from **ftc.gov/credit**. Do not contact the three nationwide consumer reporting companies individually. They are providing free annual credit reports only through **annualcreditreport.com**, 1-877-322-8228, and Annual Credit Report Request Service, P.O. Box 105281, Atlanta, GA 30348-5281.

You may order your reports from each of the three nationwide consumer reporting companies at the same time, or you can order your report from each of the companies one at a time. The law allows you to order one free copy of your report from each of the nationwide consumer reporting companies every 12 months.

A WARNING ABOUT "IMPOSTER" WEBSITES

Only one website is authorized to fill orders for the free annual credit report you are entitled to under law – **annualcreditreport.com**. Other websites

FTC Facts for Consumers Brochure: Your Access to Free Credit Reports

FTC Facts For Consumers 2

that claim to offer "free credit reports," "free credit scores," or "free credit monitoring" are not part of the legally mandated free annual credit report program. In some cases, the "free" product comes with strings attached. For example, some sites sign you up for a supposedly "free" service that converts to one you have to pay for after a trial period. If you don't cancel during the trial period, you may be unwittingly agreeing to let the company start charging fees to your credit card.

Some "imposter" sites use terms like "free report" in their names; others have URLs that purposely misspell **annualcreditreport.com** in the hope that you will mistype the name of the official site. Some of these "imposter" sites direct you to other sites that try to sell you something or collect your personal information.

annualcreditreport.com and the nationwide consumer reporting companies will not send you an email asking for your personal information. If you get an email, see a pop-up ad, or get a phone call from someone claiming to be from **annualcreditreport. com** or any of the three nationwide consumer reporting companies, do not reply or click on any link in the message. It's probably a scam. Forward any such email to the FTC at **spam@uce.gov**.

Only one website is authorized to fill orders for the free annual credit report you are entitled to under law – annualcreditreport.com.

Q: What information do I need to provide to get my free report?
A: You need to provide your name, address, Social Security number, and date of birth. If you have moved in the last two years, you may have to provide your previous address. To maintain the security of your file, each nationwide consumer reporting company may ask you for some information that only you would know, like the amount of your monthly mortgage payment. Each company may ask you for different information because the information each has in your file may come from different sources.

Q: Why do I want a copy of my credit report?
A: Your credit report has information that affects whether you can get a loan – and how much you will have to pay to borrow money. You want a copy of your credit report to:
- make sure the information is accurate, complete, and up-to-date before you apply for a loan for a major purchase like a house or car, buy insurance, or apply for a job.
- help guard against identity theft. That's when someone uses your personal information – like your name, your Social Security number, or your credit card number – to commit fraud. Identity thieves may use your information to open a new credit card account in your name. Then, when they don't pay the bills, the delinquent account is reported on your credit report. Inaccurate information like that could affect your ability to get credit, insurance, or even a job.

Q: How long does it take to get my report after I order it?
A: If you request your report online at **annualcreditreport.com**, you should be able to access it immediately. If you order your report by

FTC Facts for Consumers Brochure: Your Access to Free Credit Reports

FTC Facts For Consumers   3

calling toll-free 1-877-322-8228, your report will be processed and mailed to you within 15 days. If you order your report by mail using the Annual Credit Report Request Form, your request will be processed and mailed to you within 15 days of receipt.

Whether you order your report online, by phone, or by mail, it may take longer to receive your report if the nationwide consumer reporting company needs more information to verify your identity.

There also may be times when the nationwide consumer reporting companies receive a high volume of requests for credit reports. If that happens, you may be asked to re-submit your request. Or, you may be told that your report will be mailed to you sometime after 15 days from your request. If either of these events occurs, the nationwide consumer reporting companies will let you know.

If you request your report online at annualcreditreport.com, you should be able to access it immediately.

Q: Are there any other situations where I might be eligible for a free report?

A: Under federal law, you're entitled to a free report if a company takes adverse action against you such as denying your application for credit, insurance, or employment and you ask for your report within 60 days of receiving notice of the action. The notice will give you the name, address, and phone number of the consumer reporting company. You're also entitled to one free report a year if you're unemployed and plan to look for a job within 60 days; if you're on welfare; or if your report is inaccurate because of fraud, including identity theft. Otherwise, a consumer reporting company may charge you up to

$10.50 for another copy of your report within a 12-month period.

To buy a copy of your report, contact:
- Equifax: 800-685-1111; **www.equifax.com**
- Experian: 888-EXPERIAN (888-397-3742); **www.experian.com**
- TransUnion: 800-916-8800; **www.transunion.com**

Under state law, consumers in Colorado, Georgia, Maine, Maryland, Massachusetts, New Jersey, and Vermont already have free access to their credit reports.

Q: Should I order a report from each of the three nationwide consumer reporting companies?

A: It's up to you. Because nationwide consumer reporting companies get their information from different sources, the information in your report from one company may not reflect all, or the same, information in your reports from the other two companies. That's not to say that the information in any of your reports is necessarily inaccurate; it just may be different.

Q: Should I order my reports from all three of the nationwide consumer reporting companies at the same time?

A: You may order one, two, or all three reports at the same time, or you may stagger your requests. It's your choice. Some financial advisors say staggering your requests during a 12-month period may be a good way to keep an eye on the accuracy and completeness of the information in your reports.

SAMPLE

FTC Facts for Consumers Brochure: Your Access to Free Credit Reports

FTC Facts For Consumers **4**

Q: What if I find errors – either inaccuracies or incomplete information – in my credit report?

A: Under the FCRA, both the consumer reporting company and the information provider (that is, the person, company, or organization that provides information about you to a consumer reporting company) are responsible for correcting inaccurate or incomplete information in your report. To take full advantage of your rights under this law, contact the consumer reporting company and the information provider.

1. Tell the consumer reporting company, in writing, what information you think is inaccurate.

Consumer reporting companies must investigate the items in question – usually within 30 days – unless they consider your dispute frivolous. They also must forward all the relevant data you provide about the inaccuracy to the organization that provided the information. After the information provider receives notice of a dispute from the consumer reporting company, it must investigate, review the relevant information, and report the results back to the consumer reporting company. If the information provider finds the disputed information is inaccurate, it must notify all three nationwide consumer reporting companies so they can correct the information in your file.

When the investigation is complete, the consumer reporting company must give you the written results and a free copy of your report if the dispute results in a change. (This free report does not count as your annual free report under the FACT

Tell the consumer reporting company, in writing, what information you think is inaccurate.

Act.) If an item is changed or deleted, the consumer reporting company cannot put the disputed information back in your file unless the information provider verifies that it is accurate and complete. The consumer reporting company also must send you written notice that includes the name, address, and phone number of the information provider.

2. Tell the creditor or other information provider in writing that you dispute an item. Many providers specify an address for disputes. If the provider reports the item to a consumer reporting company, it must include a notice of your dispute. And if you are correct – that is, if the information is found to be inaccurate – the information provider may not report it again.

Q: What can I do if the consumer reporting company or information provider won't correct the information I dispute?

A: If an investigation doesn't resolve your dispute with the consumer reporting company, you can ask that a statement of the dispute be included in your file and in future reports. You also can ask the consumer reporting company to provide your statement to anyone who received a copy of your report in the recent past. You can expect to pay a fee for this service.

If you tell the information provider that you dispute an item, a notice of your dispute must be included any time the information provider reports the item to a consumer reporting company.

FTC Facts for Consumers Brochure: Your Access to Free Credit Reports

FTC Facts For Consumers **5**

Q: How long can a consumer reporting company report negative information?

A: A consumer reporting company can report most accurate negative information for seven years and bankruptcy information for 10 years. There is no time limit on reporting information about criminal convictions; information reported in response to your application for a job that pays more than $75,000 a year; and information reported because you've applied for more than $150,000 worth of credit or life insurance. Information about a lawsuit or an unpaid judgment against you can be reported for seven years or until the statute of limitations runs out, whichever is longer.

Your employer can get a copy of your credit report only if you agree.

Q: Can anyone else can get a copy of my credit report?

A: The FCRA specifies who can access your credit report. Creditors, insurers, employers, and other businesses that use the information in your report to evaluate your applications for credit, insurance, employment, or renting a home are among those that have a legal right to access your report.

Q: Can my employer get my credit report?

A: Your employer can get a copy of your credit report only if you agree. A consumer reporting company may not provide information about you to your employer, or to a prospective employer, without your written consent.

FOR MORE INFORMATION

The FTC works for the consumer to prevent fraudulent, deceptive and unfair business practices in the marketplace and to provide information to help consumers spot, stop, and avoid them. To learn more about credit issues and protecting your personal information, visit **ftc.gov/credit**.

To file a complaint or to get free information on other consumer issues, visit **ftc.gov** or call toll-free, 1-877-FTC-HELP (1-877-382-4357); TTY: 1-866-653-4261. The FTC enters Internet, telemarketing, identity theft and other fraud-related complaints into Consumer Sentinel, a secure online database available to hundreds of civil and criminal law enforcement agencies in the U.S. and abroad.

Federal Trade Commission
Bureau of Consumer Protection
Division of Consumer and Business Education

FOR THE CONSUMER	FEDERAL TRADE COMMISSION
WWW.FTC.GOV	1-877-FTC-HELP

FTC Facts for Consumers Brochure: Your Access to Free Credit Reports

EQUIFAX   **experían**   **TransUnion.**

Annual Credit Report Request Form

You have the right to get a free copy of your credit file disclosure, commonly called a credit report, once every 12 months, from each of the nationwide consumer credit reporting companies - Equifax, Experian and TransUnion.
For instant access to your free credit report, visit www.annualcreditreport.com.
For more information on obtaining your free credit report, visit www.annualcreditreport.com or call 1-877-322-8228.
Use this form if you prefer to write to request your credit report from any, or all, of the nationwide consumer credit reporting companies. The following information is required to process your request. **Omission of any information may delay your request.**
Once complete, fold (do not staple or tape), place into a #10 envelope, affix required postage and mail to:
Annual Credit Report Request Service P.O. Box 105281 Atlanta, GA 30348-5281.

Please use a Black or Blue Pen and write your responses IN PRINTED CAPITAL LETTERS without touching the sides of the boxes like the examples listed below:

A B C D E F G H I J K L M N O P Q R S T U V W X Y Z   0 1 2 3 4 5 6 7 8 9

Social Security Number: **Date of Birth:**

☐☐☐ - ☐☐ - ☐☐☐☐   ☐☐ / ☐☐ / ☐☐☐☐
                                          Month   Day   Year

Fold Here *Fold Here*

First Name   **M.I.**

Last Name   **JR, SR, III, etc.**

Current Mailing Address:

House Number   **Street Name**

Apartment Number / Private Mailbox   **For Puerto Rico Only: Print Urbanization Name**

City   **State**   **ZipCode**

Previous Mailing Address (complete only if at current mailing address for less than two years):

House Number   **Street Name**

Fold Here   *Fold Here*

Apartment Number / Private Mailbox   **For Puerto Rico Only: Print Urbanization Name**

City   **State**   **ZipCode**

Shade Circle Like This → ●

Not Like This → ⊗ ☑

I want a credit report from (shade each that you would like to receive):
○ Equifax
○ Experian
○ TransUnion

○ Shade here if, for security reasons, you want your credit report to include no more than the last four digits of your Social Security Number.

If additional information is needed to process your request, the consumer credit reporting company will contact you by mail.

Your request will be processed within 15 days of receipt and then mailed to you.

Copyright 2004, Central Source LLC

31238

Chapter 5

Understanding Your Credit Report: How to Read the Big Three

This Chapter Discusses:

★ **Personal Information**

★ **Employment Information**

★ **Scoring (Credit Score)**

★ **Public Records**

★ **Collections**

★ **Revolving Accounts**

★ **Installment Accounts**

★ **Mortgage Accounts**

★ **Inquiries**

When you receive all three reports and compare them, you'll notice they look different. This is because the **Big Three** (**Equifax, Experian** and **TransUnion**) are not associated with each other. As previously mentioned, **they are businesses that operate independently.** *Consequently, the information they receive and maintain on you varies.* Even if a creditor reports the same information to all three credit reporting agencies (CRAs), the time or manner in which the data is updated may vary. A common discrepancy, for example, is the reporting of different balances for the same exact account appearing on all three credit reports.

Over the years the CRAs have improved their formats tremendously. Therefore, the reports offered directly from the **Big Three today are actually fairly easy to read and understand**. It's the *third-party reports, such as those obtained directly from a potential lender, car dealership or mortgage broker, that may be especially confusing* – because they are designed specifically for their application processing procedures. So keep in mind that, although **the formatting of your data will vary, the information is essentially the same.**

Personal Information

Every report will contain your personal information – such as your **name**, any **aliases, date of birth, social security number** and **address history.** It's important to review this information for accuracy, as this is how your credit file is indexed. **A corrupt file with missing or inaccurate information may prevent your file from being pulled** – resulting in a **"no record found"** for your would-be creditor or employer.

This is *especially true* if the incorrect piece of information is your **social security number, name or address.** Understandably, most creditors will not take the time to investigate your claim of having a good file when they are unable to locate one in the first place.

Employment Information

Do you ever wonder how employment information is reported? It actually *comes from your creditors,* not the Social Security Administration, Internal Revenue Service or Department of Labor. Not all reports provide the name of your employer, but **if you ever complete an application for credit and include your current employer, there's a good chance the creditor may disclose this to the (CRAs).** If your credit reports do not have employment

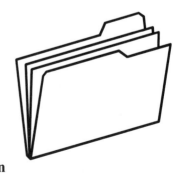

information on you, there's no need to be concerned. **This information is often deemed by most creditors to be out of date or incomplete anyway.** *Creditors who require employment verification know they should contact your workplace directly and not simply rely upon what is or isn't being reported in your credit file.*

Scoring (Credit Score)

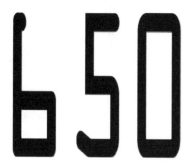

This is your infamous **three-digit credit score**, which *purports to predict the likelihood of your becoming delinquent over the next two years.* If you ordered your score with your reports, **you'll have a good starting point and an idea whether your credit is good, bad or excellent.** As you review your scores, keep in mind:

No matter what your number is and no matter what the CRAs say about you, *don't get emotional and don't panic. If your credit score is not stellar at this point* (which you probably already knew), *you can improve it with a little effort and the guidance of this book.*

Public Records

The information contained in this section of your report is **obtained from county, state and federal courts** and *includes bankruptcies, civil judgments and tax liens.* The format once again will vary, but **the data typically includes a file date, case number, case type, jurisdiction, balance and other relevant details.**

Collections

This section of your report *refers to any accounts that have been sold or assigned to collection agencies because the original creditor was unsuccessful in collecting what it was allegedly owed.* Some creditors have their own internal collection division, so you may see the original creditor listed here. **The types of data you'll see reported include the account number, date of last activity (DLA), the balance owed and the current account status** (whether or not the debt has been paid, is being paid or remains unpaid).

Revolving Accounts

The **"tradelines" (accounts)** that are listed in this section actually *revolve.* In other words: *when you charge against the account, the balance goes up and the available credit goes down. Then when you make a payment, the balance goes down and the available credit goes back up. This revolving cycle continues to repeat for the life of the account.*

Examples of revolving accounts include *credit cards, department store cards* and *gasoline cards,* and these often have the greatest impact on your credit score… but that will be discussed later.

Interpreting this section of a credit report is very easy. It usually begins with the **name of the creditor**, followed by **when the account was reported or updated**, the **date of the last activity, when the account was opened, how much credit was ever used**, the **estimated monthly payment required to keep the account current**, the **balance** and the **historical status** (showing how many 30-, 60- and 90-day late payments were recorded).

Installment Accounts

Unlike credit cards, these tradelines do not revolve. They are *opened with a fixed loan amount and come with a set monthly payment that is paid until the balance reaches zero.* Once fully paid, **the account is then closed and cannot be used again. Examples** of installment accounts include **student loans, personal loans** and **automobile loans**.

The formatting of these accounts will be similar to revolving accounts – *the primary difference is that the monthly payment is usually fixed and does not fluctuate like a credit card* – which reflects a monthly payment obligation based upon the outstanding balance at the end of each statement period.

Mortgage Accounts

All obligations that are *secured by a mortgage* **are provided here.** Accounts in this section include **purchase and refinance mortgages,** as well as **home equity loans and lines of credit.**

Inquiries

Every time you either apply for credit or a collection agency pulls your report to check up on you, the inquiry is recorded and reported for other creditors to see for two years – *after which the inquiry will simply fall off the record.*

Now that you've successfully completed this chapter, you should have a basic understanding of how to read the various sections of your credit report. Just remember, *the concept is the same for all three CRAs, but the data may be formatted and even labeled a little differently.*

Chapter 6

Repairing Your Credit Report, Part I: The Dispute Process

This Chapter Discusses:

★ FCRA Section 611
★ Inaccurate or Incomplete Information
★ FCRA Section 605
★ Outdated Negative Information
★ Negative Items That Do Not Belong to You

Now that you are familiar with your credit reports, **you may have already seen some information on them that's incomplete, very old or just not accurate**. And if these items are dragging down your credit score, getting the ominous credit reporting agencies (CRAs) to quickly and accurately fix mistakes is not always easily accomplished. But since the enactment of the **Fair Credit Reporting Act (FCRA),** consumers now have a better shot at it. **Among the many provisions that make up the FCRA, one of the more important ones is the right to have mistakes on your report corrected by simply telling the CRA to fix them** (this is known as initiating a *"dispute")*.

The CRA must attempt to contact the source creditor and write you back within about 30 days to give you one of two answers. If the source creditor verified the information as accurate, the law does not require the CRA to make any changes to your file. If the

source creditor agreed the information was inaccurate or did not bother to submit an answer at all, then the CRA must modify your report as you requested – and send you a complimentary updated copy. **This dispute process is governed by two primary sections of the FCRA (Section 611 and 605),** and they are the focus of this chapter along with explaining your rights under each of them, respectively. The next chapter ("...Part II: the Dispute Letter") will then reveal exactly how to take advantage of the information learned here.

FCRA Section 611

Section 611 of the FCRA is titled *"Procedure in case of disputed accuracy,"* and provides that *any information that is found to be "inaccurate," incomplete" or that "can no longer be verified" must be either modified according to the results of the reinvestigation or "promptly" deleted from your credit report.* **Section 611** further provides that **the CRA has only "a reasonable amount of time" to finalize a reinvestigation for you.** The Federal Trade Commission and case law have deciphered this amount of time to be 30 days in most instances.

A quick note about the use of the word "reinvestigation": The FCRA uses the word "reinvestigation" to describe the initial dispute process as if there were some type of investigation to begin with, but there wasn't! The theory is that the "Big Three" were directly involved in the drafting of the FCRA. After all, they are known to be some of the biggest lobbyists in Washington, D.C. Perhaps they wanted to give the impression that the information reported on your credit report is investigated the very first time. But as you've learned, it isn't.

An excerpt of Section 611 is provided on the next nine pages. While it may be lengthy, it is essential to this chapter because it defines many rights. ***Don't worry –*** **if you get a headache while reading it, the segment immediately following the excerpt simplifies its basic elements.**

FCRA Section 611 Procedure in Case of Disputed Accuracy

(C)   by electronic means, if available from the agency; or

(D)   by any other reasonable means that is available from the agency.

(c) *Trained personnel*. Any consumer reporting agency shall provide trained personnel to explain to the consumer any information furnished to him pursuant to section 609 [§ 1681g] of this title.

(d) *Persons accompanying consumer*. The consumer shall be permitted to be accompanied by one other person of his choosing, who shall furnish reasonable identification. A consumer reporting agency may require the consumer to furnish a written statement granting permission to the consumer reporting agency to discuss the consumer's file in such person's presence.

(e) *Limitation of liability*. Except as provided in sections 616 and 617 [§§ 1681n and 1681o] of this title, no consumer may bring any action or proceeding in the nature of defamation, invasion of privacy, or negligence with respect to the reporting of information against any consumer reporting agency, any user of information, or any person who furnishes information to a consumer reporting agency, based on information disclosed pursuant to section 609, 610, or 615 [§§ 1681g, 1681h, or 1681m] of this title or based on information disclosed by a user of a consumer report to or for a consumer against whom the user has taken adverse action, based in whole or in part on the report, except as to false information furnished with malice or willful intent to injure such consumer.

§ 611. Procedure in case of disputed accuracy [15 U.S.C. § 1681i]

(a) Reinvestigations of Disputed Information

(1) Reinvestigation Required

(A)   *In general.* Subject to subsection (f), if the completeness or accuracy of any item of information contained in a consumer's file at a consumer reporting agency is disputed by the consumer and the consumer notifies the agency directly, or indirectly through a reseller, of such dispute, the agency shall, free of charge, conduct a reasonable reinvestigation to determine whether the disputed information is inaccurate and record the current status of the disputed information, or delete the item from the file in accordance with paragraph (5), before the end of the 30-day period beginning on the date on which the agency receives the notice of the dispute from the consumer or reseller.

(B)   *Extension of period to reinvestigate.* Except as provided in subparagraph (C), the 30-day period described in subparagraph (A) may be extended for not more than 15 additional days if the consumer reporting agency receives information from the consumer during that 30-day period that is relevant to the reinvestigation.

(C)   *Limitations on extension of period to reinvestigate.* Subparagraph (B) shall not apply to any reinvestigation in which, during the 30-day period

FCRA Section 611 Procedure in Case of Disputed Accuracy

described in subparagraph (A), the information that is the subject of the reinvestigation is found to be inaccurate or incomplete or the consumer reporting agency determines that the information cannot be verified.

(2) Prompt Notice of Dispute to Furnisher of Information

    (A)   *In general.* Before the expiration of the 5-business-day period beginning on the date on which a consumer reporting agency receives notice of a dispute from any consumer or a reseller in accordance with paragraph (1), the agency shall provide notification of the dispute to any person who provided any item of information in dispute, at the address and in the manner established with the person. The notice shall include all relevant information regarding the dispute that the agency has received from the consumer or reseller.

    (B)   *Provision of other information.* The consumer reporting agency shall promptly provide to the person who provided the information in dispute all relevant information regarding the dispute that is received by the agency from the consumer or the reseller after the period referred to in subparagraph (A) and before the end of the period referred to in paragraph (1)(A).

(3) Determination That Dispute Is Frivolous or Irrelevant

    (A)   *In general.* Notwithstanding paragraph (1), a consumer reporting agency may terminate a reinvestigation of information disputed by a consumer under that paragraph if the agency reasonably determines that the dispute by the consumer is frivolous or irrelevant, including by reason of a failure by a consumer to provide sufficient information to investigate the disputed information.

    (B)   *Notice of determination.* Upon making any determination in accordance with subparagraph (A) that a dispute is frivolous or irrelevant, a consumer reporting agency shall notify the consumer of such determination not later than 5 business days after making such determination, by mail or, if authorized by the consumer for that purpose, by any other means available to the agency.

    (C)   *Contents of notice.* A notice under subparagraph (B) shall include

        (i)   the reasons for the determination under subparagraph (A); and

        (ii)   identification of any information required to investigate the disputed information, which may consist of a standardized form describing the general nature of such information.

(4) *Consideration of consumer information.* In conducting any reinvestigation under paragraph (1) with respect to disputed information in the file of any consumer, the consumer reporting agency shall review and consider all relevant information submitted by the consumer in the period described in paragraph (1)(A) with respect to such disputed information.

FCRA Section 611 Procedure in Case of Disputed Accuracy

(5) Treatment of Inaccurate or Unverifiable Information

(A) *In general.* If, after any reinvestigation under paragraph (1) of any information disputed by a consumer, an item of the information is found to be inaccurate or incomplete or cannot be verified, the consumer reporting agency shall–

   (i) promptly delete that item of information from the file of the consumer, or modify that item of information, as appropriate, based on the results of the reinvestigation; and

   (ii) promptly notify the furnisher of that information that the information has been modified or deleted from the file of the consumer.

(B) Requirements Relating to Reinsertion of Previously Deleted Material

   (i) *Certification of accuracy of information.* If any information is deleted from a consumer's file pursuant to subparagraph (A), the information may not be reinserted in the file by the consumer reporting agency unless the person who furnishes the information certifies that the information is complete and accurate.

   (ii) *Notice to consumer.* If any information that has been deleted from a consumer's file pursuant to subparagraph (A) is reinserted in the file, the consumer reporting agency shall notify the consumer of the reinsertion in writing not later than 5 business days after the reinsertion or, if authorized by the consumer for that purpose, by any other means available to the agency.

   (iii) *Additional information.* As part of, or in addition to, the notice under clause (ii), a consumer reporting agency shall provide to a consumer in writing not later than 5 business days after the date of the reinsertion

      (I) a statement that the disputed information has been reinserted;

      (II) the business name and address of any furnisher of information contacted and the telephone number of such furnisher, if reasonably available, or of any furnisher of information that contacted the consumer reporting agency, in connection with the reinsertion of such information; and

      (III) a notice that the consumer has the right to add a statement to the consumer's file disputing the accuracy or completeness of the disputed information.

(C) *Procedures to prevent reappearance.* A consumer reporting agency shall maintain reasonable procedures designed to prevent the reappearance in a consumer's file, and in consumer reports on the consumer, of information that is deleted pursuant to this paragraph (other than information that is reinserted in accordance with subparagraph (B)(i)).

FCRA Section 611 Procedure in Case of Disputed Accuracy

(D)   *Automated reinvestigation system.* Any consumer reporting agency that compiles and maintains files on consumers on a nationwide basis shall implement an automated system through which furnishers of information to that consumer reporting agency may report the results of a reinvestigation that finds incomplete or inaccurate information in a consumer's file to other such consumer reporting agencies.

(6)   Notice of Results of Reinvestigation

(A)   *In general.* A consumer reporting agency shall provide written notice to a consumer of the results of a reinvestigation under this subsection not later than 5 business days after the completion of the reinvestigation, by mail or, if authorized by the consumer for that purpose, by other means available to the agency.

(B)   *Contents.* As part of, or in addition to, the notice under subparagraph (A), a consumer reporting agency shall provide to a consumer in writing before the expiration of the 5-day period referred to in subparagraph (A)

(i)   a statement that the reinvestigation is completed;

(ii)   a consumer report that is based upon the consumer's file as that file is revised as a result of the reinvestigation;

(iii) a notice that, if requested by the consumer, a description of the procedure used to determine the accuracy and completeness of the information shall be provided to the consumer by the agency, including the business name and address of any furnisher of information contacted in connection with such information and the telephone number of such furnisher, if reasonably available;

(iv)   a notice that the consumer has the right to add a statement to the consumer's file disputing the accuracy or completeness of the information; and

(v)   a notice that the consumer has the right to request under subsection (d) that the consumer reporting agency furnish notifications under that subsection.

(7) *Description of reinvestigation procedure.* A consumer reporting agency shall provide to a consumer a description referred to in paragraph (6)(B)(iii) by not later than 15 days after receiving a request from the consumer for that description.

(8) *Expedited dispute resolution.* If a dispute regarding an item of information in a consumer's file at a consumer reporting agency is resolved in accordance with paragraph (5)(A) by the deletion of the disputed information by not later than 3 business days after the date on which the agency receives notice of the dispute from the consumer in accordance with paragraph (1)(A), then the agency shall not be required to comply with paragraphs (2), (6), and (7) with respect to that dispute if the agency

FCRA Section 611 Procedure in Case of Disputed Accuracy

       (A)   provides prompt notice of the deletion to the consumer by telephone;

       (B)   includes in that notice, or in a written notice that accompanies a confirmation and consumer report provided in accordance with subparagraph (C), a statement of the consumer's right to request under subsection (d) that the agency furnish notifications under that subsection; and

       (C)   provides written confirmation of the deletion and a copy of a consumer report on the consumer that is based on the consumer's file after the deletion, not later than 5 business days after making the deletion.

(b) *Statement of dispute.* If the reinvestigation does not resolve the dispute, the consumer may file a brief statement setting forth the nature of the dispute. The consumer reporting agency may limit such statements to not more than one hundred words if it provides the consumer with assistance in writing a clear summary of the dispute.

(c) *Notification of consumer dispute in subsequent consumer reports.* Whenever a statement of a dispute is filed, unless there is reasonable grounds to believe that it is frivolous or irrelevant, the consumer reporting agency shall, in any subsequent report containing the information in question, clearly note that it is disputed by the consumer and provide either the consumer's statement or a clear and accurate codification or summary thereof.

(d) *Notification of deletion of disputed information.* Following any deletion of information which is found to be inaccurate or whose accuracy can no longer be verified or any notation as to disputed information, the consumer reporting agency shall, at the request of the consumer, furnish notification that the item has been deleted or the statement, codification or summary pursuant to subsection (b) or (c) of this section to any person specifically designated by the consumer who has within two years prior thereto received a consumer report for employment purposes, or within six months prior thereto received a consumer report for any other purpose, which contained the deleted or disputed information.

(e) Treatment of Complaints and Report to Congress

   (1) *In general.* The Commission shall--

       (A)   compile all complaints that it receives that a file of a consumer that is maintained by a consumer reporting agency described in section 603(p) contains incomplete or inaccurate information, with respect to which, the consumer appears to have disputed the completeness or accuracy with the consumer reporting agency or otherwise utilized the procedures provided by subsection (a); and

       (B)   transmit each such complaint to each consumer reporting agency involved.

   (2) *Exclusion.* Complaints received or obtained by the Commission pursuant to its investigative authority under the Federal Trade Commission Act shall not be subject to paragraph (1).

FCRA Section 611 Procedure in Case of Disputed Accuracy

(3) *Agency responsibilities.* Each consumer reporting agency described in section 603(p) that receives a complaint transmitted by the Commission pursuant to paragraph (1) shall--

    (A)   review each such complaint to determine whether all legal obligations imposed on the consumer reporting agency under this title (including any obligation imposed by an applicable court or administrative order) have been met with respect to the subject matter of the complaint;

    (B)   provide reports on a regular basis to the Commission regarding the determinations of and actions taken by the consumer reporting agency, if any, in connection with its review of such complaints; and

    (C)   maintain, for a reasonable time period, records regarding the disposition of each such complaint that is sufficient to demonstrate compliance with this subsection.

(4) *Rulemaking authority.* The Commission may prescribe regulations, as appropriate to implement this subsection.

(5) *Annual report.* The Commission shall submit to the Committee on Banking, Housing, and Urban Affairs of the Senate and the Committee on Financial Services of the House of Representatives an annual report regarding information gathered by the Commission under this subsection.'.

(f) Reinvestigation Requirement Applicable to Resellers

    (1) *Exemption from general reinvestigation requirement.* Except as provided in paragraph (2), a reseller shall be exempt from the requirements of this section.

    (2) *Action required upon receiving notice of a dispute.* If a reseller receives a notice from a consumer of a dispute concerning the completeness or accuracy of any item of information contained in a consumer report on such consumer produced by the reseller, the reseller shall, within 5 business days of receiving the notice, and free of charge–

        (A)   determine whether the item of information is incomplete or inaccurate as a result of an act or omission of the reseller; and

        (B) if (i) the reseller determines that the item of information is incomplete or inaccurate as a result of an act or omission of the reseller, not later than 20 days after receiving the notice, correct the information in the consumer report or delete it; or

            (ii) if the reseller determines that the item of information is not incomplete or inaccurate as a result of an act or omission of the reseller, convey the notice of the dispute, together with all relevant information provided by the consumer, to each consumer reporting agency that provided the reseller with the information that is the subject of the dispute, using an address or a notification mechanism specified by the consumer reporting agency for such notices.

FCRA Section 611 Procedure in Case of Disputed Accuracy

(3) *Responsibility of consumer reporting agency to notify consumer through reseller.* Upon the completion of a reinvestigation under this section of a dispute concerning the completeness or accuracy of any information in the file of a consumer by a consumer reporting agency that received notice of the dispute from a reseller under paragraph (2)--

(A)   the notice by the consumer reporting agency under paragraph (6), (7), or (8) of subsection (a) shall be provided to the reseller in lieu of the consumer; and

(B)   the reseller shall immediately reconvey such notice to the consumer, including any notice of a deletion by telephone in the manner required under paragraph (8)(A).

(4) *Reseller reinvestigations.* No provision of this subsection shall be construed as prohibiting a reseller from conducting a reinvestigation of a consumer dispute directly.

§ 612. **Charges for certain disclosures** [15 U.S.C. § 1681j]   ***See also 16 CFR Part 610***
*****   ***69 Fed. Reg. 35467 (06/24/04)***

(a) Free Annual Disclosure

(1) Nationwide Consumer Reporting Agencies

(A)   *In general.* All consumer reporting agencies described in subsections (p) and (w) of section 603 shall make all disclosures pursuant to section 609 once during any 12-month period upon request of the consumer and without charge to the consumer.

(B)   *Centralized source.* Subparagraph (A) shall apply with respect to a consumer reporting agency described in section 603(p) only if the request from the consumer is made using the centralized source established for such purpose in accordance with section 211(c) of the Fair and Accurate Credit Transactions Act of 2003.

(C) Nationwide Specialty Consumer Reporting Agency

(i)   *In general.* The Commission shall prescribe regulations applicable to each consumer reporting agency described in section 603(w) to require the establishment of a streamlined process for consumers to request consumer reports under subparagraph (A), which shall include, at a minimum, the establishment by each such agency of a toll-free telephone number for such requests.

(ii)   *Considerations.* In prescribing regulations under clause (i), the Commission shall consider–

(I)   the significant demands that may be placed on consumer reporting agencies in providing such consumer reports;

(II)   appropriate means to ensure that consumer reporting agencies can satisfactorily meet those demands, including the efficacy of a system of staggering the availability to consumers of such consumer reports; and

SAMPLE

FCRA Section 611 Procedure in Case of Disputed Accuracy

    (III)   the ease by which consumers should be able to contact consumer reporting agencies with respect to access to such consumer reports.

    (iii)   *Date of issuance.* The Commission shall issue the regulations required by this subparagraph in final form not later than 6 months after the date of enactment of the Fair and Accurate Credit Transactions Act of 2003.

    (iv)   *Consideration of ability to comply.* The regulations of the Commission under this subparagraph shall establish an effective date by which each nationwide specialty consumer reporting agency (as defined in section 603(w)) shall be required to comply with subsection (a), which effective date--

    (I)   shall be established after consideration of the ability of each nationwide specialty consumer reporting agency to comply with subsection (a); and

    (II)   shall be not later than 6 months after the date on which such regulations are issued in final form (or such additional period not to exceed 3 months, as the Commission determines appropriate).

(2) *Timing.* A consumer reporting agency shall provide a consumer report under paragraph (1) not later than 15 days after the date on which the request is received under paragraph (1).

(3) *Reinvestigations.* Notwithstanding the time periods specified in section 611(a)(1), a reinvestigation under that section by a consumer reporting agency upon a request of a consumer that is made after receiving a consumer report under this subsection shall be completed not later than 45 days after the date on which the request is received.

(4) *Exception for first 12 months of operation.* This subsection shall not apply to a consumer reporting agency that has not been furnishing consumer reports to third parties on a continuing basis during the 12-month period preceding a request under paragraph (1), with respect to consumers residing nationwide.

(b) *Free disclosure after adverse notice to consumer.* Each consumer reporting agency that maintains a file on a consumer shall make all disclosures pursuant to section 609 [§ 1681g] without charge to the consumer if, not later than 60 days after receipt by such consumer of a notification pursuant to section 615 [§ 1681m], or of a notification from a debt collection agency affiliated with that consumer reporting agency stating that the consumer's credit rating may be or has been adversely affected, the consumer makes a request under section 609 [§ 1681g].

(c) *Free disclosure under certain other circumstances.* Upon the request of the consumer, a consumer reporting agency shall make all disclosures pursuant to section 609 [§ 1681g] once during any 12-month period without charge to that consumer if the consumer certifies in writing that the consumer

FCRA Section 611 Procedure in Case of Disputed Accuracy

          (1) is unemployed and intends to apply for employment in the 60-day period beginning on the date on which the certification is made;

          (2) is a recipient of public welfare assistance; or

          (3) has reason to believe that the file on the consumer at the agency contains inaccurate information due to fraud.

    (d) *Free disclosures in connection with fraud alerts.* Upon the request of a consumer, a consumer reporting agency described in section 603(p) shall make all disclosures pursuant to section 609 without charge to the consumer, as provided in subsections (a)(2) and (b)(2) of section 605A, as applicable.

    (e) *Other charges prohibited* A consumer reporting agency shall not impose any charge on a consumer for providing any notification required by this title or making any disclosure required by this title, except as authorized by subsection (f).

    (f) Reasonable Charges Allowed for Certain Disclosures

          (1) *In general.* In the case of a request from a consumer other than a request that is covered by any of subsections (a) through (d), a consumer reporting agency may impose a reasonable charge on a consumer

              (A)   for making a disclosure to the consumer pursuant to section 609 [§ 1681g], which charge

                  (i)   shall not exceed $8;[4] and

                  (ii)   shall be indicated to the consumer before making the disclosure; and

              (B)   for furnishing, pursuant to 611(d) [§ 1681i], following a reinvestigation under section 611(a) [§ 1681i], a statement, codification, or summary to a person designated by the consumer under that section after the 30-day period beginning on the date of notification of the consumer under paragraph (6) or (8) of section 611(a) [§ 1681i] with respect to the reinvestigation, which charge

                  (i)   shall not exceed the charge that the agency would impose on each designated recipient for a consumer report; and

                  (ii)   shall be indicated to the consumer before furnishing such information.

          (2) *Modification of amount.* The Federal Trade Commission shall increase the amount referred to in paragraph (1)(A)(I) on January 1 of each year, based proportionally on changes in the Consumer Price Index, with fractional changes rounded to the nearest fifty cents.

SAMPLE

---

[4] The Federal Trade Commission increased the maximum allowable charge to $9.00, effective January 1, 2002. 66 Fed. Reg. 63545 (Dec. 7, 2001).

Inaccurate or Incomplete Information

Once you've reviewed your reports, you're likely to find many errors – including **incomplete and inaccurate information. But stay calm,** *the credit repair process is not like a fast-paced game of pinball* (like most unscrupulous credit repair outfits would have you believe). You could go crazy and try to hit as may bumpers as you can in one round – but **there are usually specific targets you should be going for.** *You want the truly harmful information to be deleted or corrected.* So, for purposes of the dispute process, **start by looking for items or accounts that are likely to be damaging your score.**

As far as your **revolving accounts** go, if an account is still with the original creditor (it's not charged off or in collections elsewhere), then **review the payment history carefully.** If payments are reflected as timely and the balances are accurate, don't do anything with the account.

Your next step is to look for accounts that are still with their original creditors but that were reported late sometime in the past several years. Whether they are 30-, 60-, or 90-days late or more, and especially within the past 24 months – *put a mark next to those accounts.* Now if you kept your canceled checks, stubs or other receipts of payment, **look to see if in fact those payments were made timely by you.** If you don't happen to have your old checks or statements readily available, *the law does not prohibit you from relying on your own memory.* Simply **use your best recollection** as to whether you did indeed pay those accounts on time during those months in question. **If you think you may have paid those accounts on time, you'll want to tell the CRA they were "never late."** *Your score is better served if these accounts are reported current/never past due (as opposed to removed or deleted).*

The next thing to do is look for items listed as **collection accounts** or **charged-off accounts.** It's vital to understand that *it's not possible to bring a collection or charged-off account "current."* So **the best way to help your score is to have these accounts removed as if they never existed.** Look for *anything* inaccurate about these items. **Any account can be considered inaccurate under the law as long as there is some error associated with the listing** – such as an invalid account number or how the ownership of the account is listed (e.g., the account has you listed as the primary, when you were just an authorized user). And remember, **you're not legally obligated to correct a "typo" for the CRAs** – *it's their responsibility to report information about you accurately.* Make it clear that a collection or charged-off account they are reporting **does not belong to you.**

Nine out of 10 times, *you can count on being able to find errors all throughout your report.* Fortunately, the **FCRA requires that any inaccurate information be corrected "promptly,"** *within approximately 30 days from a consumer's request.* You should **keep an eye out for the following information that may be wrong:**

★ Items You Should Dispute If They Are Inaccurate:

- **Personal information** (Your name, address, phone number, social security number and birth date).

- **Employment** (Name of company, hire date, position, salary and phone number).

- Information or **accounts belonging to someone else.**

- A **late payment** when you've been paying on time.

- **Balances that are higher than they really are** (Sometimes your creditors report *only* the highest you have ever used on an account – and so your outstanding balance is proportionally "maxed out" more than it should be. **This could affect your score by more than a few points.**) **If the balance that's being reported is lower than what you have on record,** *leave it alone.*

- Debts that were **incurred by a spouse before you got married.**

- A **public record showing as active**, such as a judgment, tax or bankruptcy filing, **that was actually paid, dismissed or discharged**.

- An **account that was closed by you**, but is being reported as closed by the creditor.

- **Duplicate accounts** (This can occur when an account is turned over to a collection agency or when a good account was simply sold to a new company.)

- A **bankruptcy indication that does not include the chapter** of the bankruptcy code that it was filed under **or its disposition.**

- **Inquiries that were not authorized** by you.

Section 611 of the FCRA does not provide a detailed definition of "inaccurate." Unfortunately, *if your dispute letter* (covered in the next chapter) *simply describes an item as being "inaccurate," you will likely not receive a helpful response from the CRA.* You should either describe the item with a simple "does not belong to me" or provide the detailed correction if the details are going to improve your score.

> Let's say a collection or charged-off item lists an account number that is incorrect or incomplete by one or two digits. If you write a letter explaining that there is an error with the account number, the CRA will not delete the account or change past due payments to current ones. Instead, **the CRA will likely change the account number for you, especially if you help it by providing a number you believe is the correct one.** If that particular account number is not the one you have on record, you are better off saying: "it's not my account."

EXAMPLE

Remember, an account can be considered "inaccurate" for many reasons. Be sure to **look for errors in all places, such as dates, balances, payment history and how the account is titled** (such as "joint").

FCRA Section 605

Section 605 of the FCRA is titled *"Requirements relating to information contained in consumer reports,"* and requires items and accounts that are obsolete (outdated) to be removed, as if they never existed. Fortunately, the FCRA is specific regarding the length of time an item becomes stale (musty and crusty) under the law. Adverse information *cannot stay on your report for more than seven years.* However, the FCRA allows a few **exceptions to this general rule.**

☆ Exceptions to the FCRA Seven-Year Rule:

- ◆ *Credit inquiries* of any kind cannot remain on your report for more than *two years.*

- ◆ *Bankruptcy dispositions* can stay on for *as long as 10 years*.

- ◆ *Unpaid tax liens* can stay on your report *indefinitely.*

In their own contracts with their source members, **the CRAs specifically include disclaimers warning their subscribers that they do not and cannot guarantee that the information contained in any consumer file is full or accurate**. And our guess is that they don't offer many refunds should a subscriber unwittingly rely on an error. Kind of similar to selling a car while stating that it can't be guaranteed it will run…

An excerpt of Section 605 is provided on the next four pages so you can review precisely what your rights are under the FCRA regarding obsolete information.

FCRA Section 605 Requirements Relating to Information Contained in Consumer Reports

(4)   *Limitation on redisclosure of medical information.* Any person that receives medical information pursuant to paragraph (1) or (3) shall not disclose such information to any other person, except as necessary to carry out the purpose for which the information was initially disclosed, or as otherwise permitted by statute, regulation, or order.

(5)   Regulations and Effective Date for Paragraph (2)

   (A)   *Regulations required.* Each Federal banking agency and the National Credit Union Administration shall, subject to paragraph (6) and after notice and opportunity for comment, prescribe regulations that permit transactions under paragraph (2) that are determined to be necessary and appropriate to protect legitimate operational, transactional, risk, consumer, and other needs (and which shall include permitting actions necessary for administrative verification purposes), consistent with the intent of paragraph (2) to restrict the use of medical information for inappropriate purposes.

   (B)   *Final regulations required.* The Federal banking agencies and the National Credit Union Administration shall issue the regulations required under subparagraph (A) in final form before the end of the 6-month period beginning on the date of enactment of the Fair and Accurate Credit Transactions Act of 2003.

(6) *Coordination with other laws.* No provision of this subsection shall be construed as altering, affecting, or superseding the applicability of any other provision of Federal law relating to medical confidentiality.

§ 605. Requirements relating to information contained in consumer reports   [15 U.S.C. §1681c]

(a) *Information excluded from consumer reports.* Except as authorized under subsection (b) of this section, no consumer reporting agency may make any consumer report containing any of the following items of information:

(1) Cases under title 11 [United States Code] or under the Bankruptcy Act that, from the date of entry of the order for relief or the date of adjudication, as the case may be, antedate the report by more than 10 years.

(2) Civil suits, civil judgments, and records of arrest that from date of entry, antedate the report by more than seven years or until the governing statute of limitations has expired, whichever is the longer period.

(3) Paid tax liens which, from date of payment, antedate the report by more than seven years.

(4) Accounts placed for collection or charged to profit and loss which antedate the report by more than seven years.[2]

---

[2] The reporting periods have been lengthened for certain adverse information pertaining to U.S. Government insured or guaranteed student loans, or pertaining to national direct student loans. See sections 430A(f) and 463(c)(3) of the Higher Education Act of 1965, 20 U.S.C. 1080a(f) and 20 U.S.C. 1087cc(c)(3), respectively.

FCRA Section 605 Requirements Relating to Information Contained in Consumer Reports

(5) Any other adverse item of information, other than records of convictions of crimes which antedates the report by more than seven years.[2]

(6) The name, address, and telephone number of any medical information furnisher that has notified the agency of its status, unless--

    (A)   such name, address, and telephone number are restricted or reported using codes that do not identify, or provide information sufficient to infer, the specific provider or the nature of such services, products, or devices to a person other than the consumer; or

    (B)   the report is being provided to an insurance company for a purpose relating to engaging in the business of insurance other than property and casualty insurance.

(b) *Exempted cases.* The provisions of paragraphs (1) through (5) of subsection (a) of this section are not applicable in the case of any consumer credit report to be used in connection with

    (1) a credit transaction involving, or which may reasonably be expected to involve, a principal amount of $150,000 or more;

    (2) the underwriting of life insurance involving, or which may reasonably be expected to involve, a face amount of $150,000 or more; or

    (3) the employment of any individual at an annual salary which equals, or which may reasonably be expected to equal $75,000, or more.

(c) Running of Reporting Period

    (1) *In general.* The 7-year period referred to in paragraphs (4) and (6)[3] of subsection (a) shall begin, with respect to any delinquent account that is placed for collection (internally or by referral to a third party, whichever is earlier), charged to profit and loss, or subjected to any similar action, upon the expiration of the 180-day period beginning on the date of the commencement of the delinquency which immediately preceded the collection activity, charge to profit and loss, or similar action.

    (2) *Effective date.* Paragraph (1) shall apply only to items of information added to the file of a consumer on or after the date that is 455 days after the date of enactment of the Consumer Credit Reporting Reform Act of 1996.

(d) Information Required to be Disclosed

    (1) *Title 11 information.* Any consumer reporting agency that furnishes a consumer report that contains information regarding any case involving the consumer that arises under title 11, United States Code, shall include in the report an

---

[3]This provision, added in September 1996, should read "paragraphs (4) and *(5)*...." Prior Section 605(a)(6) was amended and re-designated as Section 605(a)(5) in November 1998. The current Section 605(a)(6), added in December 2003 and now containing no reference to any 7-year period, is obviously inapplicable.

FCRA Section 605 Requirements Relating to Information Contained in Consumer Reports

identification of the chapter of such title 11 under which such case arises if provided by the source of the information. If any case arising or filed under title 11, United States Code, is withdrawn by the consumer before a final judgment, the consumer reporting agency shall include in the report that such case or filing was withdrawn upon receipt of documentation certifying such withdrawal.

(2) *Key factor in credit score information.* Any consumer reporting agency that furnishes a consumer report that contains any credit score or any other risk score or predictor on any consumer shall include in the report a clear and conspicuous statement that a key factor (as defined in section 609(f)(2)(B)) that adversely affected such score or predictor was the number of enquiries, if such a predictor was in fact a key factor that adversely affected such score. This paragraph shall not apply to a check services company, acting as such, which issues authorizations for the purpose of approving or processing negotiable instruments, electronic fund transfers, or similar methods of payments, but only to the extent that such company is engaged in such activities.

(e) *Indication of closure of account by consumer.* If a consumer reporting agency is notified pursuant to section 623(a)(4) [§ 1681s-2] that a credit account of a consumer was voluntarily closed by the consumer, the agency shall indicate that fact in any consumer report that includes information related to the account.

(f) *Indication of dispute by consumer.* If a consumer reporting agency is notified pursuant to section 623(a)(3) [§ 1681s-2] that information regarding a consumer who was furnished to the agency is disputed by the consumer, the agency shall indicate that fact in each consumer report that includes the disputed information.

(g) Truncation of Credit Card and Debit Card Numbers

(1) *In general.* Except as otherwise provided in this subsection, no person that accepts credit cards or debit cards for the transaction of business shall print more than the last 5 digits of the card number or the expiration date upon any receipt provided to the cardholder at the point of the sale or transaction.

(2) *Limitation.* This subsection shall apply only to receipts that are electronically printed, and shall not apply to transactions in which the sole means of recording a credit card or debit card account number is by handwriting or by an imprint or copy of the card.

(3) *Effective date.* This subsection shall become effective--

(A)   3 years after the date of enactment of this subsection, with respect to any cash register or other machine or device that electronically prints receipts for credit card or debit card transactions that is in use before January 1, 2005; and

(B)   1 year after the date of enactment of this subsection, with respect to any cash register or other machine or device that electronically prints receipts for credit card or debit card transactions that is first put into use on or after January 1, 2005.

(h) Notice of Discrepancy in Address

FCRA Section 605 Requirements Relating to Information Contained in Consumer Reports

(1) *In general.* If a person has requested a consumer report relating to a consumer from a consumer reporting agency described in section 603(p), the request includes an address for the consumer that substantially differs from the addresses in the file of the consumer, and the agency provides a consumer report in response to the request, the consumer reporting agency shall notify the requester of the existence of the discrepancy.

(2) Regulations

    (A) *Regulations required.* The Federal banking agencies, the National Credit Union Administration, and the Commission shall jointly, with respect to the entities that are subject to their respective enforcement authority under section 621, prescribe regulations providing guidance regarding reasonable policies and procedures that a user of a consumer report should employ when such user has received a notice of discrepancy under paragraph (1).

    (B) *Policies and procedures to be included.* The regulations prescribed under subparagraph (A) shall describe reasonable policies and procedures for use by a user of a consumer report--

        (i) to form a reasonable belief that the user knows the identity of the person to whom the consumer report pertains; and

        (ii) if the user establishes a continuing relationship with the consumer, and the user regularly and in the ordinary course of business furnishes information to the consumer reporting agency from which the notice of discrepancy pertaining to the consumer was obtained, to reconcile the address of the consumer with the consumer reporting agency by furnishing such address to such consumer reporting agency as part of information regularly furnished by the user for the period in which the relationship is established.

§ 605A. Identity theft prevention; fraud alerts and active duty alerts [15 U.S.C. §1681c-1]

(a) One-call Fraud Alerts

(1) *Initial alerts.* Upon the direct request of a consumer, or an individual acting on behalf of or as a personal representative of a consumer, who asserts in good faith a suspicion that the consumer has been or is about to become a victim of fraud or related crime, including identity theft, a consumer reporting agency described in section 603(p) that maintains a file on the consumer and has received appropriate proof of the identity of the requester shall--

    (A) include a fraud alert in the file of that consumer, and also provide that alert along with any credit score generated in using that file, for a period of not less than 90 days, beginning on the date of such request, unless the consumer or such representative requests that such fraud alert be removed before the end of such period, and the agency has received appropriate proof of the identity of the requester for such purpose; and

July 30, 2004   25

Outdated Negative Information

As you've just read in Section 605 of the FCRA, the law provides that, for most accounts and other items, negative information cannot stay on your report for more than seven years. This includes any *trade items, such as a revolving, installment or mortgage accounts.* For example, if you were late on your car loan eight years ago and have been current ever since, there should be no evidence of the fact that you were late – *as if it never happened*. So your next step in repairing your credit report is to look for negative items that are outdated.

The **CRAs are being paid by their client subscribers to report the information they submit to them** – and they would like for the information to stay on as long as possible. *With regard to your revolving and installment accounts, the law states that a CRA cannot report "adverse information" for more than seven years.* In the case of a *collection agency, the seven years start running from the earlier of the date the collection agency received the account or 180 days since you stopped making your payments to the original creditor.* In the case of a *debt that was charged-off, it's the month the creditor reported the account as a profit and loss on the books.*

The issue is whether these dates match up to what is being reported on your credit report. It's possible a collection agency started bothering you many months before deciding to let the CRAs know.

In today's computerized age, it would seem that CRAs could easily and accurately track stale information and update reports accordingly – **but just like all of their other incorrect data, it's no surprise that many items continue to linger for years after their expiration date.** *In order to fight for your rights regarding the removal of outdated information, you need to understand when the time period starts to run.* This time period is also known as the **"statute of limitations."** The statute of limitations **begins with the date of last activity on an account** (also referred to as the *DLA* on most credit reports).

The DLA is the last time any financial activity was reported on an account. For example, **the DLA for a credit card or loan would be the date the account was paid off or closed.** But remember, *your score is affected most by your payment history over the last 24 to 36 months* – and you don't want to remove accounts that are otherwise in good standing just because they are more than seven years old. **A list of stale items you would want to look for are provided below.**

★ Items You Should Dispute If They Are Outdated:

- ◆ **Accounts that were charged off**

- ◆ **Accounts that were placed for collection**

- ◆ **Bankruptcy**

- ◆ **Tax liens for that have been paid**

- ◆ **Judgments that have been paid**

- ◆ **Overdue child support that has been paid**

Although these various **DLAs** and time limits can be confusing, it is important to know that **outdated items are the easiest and quickest ones to have deleted from your credit report.** *This is because a CRA has the unilateral power to remove items it considers to be old as well.* **Even if the DLA is less than seven years old, many times the CRA doesn't even bother to send a verification letter to the creditor.** Instead, it simply removes it. Therefore, **if you believe the DLA of an account is more that seven years old** *(even though your credit file shows it as five years old),* **you have every right to initiate a dispute and hope that the CRA will remove it without bothering to send a verification letter to the creditor.**

You won't get anywhere by sending a lengthy letter to the CRA debating the date an account was converted from active to default to charged off, etc. Remember, *an account that was charged-off or sent to a collections cannot be brought current.* The best tactic to take is to **instruct the CRA that the date of last activity was more than seven years ago** – *period* – it's the CRA's job to investigate it.

Negative Items That Do Not Belong to You

Before you take advantage of your rights under the law and write a dispute letter as discussed in the next chapter, **there's one more thing you should review on your credit report.** While this may seem obvious, one of the very first things to do is *make sure the report you received actually belongs to you.* In addition to looking for accounts with negative information, you should also be *looking for accounts and items that you don't recognize.*

If you do find a pattern of odd accounts or personal information that does not belong to you (or anyone related to you, such as a spouse), you are likely looking at "foreign accounts" or "foreign information." The CRAs refer to this phenomenon as *"merging"* or *"overlapping."* In other words, your report has been blended with another consumer's credit file. If this ever happens to you, it's imperative that you get the correct information separated from your file, **even if the foreign account is current or paid off (and even if the other person's accounts are in better condition than yours!)** *It's the stranger's future payment record that may pose a problem.*

In this situation, **disputing each account individually may be futile.** *The best tactic to take here is to write the CRA and explain the erroneous merging of your credit history with a stranger's report.* **You may actually have to show the CRA (step-by-step) what the problem is.** For example, *make a copy of your credit report, highlight or circle all of the information that is not yours and include it with your dispute letter.*

CRAs are required by law to use **"reasonable procedures"** to **assure the greatest possible accuracy of information on your report.** But the interesting thing is that when they are processing your information as it is being reported to them by their source creditors, **they do not require any corroborating evidence of accuracy.** *So it's their responsibility to verify the information and update it.*

If you are not sure about the existence or condition of any account or item on your report, or if you simply want something verified, **it is your right under the law to require the CRAs to investigate it for you.** *So don't be afraid to ask!* **Chapter 7** discusses exactly how to go about exercising all of your rights (learned in this chapter) by writing a dispute letter.

Repairing Your Credit Report, Part II: The Dispute Letter

This Chapter Discusses:

★ **Verification Forms Used by CRAs**

★ **Fill-In Dispute Forms**

★ **Picking Your Battles**

★ **Writing Your Own Dispute Letter**

★ **Sample Dispute Letters**

★ **Sending Your Dispute Letter**

★ **What's Included in a CRAs Response to a Dispute**

Getting negative information removed from your credit report is the most important step to improving your score in the short term. As mentioned previously, **credit reporting agencies (CRAs) have absolutely no obligation to notify you if and when negative information has been reported about you.** Their only obligation when information comes to them is to use **"reasonable procedures to ensure accuracy."** *But the law does not provide any definitions for these procedures, such as a checklist of what needs to be done.* If the law were to require CRAs to verify every piece of information that comes to them, they would go out of business.

Verification Forms Used by CRAs

So the FCRA attempts to even the playing field for us through the dispute process. As it is, this process keeps the CRAs so busy that they tried to streamline it by designing and providing both their own dispute forms for consumers as well as their own verification forms for their source creditors.

Not surprisingly, verification forms are simple for creditors to complete and easy to return. Because the CRAs have only about 30 days to respond to your dispute, either to tell you that an item was corrected or that it was verified, *creditors have only a few weeks time to turn around the verification forms to the CRAs.* But guess what – not all source creditors return these forms within the time allotted, or at all. Consequently, many disputes result in the deletion or correction of items for this reason alone. **A copy of an actual verification form appears on the next page so you can see the manner in which this information is verified.**

CRA Verification Form

Consumer Dispute Verification

Control 33004985

Date 4/17/07   5/13/07

CREDIT REPORTING AGENCY
1234 FANTASY AVE
ANYTOWN, USA 886995904

Your Account Number:
To Comply with FCRA, please respond within 5 working days.
Name: JOHN DOE CONSUMER
Addr: 1234 MAKE BELIEVE WAY
ANYTOWN, USA 993840948
Prev:

SSN/DOB: 123456789
Spouse/SSN: JANE
Consumer States: Not Mine – Fraudulent Inquiry (D)

SAME
☐ Name:
☐ Addr:
☐ Prev:
☐ SSN/DOB:
☐ Spouse/SSN:

Please check the "SAME" box for each identification item appearing on the CDV which is identical to your records. Provide differing information in the shaded area.

Subscriber Name	Subscriber Code	Date Opened	Present Status / Balance Owing	Amount Past Due	High Credit	MOP Payment History 1-13 Months 14-25 Months	Type Acct & MOP ECOA
Credit Limit/Amount	Terms	Date Last Payment	Maximum Delinquency / Date / Amount	Maximum Delinquency / Amount / Date / MOP	High Credit Amount / MOP	Month Rev / 30 Day / 60 Day / 90 Day / Derog	
Type Loan	Balloon Payment/Date Due,Collateral,Sold To,Original Creditor	Account Condition/Payment Status	Status Date/Closed				
MAKE BELIEVE CREDITOR RENTAL AGREEMENT	UNK	INQUIRY			06/01/05		REN

Verified As Reported ☐
Consumer Claims ☐
Change Data As Shown ☐
Delete Account ☐

Reason for change/comments _____

Authorized Signature _____ Title _____ Date _____ Phone _____

**** NOTICE ****
In order to comply with the FCRA and maintain file integrity, we need your assistance. To avoid permanent deletion of this trade information, please complete and return this form immediately. Once this information is deleted, your tapes cannot reappend this data to our file.

When you sign this form, you certify that you have verified the accuracy of the entire item, and your computer and/or manual records will be adjusted to reflect changes noted above.

SAMPLE

Fill-In Dispute Forms

If you request your reports online, the CRAs usually provide a page where you can dispute items. This dispute screen will summarize your accounts and offer multiple choice dispute possibilities for each of them. An example of the type of descriptions you may choose from are listed below.

☆ An Example of a Multiple Choice Dispute Description:

[ ] The item/account is not mine.

[ ] The account status is incorrect (past due indications are incorrect).

[ ] The item/account is too old to be included on my report.

When you attempt to dispute an item using the online submission, *a note may pop up that asks if you are absolutely sure you really intend to dispute this item* and then requires you to click "yes" in order to proceed. This safeguard clause is more like a subtle message making you think that you may not be legally allowed to dispute an item that the CRAs see as correct or valid. **Don't let this intimidation tactic scare you.** Remember, *you have a legal right to dispute any item or information you believe to be inaccurate.*

If your reports are sent to you through the mail, one of the documents included in the package is a *dispute form.* The CRAs will suggest you complete this pre-typed form if you see anything inaccurate on your report. Again, these forms are pretty simplified and the CRAs' reasons for providing them are twofold: **First, they are getting credit for further promoting their compliance with the dispute process required by law; and, second, they are promoting their own forms for their own convenience.** With these forms, representatives are trained to quickly read and transfer the information on to their creditor verification forms. **It's OK to use the forms that come with your reports through the mail or online if your disputes are simple and there is a line or box to provide the precise issue you need resolved.** *However, many times there is not an appropriate space or enough choices to select from for all types of dispute issues you need to address.* And, with regard to the form sent to you through the mail, **be careful that you don't provide the CRAs with more personal information than they are entitled to** – just because they may ask for it. The bottom line is – *if these fill-in dispute forms are not ideal for your situation, then write your own letter.*

Picking Your Battles

Before you expel all of your energy on trivial matters, *use your common sense when picking certain battles,* because there are plenty of inaccuracies that will not have an impact on your credit rating.

For example, if you have collection accounts that need to be removed from your file, you shouldn't waste your time worrying about whether your report properly reflects your address as "Apartment # 01" instead of "Unit 1." Or if your name is actually Jon, but it's being reported as "John," "Johnny," "Jonathon" or "Jonathan" – you can deal with innocuous issues when you don't have any major pressing problems. By the way, statistics show that, **aside from using a middle initial, consumers claim they usually use only one form of their name when it comes to important or formal documents, such as credit applications.** So how the CRAs can claim they are only reporting what they've been told to report is a big mystery.

It's theorized that the portions of your credit report that don't affect your score are not scrutinized as carefully by the representatives at the CRAs – and this is likely due to the fact that their liability is not as great for these types of mistakes. So if your gut tells you to ignore something – go ahead – if you change your mind, you can always dispute it later on down the road.

So let's focus on the important personal information. **It's imperative that certain information be precise**, such as your **social security number (SSN)** and **date of birth (DOB).** *In the case where the CRAs provide "other" social security numbers associated with your identity, it can seem that you have a backup SSN for devious purposes.* Therefore, you need to instruct the CRAs to delete the incorrect one.

An incorrect DOB can also pose a problem if you're relying on your report for a loan, a job, or insurance coverage. In other words, if your report says you are 30 years older than you really are, there might be a delay in getting an approval because additional documentation will most likely be requested to verify your true age. **There have even been cases where a CRA erroneously reported that an applicant was deceased.** *Even though the applicant is right in front of them (alive and well) and all accounts are kept current, creditors become suspicious and will often suspend the processing of an application until the matter has been investigated.*

Writing Your Own Dispute Letter

If you choose to write your own letter, **once you have all of your items organized, be sure to include each dispute in one correspondence.** Don't worry if you have a lot to list, *you can arrange your letter in different ways and on multiple pages.*

For example, you can list each account in the left column and indicate in the right column what the problem is in a few words ("date of last activity more than seven years ago," "not my account," "never late/always paid on time," etc.). Or you can choose to describe your dispute first and then list the accounts that apply, such as "the following accounts do not belong to me..." *Whatever you do, keep it simple!*

It's best if you include all of your disputes in your initial letter. However, *if you do forget to include something in your first letter, then you should wait at least 30 days to send your second letter.* If the CRAs receive more than one correspondence from you (or a letter within a few days of an online dispute) before their verification process is complete, then you will actually provide them with an excuse to postpone their investigation of your initial disputes. And they will usually let you know that in a letter back to you explaining that their first investigation has been postponed because you added something new. **So just wait 30 days – and by then you** *should have also received your first corrected report.*

Sample Dispute Letters

Over the next several pages, there are **examples of four different types of dispute letters** that can be used to address the *most common inaccuracies encountered on your credit file.* For your convenience, **each of these letters has also been included on the enclosed CD-ROM** in a format that can be easily imported into most word processors, modified to accommodate your specific situation, and then printed in a final format. **Below is a list of the following letters found in this section...**

☆ The Four Types of Dispute Letters Provided on the Following Pages

- Dispute *an account that is not yours* or *has never been paid late*

- Dispute an account that is past the *seven-year date of last activity (DLA) limit*

- Dispute being listed as an *authorized user on someone else's account*

- Dispute an *inquiry that was not authorized* or *occurred more than two years ago*

Dispute an Account That Is Not Yours or Has Never Been Paid Late

Your Name
Your Address

Today's Date

Equifax-Experian-TransUnion
Address
Fax Number: *(if available)*

Re: My Name:
        My Social Security Number:
        My Date of Birth:
        My Current Address:

Dear Sir/Madam,

Please be advised you are reporting erroneous and incorrect information on my credit report, specifically as follows:

The following *item(s)/account(s)* do not belong to me, please remove them immediately as if they never existed:

Creditor/Item (as listed by you)   Account Number (as listed by you)

_____   _____

_____   _____

The following *item(s)/account(s)* were always current; I never paid them late. Please change the status to show current, timely payments:

Creditor/Item (as listed by you)   Account Number (as listed by you)

_____   _____

_____   _____

Please make these changes as soon as possible. I look forward to receiving a corrected report from you within the next 30 days.

Sincerely yours,

Signature
_____
Printed Name

Dispute an Account That Is Past the 7-Year Date of Last Activity Limit

Your Name
Your Address

Today's Date

Equifax-Experian-TransUnion
Address
Fax Number: *(if available)*

Re: My Name:
          My Social Security Number:
          My Date of Birth:
          My Current Address:

Dear Sir/Madam,

Please be advised you are reporting erroneous and incorrect information on my credit report, specifically as follows:

The date of last activity for the following *item(s)/account(s)* was more than 7 years ago, please remove them immediately as if they never existed:

Creditor/Item (as listed by you)   Account Number (as listed by you)

_____   _____

_____   _____

SAMPLE

Please delete these *item(s)/account(s)* as soon as possible. I look forward to receiving a corrected report from you within the next 30 days.

Sincerely yours,

Signature
_____
Printed Name

Dispute Being Listed as an Authorized User on Someone Else's Account

Your Name
Your Address

Today's Date

Equifax-Experian-TransUnion
Address
Fax Number: *(if available)*

Re: My Name:
        My Social Security Number:
        My Date of Birth:
        My Current Address:

Dear Sir/Madam,

It has come to my attention that my credit file with you shows me as an authorized user on an account that I am not an authorized user on. The original creditor has verified that I am not an authorized user on this account. The account you need to delete from my credit file as if it never existed is as follows:

Creditor/Item (as listed by you)	Account Number (as listed by you)
_____	_____
_____	_____

Please delete this account as soon as possible. I look forward to receiving a corrected report from you within the next 30 days.

Sincerely yours,

Signature

_____
Printed Name

Dispute an Inquiry That Was Not Authorized or Occurred More Than 2 Years Ago

Your Name
Your Address

Today's Date

Equifax-Experian-TransUnion
Address
Fax Number: *(if available)*

Re: My Name:
       My Social Security Number:
       My Date of Birth:
       My Current Address:

Dear Sir/Madam,

Please be advised you are reporting erroneous and incorrect information on my credit report, specifically as follows:

The following inquiries were not authorized by me, please remove them immediately as if they never existed:

Creditor / Person / Organization (as listed by you as an inquiry)

_____

_____

The following inquiries were made more than 2 years ago, please remove them immediately as if they never existed:

Creditor / Person / Organization (as listed by you as an inquiry)

_____

_____

Please delete these inquiries as soon as possible. I look forward to receiving a corrected report from you within the next 30 days.

Sincerely yours,

Signature

_____
Printed Name

SAMPLE

Sending Your Dispute Letter

When embarking on the task to correct your credit report, **it's important to correct the information with all three major CRAs.** Even if one or more of your reports does *not* include an error that appears on another, **it can't hurt to let all three know about the mistake you discovered.** *It may very well be that a particular error is a more recent mistake and has not reached all reports yet.*

Even if you have not had the chance to acquire all three of your credit reports, you should still send a dispute letter to all three CRAs. As a consumer, it's understandable that you would suppose that all CRAs would reflect similar if not identical information – *so there's nothing wrong in disputing a particular error with all of them.* **Once you begin the dispute process with one CRA, it shouldn't take you much more effort to dispute that same information with the other CRAs.** If a CRA can't locate such an error, it will send you back a letter thanking you for your request, but stating that its records simply do not include a particular item or indication to which you are referring.

Whether you draft your own dispute or use a form provided by a CRA, some credit repair experts recommend you always send your correspondences using *only* certified mail, return receipt requested. *This is sound advice.* However, overall, it's rare that a CRA claims it never received a letter. Worse case scenario: *If you must send the same letter again, then by all means, send it certified.* On the other hand, if you have *a more pressing legal issue*, such as *identity theft*, then **you may want** to *send all correspondence via certified mail.*

You can also contact the CRA by phone to see if your dispute was received. *When speaking to a CRA, just be sure you don't give the representative any information you don't want him or her to know or report about you.* The following is a list of phone numbers you can call to check on the status of your dispute letters...

★ The Big Three's Customer Service Numbers

♦ **Equifax:** (800) 685-1111

♦ **Experian:** (888) 397-3742

♦ **TransUnion:** (800) 916-8800

Once a CRA receives your dispute, it will usually send you **an interim response**, letting you know it received your letter and that it will send you an update as soon as the verification process is complete. Depending on how many accounts you've disputed and how fast the source creditors return the verification forms, *you may actually receive a response and updated credit report sooner than 30 days,* but you should allow up to a full 40 days. **If you don't receive a corrected report or any correspondence from the CRA within 40 days, then you can assume your dispute was not properly acknowledged and you should resend it.**

What's Included in a CRA's Response to a Dispute

Once you receive your updated reports, read through them carefully. *On the first or second page, there should be a paragraph that tells you about the information that was reinvestigated upon your request* – **underneath will be listed the accounts and the results of the reinvestigation.** This is where you'll encounter one or more of the three possible outcomes to the dispute process, and each of them is defined on the following page.

The Three Possible Outcomes of Disputed Items on Your Credit Report:

★ Deleted

The accounts that were **deleted** are just that: **removed as if they never existed**.

★ Verified - No Change

The accounts that were allegedly **verified and not changed** will reflect words such as **"verified, no change,"** in which case the accounts will continue being reported in the body of the report just as they were before.

★ Updated

The accounts that indicate they have been **"updated"** are **a little more confusing.** This could mean one of several things, including:

♦ *Late or past due indications were actually removed;*

♦ *The source creditor reviewed the account and made an adjustment so small or innocuous that you can't see any change on your report,* or;

♦ *The source creditor returned the form along with a submission on your file* (just as source creditors do once every few months anyway) to update your account. **Unless you see the adverse information removed** (i.e., late payments now showing as current), **don't go crazy trying to figure out how an account was "updated" because you might not be able to tell.** If it was not changed according to your specifications, send the CRA a follow-up letter.

Chapter 8

Repairing Your Credit Report, Part III:
When Things Don't Go Your Way

This Chapter Discusses:

★ **Sending a Second Dispute Letter**
★ **100-Word Consumer Statement**
★ **Speak to a Professional If Necessary**
★ **The Reality of Suing a Credit Reporting Agency**

After you've spent some time reviewing your credit report and have carefully worded your dispute letter to take care of everything with one stroke of your mighty pen, within a month or so, you should have received your first response. The chance is good that you will see corrections and deletions as you requested them. So now you can see how, with a little time and effort, this dispute process works to your advantage. But, be prepared - there's the likelihood that one or more of the credit reporting agencies (CRAs) will notify you in the same response package that an **item you were disputing was verified as accurate, in which case the particular item in question would remain on your report with no change**. *So what do you do now?*

Sending a Second Dispute Letter

When you receive your initial updated reports, don't be discouraged if the CRAs do not correct all of the items you asked them to. *Your next step is to write them again.* This time, *direct your letter to their attorney.*

If you can't find out the names of the attorneys who work for the CRAs, you'll just have to send your letter to the attention of their legal department. You can ask that the letter be given to a real attorney, but it's their legal assistants who actually read them. *Your main query to them is to ask why they removed or updated some of the inaccurate accounts you instructed them to, but not the others.* **And then kindly provide them with a list of the remaining inaccurate items.** You may actually receive a letter back from a representative who works in the legal department – but it won't be from one of the attorneys; **CRAs usually reserve those letters when responding to another attorney or federal authority.**

In this second letter, you also have the right to ask the CRA's legal department to send you some additional information.

☆ Three Things to Request When a Disputed Item Is Not Corrected

- ♦ **A copy of the completed verification form used**

- ♦ **The contact information for the creditor's representative who responded to the verification form including name, title and phone number**

- ♦ **A copy of the documents relied on as evidence of the debt**

A **sample letter for writing to their attorneys is provided on the next page** and also on the enclosed CD-ROM…

Second Dispute Letter When a CRA Refuses to Update Your Credit Report

(Outside of envelope must say: "Attn: Legal Dept." and highlight these words.)
Your Name
Your Address

Today's Date

Equifax-Experian-TransUnion
Address
Fax Number: *(if available)*

Attn: Legal Department

Re: My Name:
       My Social Security Number:
       My Date of Birth:
       My Current Address:

Dear Counselor,

Please be advised this is my second notification to you that you are reporting erroneous and incorrect information on my credit report. You have refused to make the necessary changes to correct my report. I now consider your actions and inactions as reckless and malicious. I demand that you make the following changes immediately, and forward me a copy of my corrected report as soon as possible.

Creditor / Item (as listed by you)	Account Number (as listed by you)	Correction Needed
_____	_____	_____
		_____
_____	_____	_____
		_____

Sincerely yours,

Signature

_____
Printed Name
cc: Federal Trade Commission
    Attorney General of *your state*
    Your Attorney's Name

> ***Keep fighting!*** Ironically, after receiving an initial response and updated report, some consumers are afraid to further "bother" the CRAs again – for fear they will be retaliated against and the information they already corrected will be reinstated – **Don't worry, *it won't be re-implanted for that reason alone*!**

Oftentimes, a second, stronger letter will get more results. But when CRAs continue to refuse to honor your requests to correct or delete information according to your directions, then they may try to appease you by **using your second letter as a "consumer statement."** What they'll do is include an entry alongside the item, such as: *"Account information disputed by consumer (Meets requirements of the Fair Credit Reporting Act)."* **But don't let this fool you –** *a notation that you dispute an account has absolutely no affect on your credit score.*

Unfortunately, **a third correspondence sent directly by you probably won't do much good** at that point. *The CRAs will likely send you a response letter using a firm tone explaining that they will no longer be reinvestigating the matter on your behalf because they now consider your requests to be "frivolous" and "irrelevant"* under the law and allude to the fact that you are now wasting their time. One recourse is to ask the Federal Trade Commission to intervene by explaining your plight, but getting results this way will take some time, usually several months. Another recourse is to hire an attorney.

> **If you need assistance and can't afford to hire an attorney, you can call the Federal Trade Commission toll-free: 1-877-FTC-HELP (1-877-382-4357).** You can also **visit the FTC online** at www.ftc.gov or mail a letter to:
>
> Federal Trade Commission
> 600 Pennsylvania Avenue, N.W.
> Washington, D.C. 20580

100-Word Consumer Statement

The law allows you to **include a "consumer statement" on your report of up to 100 words to explain your side of the story if your dispute is not resolved in your favor.** This provision is found in Section 611 of the Fair Credit Reporting Act (FCRA). **But the reality is *this statement is practically useless; it does not affect your credit rating*.** Nonetheless, many consumers are encouraged by the CRAs to add a statement, especially when they see you've tried in vain to have something updated on your report.

In essence, the 100-word statement is used by CRAs to appease you, as if they are affording you some rights as a consumer by "allowing" you to explain away a debt. It's up to you, but adding a consumer statement has rarely proven to be effective.

☆ Three Reasons Why Submitting a 100-Word Statement May Be Futile

- *A statement submitted by you in no way affects your credit score or your creditworthiness.*

- The chances of an existing or would-be creditor actually reading a 100-word dissertation from you are slim at best.

- You are better off explaining to a potential creditor or employer *in person* as to the reason why there are errors on your credit report (including the fact that you made several attempts to have an item deleted or corrected because you were in the right).

Now, adding a 100-word consumer statement is your legal right under the FCRA. So if you do decide to write a statement, make it brief; get your point across without whining or making up apparently ridiculous excuses that might further damage your credibility when applying for a loan or a job. There's nothing in the law that prohibits you from submitting a statement that simply reads: "I do *not* owe this debt." And **this will look more legitimate if used sparingly,** *not with every account listed on your file.* **It's best to explain away adverse information resulting from situations that were not necessarily within your control.** An example of these appears below.

★ Adverse Information Worth Explaining in Your Statement

- *Medical bills* that are showing as collection accounts because insurance has not covered them yet.

- A *bankruptcy* that was dismissed, but your debts were not discharged.

- **Severe account changes resulting from identity theft**, death, major medical problems or divorce.

One good place for a 100-word consumer statement is next to medical debt. Oftentimes, a medical visit or procedure that should have been covered by insurance is not paid because of a miscommunication (such as the use of another family member's name, or a social security number typo). So the insurance company does not pay the bill quickly enough, or you have to fight the company to pay it. As many consumers have learned, **hospitals and doctors send overdue bills to collection agencies within just a few weeks, and even when you are still an active patient at their facility!** *The good news is that when an insurance company eventually pays the bill, the law requires the collector to remove the account from your report.*

Speak to a Professional If Necessary

This book provides you with some important information on raising your credit score and knowing your legal rights regarding how your credit file is maintained. But even if you've done your best to resolve some issues on your own, *there are times when it's appropriate and even recommended to seek the assistance of an expert, such as an attorney, accountant or tax professional*.

In recent years, alternatives to licensed professionals have sprung up like mushrooms on cow manure – the so-called *do-it-yourself kits* and *legal document services.* Relying on a three-page kit or fly-by-night service to repair your credit is not how you should handle such an important part of your life. **You'd be better off investing your money and time educating yourself and/or seeking the help of an attorney.**

If you do keep running into a brick wall even after following the procedures in this *American Credit Repair* volume, and you feel your credit report rights have been violated, you may want to consider filing a lawsuit. The first step is to find a lawyer who has a lot of experience in the area of debtor/credit issues and/or consumer rights.

When it comes to consumer rights attorneys, they fall into two basic categories: *litigators* and *non-litigators*. **A litigator is an attorney who has many years of experience in the courtroom.** *A non-litigator (also known as a transactional attorney) is not usually in the courtroom very often*, either because the attorney prefers to settle matters before they get to court or he or she just doesn't have much experience handling trials. Either brand of attorney can start writing letters on your behalf. However, if you still don't get the results you need, you may have to take the CRA to court, and this is when you need to carefully consider an attorney's credentials, experience and reputation.

★ Three Tips to Know Before Hiring an Attorney

- From the moment you walk into the attorney's office, **pay attention to how the office is run.** *Is the staff friendly, helpful and professional? Or are they running around frantic, letting the phone ring off the hook or complaining under their breath?*

- During your initial consultation, **ask the attorney questions and see if he or she addresses all of your concerns and is realistic about the outcome of your case.** Keep in mind: There will always be pros and cons to bringing a lawsuit, and there's even a possibility you could lose and therefore be held responsible for the other side's costs expended to defend your suit.

- **Read through the attorney's retainer agreement carefully.** Take it home if you feel you need more time to peruse it. *If the attorney is not willing to provide you with a copy of the written fee agreement ahead of time, then you should interview another attorney.*

The Reality of Suing a Credit Reporting Agency

CRAs are frequently sued by consumers as well as federal authorities for violations of the FCRA. In order for a consumer to prevail in a suit against a CRA, the consumer usually has to demonstrate that the *CRA continually knowingly or negligently reported inaccurate information.*

☆ In Order to Prevail Against a CRA, You Must Prove the Following:

- **The CRA was repeatedly asked to correct erroneous information;**

- **The CRA was willfully noncompliant or negligent** (either the CRA ignored the requests or did not pay close attention to information that was clearly suspect);

- **Damages were suffered by the consumer due to the CRA's actions or inactions** (e.g., loss of money, time, wages, favorable interest rate); and

- **The suit was brought (filed) within two years of the violation.**

If you win your case, the FCRA says that **the CRA may be responsible for $1,000 in statutory (automatic) damages.** You may also be awarded actual damages, which include lost wages and court costs as well as some of (if not all) your attorney's fees.

Although it's rare, you can be awarded money based on an intentional infliction of emotional distress – which is not always easy to prove. In the case of willful misconduct, *it's even possible for a judge or jury to impose punitive damages, in an effort to punish a CRA for truly malicious or outrageous conduct.* You may have heard about such large monetary awards in the media – but they are extremely rare, and your attorney might advise you not to count on such damages.

Unfortunately, *lawsuits can take months and even years to run through the judicial system.* However, **a good attorney can at least offer you some means of damage control in the meantime** by writing letters on your behalf to your existing creditors, potential lenders and employers.

Chapter 9

Collection Agencies:
How to Deal with These Bad Guys

This Chapter Discusses:

★ **How a Collection Agency Operates**

★ **The Fair Debt Collection Practices Act (FDCPA)**

★ **Validation of the Alleged Debt**

★ **Drafting a Verification Request Letter**

★ **Stop Calling Me**

★ **Stop Calling My Employer**

★ **How to Settle with a Collection Agency**

Congress enacted a set of laws for the purpose of curbing abusive, deceptive, and unfair debt collection practices known as the Fair Debt Collection Practices Act (FDCPA). This chapter focuses exclusively on this law, because **it applies to *collection agencies*, not to original creditors or lenders.**

Overall, original creditors do not warrant the reputations earned by collection agents who tend to be egregiously abusive and deceptive with consumers. This chapter is intended for those of you **who are being harassed by collection agencies,** as well as for those of you **whose credit reports are being damaged by collection accounts.**

How a Collection Agency Operates

As most of us know, *creditors use collection agencies basically as hired guns – the bad-guy role is turned over to them when payments have been defaulted.* Original creditors will first use their **in-house collection department for a while (usually three to four months) in order to try to collect overdue payments from their customers.**

However, since most original creditors usually care about their reputations, it's often not cost effective to use their in-house staff to chase bad debts. *So once they realize it's not going to be quick or easy to collect past due payments, they will stop hounding you directly and get an outside collection agency to start harassing you instead.*

Collection agencies either work directly for an original creditor by earning a percentage of the money that finally gets paid through their efforts or they buy the debt outright (usually for a deep discount), in which case they keep all of the money they collect. *Either way, they make money only when you pay them.* Consequently, collection agencies will attempt to locate you using all means available to them. **With the age of the Internet, it's not difficult to find someone. In an effort to locate you, or to get you to return their calls, they will try to contact your** *employer, relatives, friends and neighbors.* And once they get your attention, they will try to embarrass, intimidate or scare you into paying them.

The Fair Debt Collection Practices Act (FDCPA)

In response to all the many abusive tactics practiced by collection agencies up until 1977, Congress passed the **Fair Debt Collection Practices Act (FDCPA)**. Among the many rights afforded consumers within this law is the right to be treated fairly by a debt collector. **Certain debt collection methods and activities are strictly prohibited.** Since it's important that consumers understand these rules, the **Federal Trade Commission** has published the brochure provided on the next four pages.

FTC Facts for Consumers Brochure: Fair Debt Collection

FTC Facts
For Consumers

focuson CREDIT

FEDERAL TRADE COMMISSION
FOR THE CONSUMER

www.ftc.gov ■ 1-877-ftc-help

March 1999

Fair Debt Collection

If you use credit cards, owe money on a personal loan, or are paying on a home mortgage, you are a "debtor." If you fall behind in repaying your creditors, or an error is made on your accounts, you may be contacted by a "debt collector."

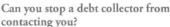

You should know that in either situation, the Fair Debt Collection Practices Act requires that debt collectors treat you fairly and prohibits certain methods of debt collection. Of course, the law does not erase any legitimate debt you owe.

This brochure answers commonly asked questions about your rights under the Fair Debt Collection Practices Act.

What debts are covered?
Personal, family, and household debts are covered under the Act. This includes money owed for the purchase of an automobile, for medical care, or for charge accounts.

Who is a debt collector?
A debt collector is any person who regularly collects debts owed to others. This includes attorneys who collect debts on a regular basis.

How may a debt collector contact you?
A collector may contact you in person, by mail, telephone, telegram, or fax. However, a debt collector may not contact you at inconvenient times or places, such as before 8 a.m. or after 9 p.m., unless you agree. A debt collector also may not contact you at work if the collector knows that your employer disapproves of such contacts.

Can you stop a debt collector from contacting you?
You can stop a debt collector from contacting you by writing a letter to the collector telling them to stop. Once the collector receives your letter, they may not contact you again except to say there will be no further contact or to notify you that the debt collector or the creditor intends to take some specific action. Please note, however, that sending such a letter to a collector does not make the debt go away if you actually owe it. You could still be sued by the debt collector or your original creditor.

FTC Facts for Consumers Brochure: Fair Debt Collection

2 FTC Facts For Consumers

May a debt collector contact anyone else about your debt?

If you have an attorney, the debt collector must contact the attorney, rather than you. If you do not have an attorney, a collector may contact other people, but only to find out where you live, what your phone number is, and where you work. Collectors usually are prohibited from contacting such third parties more than once. In most cases, the collector may not tell anyone other than you and your attorney that you owe money.

What must the debt collector tell you about the debt?

Within five days after you are first contacted, the collector must send you a written notice telling you the amount of money you owe; the name of the creditor to whom you owe the money; and what action to take if you believe you do not owe the money.

May a debt collector continue to contact you if you believe you do not owe money?

A collector may not contact you if, within 30 days after you receive the written notice, you send the collection agency a letter stating you do not owe money. However, a collector can renew collection activities if you are sent proof of the debt, such as a copy of a bill for the amount owed.

> *Debt collectors may not harass, oppress, or abuse you or any third parties they contact.*

What types of debt collection practices are prohibited?

Harassment. Debt collectors may not harass, oppress, or abuse you or any third parties they contact.

For example, debt collectors may not:

- use threats of violence or harm;

- publish a list of consumers who refuse to pay their debts (except to a credit bureau);

- use obscene or profane language; or repeatedly use the telephone to annoy someone.

False statements. Debt collectors may not use any false or misleading statements when collecting a debt. For example, debt collectors may not:

- falsely imply that they are attorneys or government representatives;

- falsely imply that you have committed a crime;

- falsely represent that they operate or work for a credit bureau;

- misrepresent the amount of your debt;

- indicate that papers being sent to you are legal forms when they are not; or

- indicate that papers being sent to you are not legal forms when they are.

FTC Facts for Consumers Brochure: Fair Debt Collection

FTC Facts For Consumers 3

Debt collectors also may not state that:
- you will be arrested if you do not pay your debt;
- they will seize, garnish, attach, or sell your property or wages, unless the collection agency or creditor intends to do so, and it is legal to do so; or
- actions, such as a lawsuit, will be taken against you, when such action legally may not be taken, or when they do not intend to take such action.

Debt collectors may not:
- give false credit information about you to anyone, including a credit bureau;
- send you anything that looks like an official document from a court or government agency when it is not; or
- use a false name.

Unfair practices. Debt collectors may not engage in unfair practices when they try to collect a debt. For example, collectors may not:
- collect any amount greater than your debt, unless your state law permits such a charge;
- deposit a post-dated check prematurely;
- use deception to make you accept collect calls or pay for telegrams;
- take or threaten to take your property unless this can be done legally; or
- contact you by postcard.

What control do you have over payment of debts?
If you owe more than one debt, any payment you make must be applied to the debt you indicate. A debt collector may not apply a payment to any debt you believe you do not owe.

You have the right to sue a collector in a state or federal court within one year from the date the law was violated.

What can you do if you believe a debt collector violated the law?
You have the right to sue a collector in a state or federal court within one year from the date the law was violated. If you win, you may recover money for the damages you suffered plus an additional amount up to $1,000. Court costs and attorney's fees also can be recovered. A group of people also may sue a debt collector and recover money for damages up to $500,000, or one percent of the collector's net worth, whichever is less.

Where can you report a debt collector for an alleged violation?
Report any problems you have with a debt collector to your state Attorney General's office and the Federal Trade Commission. Many states have their own debt collection laws, and your Attorney General's office can help you determine your rights.

FTC Facts for Consumers Brochure: Fair Debt Collection

4 FTC Facts For Consumers

The FTC works for the consumer to prevent fraudulent, deceptive, and unfair business practices in the marketplace and to provide information to help consumers spot, stop, and avoid them. To file a complaint or to get free information on consumer issues, visit ftc.gov or call toll-free, 1-877-FTC-HELP (1-877-382-4357); TTY: 1-866-653-4261. The FTC enters Internet, telemarketing, identity theft, and other fraud-related complaints into Consumer Sentinel, a secure, online database available to hundreds of civil and criminal law enforcement agencies in the U.S. and abroad.

Federal Trade Commission
Bureau of Consumer Protection
Office of Consumer and Business Education

| FOR THE CONSUMER | FEDERAL TRADE COMMISSION |
| WWW.FTC.GOV | 1-877-FTC-HELP |

Validation of the Alleged Debt

In addition to using abusive tactics, **collectors are also notorious for trying to collect more than they are entitled to** or *from the wrong consumer altogether.* Oftentimes, **their records are just plain unreliable** – due to the fact that collection accounts are bought and sold so often. So among the rights afforded consumers within the FDCPA is the right to have a debt verified for accuracy.

As discussed in **Chapter 7,** the process of **validating an account or item on your credit report** simply **requires the CRA to contact the source creditor and rely on a response from the creditor as to whether the account is accurate or not.** When dealing directly with a collection agency, the law under the FDCPA requires a slightly more involved validation process. And of course, **the consumer must initiate this validation procedure.**

The FDCPA requires you to put your request in writing within 30 days of receiving your first collection letter from an agency. The collector must then respond back to you in writing, showing that the debt is your responsibility and that it is entitled to collect the monies either on behalf of the creditor or as the new owner of the account. And *until the collector provides you with this evidence, it has to cease all collection activity.* **If the collector cannot validate the debt with at least some cursory evidence, it must permanently cease all attempts to collect the debt and remove all indications of the collection account from your credit report.**

If you receive a letter or phone call from an attorney or law firm trying to collect from you, there are two possible scenarios happening: Either **the debt was referred to the attorney to try to collect from you and he or she is in the role of any other collection agency** or **the attorney was hired to file suit against you if he or she is unable to immediately collect the debt.** *Under the FDCPA, until a lawyer hired by a creditor and/or collection agency actually sues you, he or she is considered a "collector" under the law and must follow most of the same rules a collection agency does.*

⭐ **Here Is an Excerpt from the FDCPA Regarding Validation of Debts**

> **FDCPA Section 809.** Validation of debts [15 USC 1692g] (b) If the consumer notifies the debt collector in writing within the thirty-day period described in subsection (a) that the debt, or any portion thereof, is disputed, or that the consumer requests the name and address of the original creditor, the debt collector shall cease collection of the debt, or any disputed portion thereof, until the debt collector obtains verification of the debt or any copy of a judgment, or the name and address of the original creditor, and a copy of such verification or judgment, or name and address of the original creditor, is mailed to the consumer by the debt collector.

If a collection agency proceeds to attempt to collect a debt it cannot verify, or if it does not remove the account from your credit report, it is in violation of the FDCPA – *which provides that the collection agency may be liable for statutory (automatic) damages to you up to $1,000.*

Even if a collection agency is not harassing you by phone or mail, **the FDCPA verification requirement is important to know if you have collection accounts on your credit reports.** Although a collection account, especially an old one, does not have as much weight with your credit score as compared to an original creditor in default or charged-off status, **the deletion of a collection account or two can raise your score several points.**

Drafting a Verification Request Letter

Whether your goal is to get the collection agency off your back or to have the account removed from your credit report, *you need to write a letter or two.*

The **Federal Trade Commission** has stated that **the mere itemization of an account** (such as information on a letterhead or a computer printout) **is not enough to show validation of a debt.** So you need to make it clear to the collector that you need more than just the collector's word that *the debt is legitimate and accurate.* **Therefore, you need to provide a request for the following information in your letter...**

The Three Items of Verification to Request from a Collection Agency:

✰ A Document Proving the Agency Is Entitled to Collect the Debt

This would be a buy/sell contract or assignment agreement between the original creditor and the collection agency – or between the previous collection agency and the latest one.

✰ Origination Documents

These are the original documents showing your signature on the credit card, loan application or agreement for services. **A copy of your contract with the original creditor** also establishes whether the account was legally assignable or transferable to another creditor or collection agency in the first place.

✰ Usage History

You are entitled to see some type of statement itemizing a credit card or medical bill *or payment history* for a loan.

Also ask for a copy of the agency's state and local licenses giving it authority to act as a collector in your state. Many times, an agency that is trying to collect from you is actually located in another state. **If it's not readily apparent where the collector is located, do some research on your own.** *If you discover the agency's office is out of state, include in your letter a request for a copy of its license to do business in your state.* **If it doesn't have one, your state laws may prohibit the agency from trying to collect from you –** *in which case, tell the agency that if it continues trying to collect from you, you will report it to your state authorities.*

State Licensing Requirements for Collection Agencies

Alabama	License Required
Alaska	License and Bond Required
Arizona	License and Bond Required
Arkansas	License and Bond Required
California	No License Required
Colorado	License and Bond Required
Connecticut	License and Bond Required
Delaware	License Required
District of Columbia	No License Required
Florida	License Required
Georgia	No License Required (Only a Bond Is Required)
Hawaii	License and Bond Required
Idaho	License and Bond Required
Illinois	License and Bond Required
Indiana	License and Bond Required
Iowa	License Required in Certain Instances
Kansas	No License Required (Certificate of Authority Required in Some Instances)
Kentucky	No License Required If Collection Agency Is Paid By Creditor, Not Debtor
Louisiana	No License Required
Maine	License and Bond Required
Maryland	License and Bond Required
Massachusetts	License and Bond Required
Michigan	License and Bond Required
Minnesota	License and Bond Required
Mississippi	No License Required (Certificate of Authority Required in Some Instances)
Missouri	No License Required (Certificate of Authority Required in Some Instances)

Montana	No License Required (Certificate of Authority Required in Some Instances)
Nebraska	License and Bond Required
Nevada	License and Bond Required
New Hampshire	No License Required (Certificate of Authority Required in Some Instances)
New Jersey	No License Required (Only a Bond Is Required)
New Mexico	License and Bond Required
New York	License and Bond Required Only in the City of Buffalo
North Carolina	License and Bond Required
North Dakota	License and Bond Required
Ohio	No License Required (Certificate of Authority Required in Some Instances)
Oklahoma	No License Required
Oregon	License and Bond Required (Out of State Agencies May Be Exempt)
Pennsylvania	No License Required (Certificate of Authority Required in Some Instances)
Rhode Island	No License Required (Certificate of Authority Required in Some Instances)
South Carolina	No License Required (Certificate of Authority Required in Some Instances)
South Dakota	No License Required (Certificate of Authority Required in Some Instances)
Tennessee	License and Bond Required
Texas	No License Required (Only a Bond Is Required)
Utah	No License Required (Only a Bond Is Required)
Vermont	No License Required
Virginia	No License Required (Certificate of Authority Required in Some Instances)
Washington	License and Bond Required
West Virginia	License and Bond Required
Wisconsin	License and Bond Required
Wyoming	License and Bond Required

When dealing directly with a collection agency, *if it doesn't already have your current address, you may not want it to have it.* In this case, **when you ask the agency to send you verification of the debt, you may want to consider providing a fax number, a post office box number or even a previous address from which your prior mail may still be forwarded.** If your mail is not being forwarded anymore, then **you can request the post office** *to forward your mail for another 30-90 days,* **giving you enough time to receive it. If the agency is nearby, you can go and pick up the copies of the documents it has on file for you** – but it stands to reason that you may not want to show up in person if you lose your confidence to present yourself without getting nervous or without giving out more information than you should.

Remember, if a collection agency cannot verify a debt, it is prohibited by law from doing any of the following...

★ **Collecting the Debt (including filing a lawsuit against you)**

★ **Contacting You About the Debt**

★ **Reporting the Debt to the CRAs**

Since a collection agency has **only 30 days to respond** to your verification request, *you should send one copy of your correspondence by way of a mail method that requires a signature upon receipt.* **If you don't hear back from the collector within 30 days of your letter, write again –** *immediately!* **Inform the agency that it has not provided you with the necessary documents as required by law and that it is in violation of the FDCPA** [specifically, section 809(b)]. **Demand that the agency cease all collection activities and remove the account from all three CRAs** *– as if it never existed.* For your reference, **a sample verification request letter is provided on the next page and also on the enclosed CD-ROM.**

Verification Request Letter

Your Name
Your Address

Today's Date

Collection Agency Name
Address
Fax Number: *(if available)*

Re: *My/Our* Name: *(include both spouses if appropriate)*
        Your Reference Number: *(try not to provide your social security number)*
        Alleged Original Creditor:
        Alleged Original Account Number:

Dear Sir/Madam,

It has come to *my/our* attention that you are attempting to collect monies for the alleged above-referenced matter. *I/We* do not recognize the account in question. Pursuant to the Fair Debt Collection Practices Act, *I/we* request verification of the debt including the following information:

Copies of all information regarding the above-referenced debt, including statements, reports, ledgers, correspondence, notes, origination documents (including any and all application and usage/activity signatures) and documents relating to any assignment of such account to and/or from any third party or parties. Please label all quantitative entries, such as, dates, payments, credits, finance charges, penalty fees, collection commissions, and attorney fees.

Also, please provide *me/us* with a complete description of your client's identity, including its full name, address, state and local license(s) and state and federal tax numbers.

Until you provide *me/us* with the above information, please cease all collection efforts and remove all indications of negative information regarding this matter from all credit reports.

Time is of the essence. *I/We* expect to receive these documents within the next 7 days.

Sincerely yours,

Signature

_____
Printed Name

Stop Calling Me

No matter what the results are of a verification process, or even if you never bothered to ask the collection agency for verification, **you have the right to tell it to stop calling you, *period.*** Section 805(c) of the FDCPA simply provides that *if you instruct a collection agency in writing to stop contacting you, it must stop everything (including letters).*

Once the agency receives your letter, the law **allows it to send you one more letter** in case it wants to tell you that it is agreeing to stop collection efforts, or it plans on using **legal remedies** to collect the money you owe, **such as filing a lawsuit against you** or **repossessing property used to secure the debt.**

A sample letter to assist you in getting a collection agency to stop calling you has been provided on the following page and on the **enclosed CD-ROM.**

Stop Calling Me Letter

Your Name
Your Address
My Telephone Number: _____

Today's Date

Collection Agency Name
Address
Fax Number: *(if available)*

Attn: Legal Department

Re: Alleged Original Creditor:
        Reference Number: _____   *(usually provided on collection letter – otherwise try to obtain an account or reference number when they call – use last four digits of your social security number if necessary)*

Dear Sir/Madam,

I have repeatedly asked you to stop calling me. Pursuant to the Fair Debt Collection Practices Act, each time you call me once I have asked you to stop, you are in violation of federal law.

If you call me again, you may be responsible for statutory damages, court costs and my attorney's fees.

Therefore, immediately remove my telephone number from your files. I trust you will not attempt to contact me, or anyone I know, again.

Sincerely yours,

Signature
_____

Printed Name
cc: Federal Trade Commission
    Attorney General for *your state*

Stop Calling My Employer

There is one more important provision in the FDCPA, Section 805(a)(3), that **prohibits a collection agency from calling your place of employment once you notify it that your employer prohibits such contact.** This directive does not have to be in writing – **the law allows you to simply tell the agency over the phone when it calls you at work.**

Now, *even though you're not required to notify the collection agency in writing, it's a good idea to go ahead and do it anyway.* This way you'll have documented proof of your attempt. The next page depicts a sample letter that will assist you in getting a collection agency to stop calling you at work. As always, a copy can also be found on the **enclosed CD-ROM.**

Stop Calling My Employer Letter

Your Name
Your Address
My Employer's Telephone Number: _____

Today's Date

Collection Agency Name
Address
Fax Number: *(if available)*

Attn: Legal Department

Re: Alleged Original Creditor:
        Reference Number: *(usually provided on collection letter – otherwise try to*
        obtain an account or reference number when they call –
        use last four digits of your social security number if
        necessary)

Dear Sir/Madam,

I have repeatedly asked you to stop contacting my employer. Pursuant to the Fair Debt
Collection Practices Act, each time you contact my employer once I have asked you to stop, you
are in violation of federal law.

If you contact my employer again, you may be responsible for statutory damages, court costs and
my attorney's fees.

Therefore, immediately remove my employer's telephone number from your files. I trust you
will not attempt to contact my employer, or anyone I know, again.

Sincerely yours,

Signature
_____
Printed Name
cc: Federal Trade Commission
     Attorney General for *your state*

SAMPLE

How to Settle with a Collection Agency

Even though you can require a collection agency to cease all contact with you, if it can verify the debt to you (and to the CRAs), **you may have to face the fact that the account is going to hang around on your report for a while.**

An effective way to have the account deleted from your credit file is to **negotiate its removal with the collector through** *settlement negotiations.* And **the older the account is, the more likely the collector will accept a less than full portion of the total debt amount.** You can even settle with a lawyer who has already sued you on behalf of a creditor (although you will probably pay a relatively higher portion of the total obligation if the creditor already has a judgment against you).

You can make your **offer to settle** an account **over the phone** or **by writing to the agency.** *Start with a reasonable offer.* Depending on the total amount of debt, an initial offer of a lump-sum payment of, say, somewhere between 20-30% of the total outstanding balance is a good place to start. *Never ask creditors to give you their offer first, otherwise you'll be bidding against yourself.* **Put in writing that you will send the settlement amount in exchange for the delinquency or collection account being removed from your credit report.**

Because they are paid on commission, representatives at the collector's office will want as much of the full amount as they can get. They might tell you that if you can pay the account in full, they will gladly update your report to show that the account has been paid in full. **Counter by telling them this is not good enough, you want the account completely deleted from your report, no matter what settlement amount you agree on.**

Their initial response is likely to tell you that they can't do that, and they might even say that they are legally forbidden to delete legitimate debts. *This is nonsense* – it's only their internal policy; **there is no law prohibiting them from deleting an account from your credit file.** Try to negotiate *directly with a supervisor* for the removal of the collection indication from your credit report, and *get it in writing.*

You can even ask them to tell the original creditor to remove the charge off or default indication from your credit report as well. Again, they'll give you a reason why they can't do this. They'll claim they don't have any influence over the original creditor. **Tell them you know that if their agency obtained the account directly from the creditor, they should have some power to get all indications of the account removed.**

The truth is that **it takes time** (and, hence, money) **for an account representative who works on commission to initiate the removal of the account from your credit file.** Again, if a representative won't guarantee the removal from your credit report, request to speak to a supervisor. **If the supervisor is just as stubborn and won't guarantee to remove the account from your credit report, then initiate your own dispute through the CRAs and ask the supervisor if he or she will at least be willing to ignore the verification forms that will arrive in a few weeks** – of course, this tactic will take **up to 45 days,** assuming the collection agency will stick to its end of the bargain.

If the collection agency *fails* to live up to its end of the bargain and does not remove an account from your credit report after you've paid it in full, you can also try disputing it sometime down the road – because *if an account is paid off, it's more likely the agency might ignore the CRA's verification letter.*

Granted, negotiating with a collection agency isn't the easiest thing in the world. So to further assist you, **a summary of some helpful hints have been provided.**

Helpful Hints for Negotiating with a Collection Agency:

★ Contact the Agency at the End of the Month

The best time to negotiate with a collection agency may be **a few days before the end of the month** in order for the agency to meet its commission quota – *and after the agency had your account for more than two to three months in its office.* Promise the agency that you can send the check overnight to be received by a certain date, such as the 30th or 31st.

★ Offer One Large Lump-Sum

Collection agencies want as much money upfront as possible. **Don't mess around with smaller installment payments.** Just *offer as much as you can afford to pay in exchange for having the agency remove the account from your credit file.*

★ Make Up a Good Story

Whatever lump-sum you can afford to make, **tell the collection agency it's the best you can do** *(i.e., you just lost your job, you're going into the hospital for major surgery and may not be able to revisit the issue for several weeks or you just got your tax refund and are tempted to spend it on something other than past due bills).*

★ Submit Your Offer in Writing

Although they never admit to this, **most collection agencies know what you want, but will not negotiate those types of terms verbally over the phone.** You see, *the secret backdoor can only be opened with a serious written offer.* So ask for a fax number or overnight mailing address to submit an offer in writing.

Now, instead of drafting your own letter, you can also try to ask the collector to send you a formal letter it has previously drafted. After all, it's not as if the agency hasn't done this a thousand times before. Just be sure to *read the letter carefully* – make certain everything is agreeable to you, including dates and amounts, and don't be afraid the let it know if you don't understand or agree with something. And if necessary, **ask the agency to re-write it.** Remember, it could care less about your credit report; it just wants to get paid and will do almost anything to collect some cash.

Caution! No matter what type of arrangements you make, *you should only pay a collection agency with a money order or certified funds* – as opposed to sending a personal check or making a credit card payment over the phone. **One of the most successful schemes used by collection agencies is to convince consumers to give them a checking account or credit card number over the phone so they can automatically deduct future payments.** An agency will claim that it won't be able to stop any legal action against you unless it receives your payment over the phone right away. *Don't fall for it!* If it has waited all this time to collect on your account, then it can wait another day for an overnight payment.

After you send in your payment, let a week or so go by and then **call the collection agency to make sure your arrangements were finalized.** You want to do two things: first, *make sure it received your payment and that it has been properly*

credited to the account. Second, *ask the agency to send you a* **"Release Letter."** It may tell you some excuse about how you need to wait 30 days to process your request, to make sure your check clears, etc., etc. But **keep calling the agency once a week until you receive it.** *Its letter should clearly spell out the fact that the debt in question has been paid in full and that you are no longer obligated on the account.* Keep this letter for your records in a safe place for the next several years…

To further help you with your negotiations, **five sample settlement letters have been provided on the following pages.** Each letter applies to a different type of payment arrangement, so please read them carefully. You can personalize and print originals from the **enclosed CD-ROM.**

Offer to Settle Less for Than You Owe (No Credit Report Removal)

(Before you use this letter - try to have them fax you an offer of 50% or better.)
Your Name
Your Address
My Fax No.: *** important ***

Today's Date

Collection Agency Name
Address
Fax Number: *(if available)*

Attn: Legal Department

Re: Settlement Offer :
              Alleged Original Creditor:
              Alleged Outstanding Balance:
              Reference Number: *(usually provided on collection letter – otherwise try*
                                                  to obtain an account or reference number when
                                                  they call – use last four digits of your social security
                                                  number if necessary)

Dear Collection Manager,

My attempts to resolve this debt matter with your office have been unsuccessful. This
account is in dispute and you have failed to provide me with all the documents I
requested.

As I am anxious to dispose of this entire matter as soon as possible, I am offering a one-
time, lump sum payment of $ _____ *(offer less than 50% or whatever amount you
can afford to mail today)* as a full and final settlement of this account. Payment will be
made in the form of a money order and sent to you via overnight mail. This payment will
be received in your office on or before ___*date*___ *(must be a Monday through Friday
to ensure overnight delivery)*. Of course this is conditioned upon your written approval
on your letterhead that you must fax to me on or before ___*date*___ *(must be two days
prior to the date you promised your payment is to be received)*.

In case this account was not sold, but assigned to you for the purposes of collection only,
I am also sending a copy of this letter to the alleged original creditor for their review.

Sincerely yours,

Signature

_____
Printed Name
cc: *original creditor*

Lump-Sum Payoff in Exchange for Removing Account from Credit Report

Your Name
Your Address

Today's Date

Creditor or Collection Agency Name
Address

Re: *My/Our* Name: *(include both spouses if appropriate)*
      Your Reference Number: *(try not to provide your social security number)*
      Original Creditor:
      Original Account Number:

Dear Sir/Madam,

Thank you for agreeing to settle the above-referenced account and to remove any and all derogatory information from all of the major credit bureaus including, but not limited to, Experian, Equifax and TransUnion. To that end, enclosed find *my/our check/money order* number _____ in the amount of $ _____ , as the total amount we agreed on to settle and finalize this account. As we discussed, and you agreed, this payment is to be received in your office no later than __date__.

(Try to get the creditor or collection agency to send/fax you a letter of settlement first.)
For your reference, enclosed please find a copy of your letter dated __date__ further reflecting this arrangement.

If this particular payment and/or terms cannot be accepted as part of our settlement arrangement, for any reason (including, but not limited to, information on the check is inaccurate and/or unacceptable, you did not receive this payment in accordance with our arrangement, or you received this check in error), please return the un-endorsed check to *me/us* as soon as possible. If the check is negotiated by you, and/or you do not return the check to *me/us* within 2 weeks of your receipt, *I/we* will presume this settlement arrangement is confirmed and further agreed to by you.

I/We anticipate this payment is accurate, and look forward to finalizing this arrangement.

Also, within the next 21 days, please send *me/us* a release on your letterhead confirming this account now has a zero balance and that the credit bureaus have been updated.

Sincerely yours,

Signature

_____
Printed Name

Lump-Sum Payoff for Less Than You Owe (No Credit Report Removal)

Your Name
Your Address

Today's Date

Creditor or Collection Agency Name
Address

Re: *My/Our* Name: *(include both spouses if appropriate)*
        Your Reference Number: *(try not to provide your social security number)*
        Original Creditor:
        Original Account Number:

Dear Sir/Madam,

Thank you for agreeing to settle the above-referenced account for an amount that is lower than the outstanding balance you have on record. To that end, enclosed find my *check/money order* number _____ in the amount of $ _____ , as the total amount we agreed on to settle and finalize this account. As we discussed, and you agreed, this payment is to be received in your office no later than __date__.

(Try to get the creditor or collection agency to send/fax you a letter of settlement first.)
For your reference, enclosed please find a copy of your letter dated __date__ further reflecting this arrangement.

If this particular payment cannot be accepted as part of our settlement arrangement for any reason (including, but not limited to, information on the check is inaccurate and/or unacceptable, you did not receive this payment in accordance with our arrangement, or you received this check in error), please return the un-endorsed check to *me/us* as soon as possible. If the check is negotiated by you, and/or you do not return the check to *me/us* within 2 weeks of your receipt, I will presume this settlement arrangement is confirmed and further agreed to by you.

I/We anticipate this payment is accurate, and look forward to finalizing this arrangement.

Also, within the next 21 days, please send *me/us* a release on your letterhead confirming this account now has a zero balance.

Sincerely yours,

Signature
_____
Printed Name

SAMPLE

Installment Payments to Settle Debt

(Send a copy of this letter with each payment you make.)

Your Name
Your Address

Today's Date

Creditor or Collection Agency Name
Address

Re: *My/Our* Name: *(include both spouses if appropriate)*
          Your Reference Number: *(try not to provide your social security number)*
          Original Creditor:
          Original Account Number:

Dear Sir/Madam,

Thank you for agreeing to settle the above-referenced account for an amount that is lower than the actual outstanding balance. As we discussed, and you agreed, *I/we* will send ___*how many*___ installment payments, specifically as follows:

        1. $ _____ by ___*date*___
        2. $ _____ by ___*date*___
        3. $ _____ by ___*date*___

for a total of $ _____ to be received in your office by the final date listed above. For your reference, *I/we* have enclosed a copy of your letter dated ___*date*___ further reflecting this arrangement. *(Try to get the creditor or collection agency to send a settlement letter first.)*

To that end, enclosed find *my/our first-second–third...final* installment in the form of a money order number _____ in the amount of $ _____ .

If this particular payment cannot be accepted as part of our settlement arrangement, for any reason (including, but not limited to, information on the money order is inaccurate and/or unacceptable, you did not receive this payment in accordance with our arrangement, or you received this money order in error), please return the un-endorsed money order to *me/us* as soon as possible. If you cash the check, and/or you do not return the check to *me/us* within 2 weeks of your receipt, *I/we* will presume this settlement arrangement is confirmed and further agreed to by you.

Include with final instalment letter only: Also, within the next 21 days, please send *me/us* a release on your letterhead confirming this account now has a zero balance and that you have removed all indications of it from *my/our* credit reports.

Sincerely yours,

Signature
_____
Printed Name

SAMPLE

Verify the Debt Has Been Paid Off

Your Name
Your Address

Today's Date

Collection Agency
Address
Fax Number: *(if available)*

Attn: Legal Department

Re: *My/Our* Name: *(include both spouses if appropriate)*
        Your Reference Number: *(try not to provide your social security number)*
        Original Creditor:
        Original Account Number:

Dear Sir/Madam,

On or about __date__ *I/we* sent in our *final/one-time* payment to settle the above-referenced account in accordance with the terms we discussed and agreed upon. *My/Our* payment *was in the form of a money order/our check has since cleared the bank* and *I/we* have waited more than 21 days to receive a Formal Release from your company. *I/We am/are* enclosing a copy of *my/our* previous correspondence.

Accordingly, within the next 5 days, please send *me/us* a Letter of Satisfaction on your letterhead releasing *me/us* from any further obligation on this account. Also, as you agreed, please make sure this account has been removed from *my/our* credit reports, and send *me/us* verification of that as well.

Sincerely yours,

Signature

_____
Printed Name
cc: Federal Trade Commission

Chapter 10

How to Deal with Secured Accounts:
Plus Student Loans & Tax Liens

This Chapter Discusses:

★ **Repossession**
★ **Foreclosure**
★ **Student Loans**
★ **Tax Liens**

As Americans, many of us are accustomed to the finer things in life: cars, homes, formal educations and an occasional tax refund check. Unfortunately, *if you can't keep up your end of the bargain as a consumer, you may lose the right to retain some of these finer things,* finding yourself in a situation where you can no longer take these possessions for granted. **This chapter explains exactly how to deal with some of life's most difficult financial situations including repossession, foreclosure, student loans and tax liens.**

Repossession

If you are late on your payments for a vehicle or boat, you take the chance of having your ride repossessed. *Once you miss a payment* the lender will send you notice of your past due amount, along with all the interest and fees you are accruing. Unfortunately, **there's really little benefit to ignoring them because they won't wait around much longer for you to make a payment.** So you have two realistic options to choose from.

The Two Options for Dealing with a Repossession:

★ Call Your Lender

Your finance company may accept partial payments for a time period, or it may have a program where you can have one or two months' worth of obligation transferred to the end of the loan. So call and ask!

★ Consider Voluntary Repossession

If you receive a warning and you know you cannot make good on your payments, you need to face the fact that your vehicle will be repossessed in the near future. *In this case, you can consider voluntary repossession.* **Gather your courage and make a call to the creditor, indicating where and when you'll have the vehicle and keys available.** The **benefit of this** is simply *to avoid the embarrassment* of having the creditor's goons track you down *and take your vehicle before you've removed your personal belongings.*

Sadly, even if you have your vehicle voluntarily repossessed, *it* **is still indicated on your credit report as a form of repossession** – *and your score will be hit just as hard* as if the goons had to chase you. And regardless whether your repo is voluntary or involuntary, **you may still be financially obligated to the lender.** You'll know exactly how much after your lender sells your car, which it usually does, at a public auction. You can actually show up and compete with the others in attendance who are bidding on your car. Of course this is not practical for most consumers because you have to come up with the price in cash – even though someone is probably getting a pretty good deal. The deal is so good that **the lender usually does not recover the full outstanding amount, which is now compounded with fees, interest, towing, storage and auction expenses.** The *difference between the sale price and the debt you now owe* is often referred to as a *"deficiency balance."* **(You can also owe a deficiency balance if you had leased the vehicle.)** Your lender might then send you a friendly notice of this revised outstanding amount. But more than likely, a not-so-friendly collection agency will now be contacting you.

Now, if you think you will be able to redeem yourself days before the tow truck actually arrives, *most lenders have some kind of internal policy to help you out.* For example, they might excuse a month's payment by extending the length of your loan by one more month (for example if you had a 60-month loan, and two payments were deferred, the loan may be extended to 62 months). **Give them a call.** *If they approve your request, they will likely do so in writing and mail you a letter with a new contract for you to sign and/or a new loan coupon book.* **You are more apt to get approval for such an arrangement if you can convey your financial problems to your lender before your delinquency is too far gone.**

Just remember, as obvious as this may sound, *this is a secured debt* – if you become delinquent by 60 days or more, your chance increases that you won't find your car in the driveway the next morning. Repossession is a possible consequence for any secured debt. *Creditors are legally allowed to confiscate personal property you use as collateral for any debt.*

As far as your credit report is concerned, *don't just skip over the part about your repossession just because you don't want to face it anymore.* Start by **looking at the balance that's showing.** Because of all the **alleged costs added and subtracted** from the loan, **there's a good chance that the balance on your credit report is not the same balance the collection agency is trying to collect from you or the actual balance that legally remains –** *and it may vary by several thousands of dollars!*

If this is the case, it may be inaccurate and you should **dispute this item with the credit reporting agencies directly.** As with any collection matter – if the creditor no longer has an account as an active issue, the chances of it being able to locate all the necessary documents in order to verify the debt lessens as time goes by.

Foreclosure

Depending on the state where you live, having your home foreclosed on can happen in as little as a few weeks following delinquent mortgage payments. *So don't fool around.* If you are late at this very moment on your mortgage, even by just a few weeks, you should put down this book and go out and get yourself a copy of *American Foreclosure.* That volume is an invaluable tool if you find yourself nearing foreclosure when it's suddenly important to learn **"Everything U Need to Know…"**

When you begin missing payments on your mortgage, your first objective is to review your entire financial situation. As basic as this sounds, *you need to establish your priorities.* **Take the time to carefully and accurately list your monthly financial responsibilities.**

Understandably, many homeowners have a tendency to keep up with their smaller bills instead of their larger ones, simply because it's easier and provides a sense of accomplishment to have at least some bills paid. That's great, but *would you rather lose your cell phone or your house?* Your entire mortgage payment should be a top priority (second only to food and healthcare). And unfortunately, **it's pointless to even consider making a partial payment unless you can convince your mortgage lender to agree (in writing) to accept less than what is owed.** *Otherwise, if your payment is short by as little as $1, your lender will have the right to consider the loan to be in default which brings you one step closer to foreclosure.*

As discussed in further detail in *American Foreclosure*, **the foreclosure process and time frames vary from state to state.** But *most steps are basic.* **Once you miss a payment, your lender will surely send you a reminder of your missing payment** and compute your late fees to date. **If you can't bring your mortgage current within a few more weeks, your lender will soon instruct you that your account is slated for foreclosure proceedings.**

At this point, it's likely the lender will refuse to accept payments in the form of personal checks. **You may only be able to "cure" the default and reinstate the loan by sending certified funds for the *entire* past due amount. If you are unable to accomplish this, then the next process is for the lender to file a document with the court and apply for an order to sell your house at an auction.**

When a home is secured with a ***deed of trust*** (as opposed to a mortgage), as allowed by some states, ***the foreclosure process moves much faster*** – because your lender does not have to go through the many hoops of a court proceeding; **deeds of trust allow for a non-judicial process that does not involve a court.**

Once your lender commences foreclosure proceedings, it will usually publish a notice of sale in your local newspaper. Up until the time the lender actually sells your house, you have a chance to convince the lender to reinstate your loan. But *to accomplish this at this point really takes a miracle as mentioned above – still it can be done!*

The final step is when the lender "accelerates" your loan. *The only way to recover your home at this point is to pay the entire mortgage balance and within just a few short days, if not sooner!*

One way to get out of this situation is to sell your house fast. **The trick here is to advertise the home for sale, show it to prospective buyers, accept an offer and finalize the sale** (at a "closing") **all before your home is auctioned off to the highest bidder to someone other than you.**

Student Loans

Student loans are in a class of their own. Many students don't realize how much grief it's possible to encounter later on in life because they took out a few student loans years ago when they were much younger and carefree. **There are many professionals out there who are still paying off student loans 30 plus years since receiving their fancy degrees.**

A higher education is certainly a good thing. And America has put much effort into promoting education to its citizens and **affording them all an equal opportunity to attend college.** *Many attendees figure they're going to get that great job and, hence, the money to re-pay the student loans from the proverbial "bucket" of riches they'll make.* Unfortunately, after four years of undergraduate and then graduate school (or other specialized training), the debt can become overwhelming – especially if you took out loans for living expenses as well.

The first thing you need to decipher regarding student loans is the *type* **of student loan it is.** *Loans provided for technical or other specialty schools are often financed by the school directly* **– in which case, you may be able to treat these debts like any other revolving debt or personal loan, and negotiate them or even include them in bankruptcy.** *But these are not the loans referred to here.* Even if your loan appears to be sponsored by one of the more popular, well-known private banking institutions, *more than likely the loan is insured by the federal government.* And the government has had to come up with a fine balance of lending and collecting.

In all fairness to the federal student loan programs, they do try to give all borrowers as many breaks as they need in an effort to help them get to the point where they can pay the loans off. *If you do fall behind in your payments, it's really a shame if you don't communicate with your lenders.* **They offer several respite methods you can often benefit from no matter how long you've been out of school, such as a reduced payment arrangement, forbearance or deferment.** *Many times, you simply have to notify their office that you are having difficulty making your payments, and they will actually walk you through the options available to you.* It's even possible to have your loan or loans brought current from a collection status. **It's when you ignore your lenders or collectors** (and usually after a long period of time) **that they will get impatient with you and use their muscle.**

Once you default on a student loan, it may stay with the loan department for a while (up to several months or years), **or it may go to a collection agency or it may be turned over to a litigation attorney.** This all really depends on **how much you owe**, **how far past due you are** and **what the records reveal about your efforts to communicate with the original lender or subsequent collector.**

One important fact to understand is that IRS can get involved at any time. Because of its omnipotence (and the simple fact that it is a part of the same system as the federal loan insurers), *the IRS can stronghold any and all tax return refunds you may be entitled to until the debt is paid in full, including additional interest, fees and penalties.*

If you know ahead of time that the IRS is going to keep any tax return refunds, or it has already done so in the past and you still have a balance on your student loan accounts, **you can keep more money in your pocket by asking your employer to increase your number of exemptions.** Your employer will ask you to complete a new W-4 Form, but *you do not have to provide an explanation for the increase.* **It may be a good idea to ask your accountant or tax advisor to help you calculate the precise number of exemptions you'll need** to bring you close to flush on your tax return so that you owe a few dollars each year, instead of having a large refund that you are never going to see.

TIP

If you do get your student loan account deferred, **it's important to know how the account is being reported on your credit files.** If the account is **reported as a default,** but it is now in a **forebearance or deferment status**, *you need to let the CRAs know that by* **using a dispute letter.** And remember, **don't give the CRAs**

any extra information that might just confuse them. ***Simply tell them in your letter:*** "My student loan account number *** is not in default – it is in a deferment status. Please correct this indication and mail me a copy of my updated credit report within 30 days... Thank you."

If you need further assistance regarding your student loans, **contact the Federal Student Aid Information Center** at: **(800) 433-3243.** ***Don't be afraid to call!***

Tax Liens

As mentioned earlier, **taxes are one of those things that don't show up on your credit report until they are in a delinquent status and/or until a lien has been filed against you.**

If you are behind in your federal taxes, whether personal or business, there's a good chance the IRS is after you. And if the IRS is one of several debt issues you are facing, **you should consider putting it on the top of your list** – *and start dealing with it as soon as possible!* **While other creditors can make your life miserable, *the IRS can completely wipe you out and for a long time to come.***

Even if you are able to pay an outstanding tax obligation, the law allows it to remain on your report for seven more years. And an unpaid tax lien can stay on your report infinity – literally, for as long as you live – and maybe even after that. But what is even more disconcerting is that **the IRS has a right to affect many, many aspects of your life and the first way they begin is by filing a lien against something you own so they can levy it if necessary.**

A *lien* **represents the** *security* **for a tax debt and the action used to** *seize* **your property in order to partially or fully satisfy the lien is called a** *levy.* ***If there is an IRS lien being reported on your credit file, it's because they have already put a lien on some property that you own, oftentimes your home*** – in which case your property is automatically encumbered and you cannot sell your home until the IRS is paid.

You can't even refinance or get a home equity loan to pay the IRS. Behind your current mortgage, *the IRS is now the next to be paid.* And in some circumstances, although rare, **the IRS *can* go as far as to force you to sell your home to pay it.**

Many aspects of your life are reachable by the IRS – including bank accounts, income, the cash value of life insurance, real estate, vehicles, money owed to you by others, inheritances, proceeds from lawsuits, social security benefits and even retirement accounts. And if you owe the IRS for business taxes, it can even ruin your chances of future income by **seizing your business bank accounts and business assets.** And, because the IRS is all powerful, it doesn't have to follow your state's laws you may think are protecting you. *There is no protection from the IRS.*

Similar to other creditors, you can enter into installment arrangements to get your taxes paid off. And *just like other collection accounts, you should have a plan.* Small token payments may only confuse things for you and the IRS. And don't sign anything just because the IRS or a representative asks you to – or because you think you are doing something that is necessarily going to help your situation. Start by getting a copy of a publication put out by the IRS called a **"Taxpayer Bill of Rights."** *If there is any doubt that you can realistically pay off the IRS without putting you or your family's security in jeopardy, contact an attorney or accountant immediately.* The money you spend for professional representation will be worth it.

A formal method of submitting a settlement offer to the IRS is called an "Offer in Compromise" (OIC). Because an OIC is **quite tedious** and **requires complete, accurate and truthful disclosure about several aspects of your financial life,** *it is a serious undertaking.* Therefore, it's best to hire an accountant or attorney who has a lot of experience in this area.

As far as how much it will cost you to hire a good accountant or attorney, it depends on whom you choose. **Make sure you know and understand the fee schedule before you hire him or her.** And if your head spins when you learn of the fee, **don't hesitate to ask for a reduction; the worst the accountant or attorney can say is "no."** *Just keep in mind: It may cost you more in interest, fees and penalties if you don't hire someone qualified to handle the IRS.*

Bankruptcy:
The Pros and Cons of Filing

This Chapter Discusses:

★ The Term "Bankruptcy"

★ Chapters 7, 11 and 13

★ Hiring a Bankruptcy Attorney

★ How Bankruptcy Affects Your Credit Report

This chapter is written as an overview of the workings of bankruptcy *and discusses the pros and cons of filing.* **If you are at the point where you've already been sued and you're facing wage garnishment or the seizure of your assets,** *contact a bankruptcy attorney immediately.* If for some reason you don't qualify to file, an attorney might be able to provide you with some valuable references or advice regarding options to handle your existing judgments.

The Term "Bankruptcy"

Several theories exist as to where the term **"bankruptcy"** originated. Some say it comes from two ancient Latin words: *bancus* (meaning **"bench"**), and *ruptus* (meaning **"broken"**). In Roman times, it was on a bench or table situated in public places where bankers conducted business. When a banker ran out of money, he would break his bench to notify the public that he was no longer in business. Its literal meaning is **"broken bench."**

Another story describes how creditors **would gather around a worker's bench** to divy up the assets of a delinquent debtor – and then **break his workbench as punishment and a warning to other debtors**. And still other versions claim the origin is French or Italian for **when a moneyman would run off with funds entrusted to him**, fleeing so quickly, he was unable to gather the base of his table that was secured to the ground, hence, **breaking it.**

Whatever the true origins, today *bankruptcy simply does not have the stigma it once did.* **Our attitudes, as well as our laws, have changed dramatically regarding bankruptcy and the rights of those who file.**

Chapters 7, 11 and 13

Bankruptcy matters are placed under federal jurisdiction by the United States Constitution (specifically **Article 1, Section 8**). And *bankruptcy cases are always filed in* United States Bankruptcy Court. But, **bankruptcy cases in many jurisdictions are affected by individual state guidelines,**

such as the definition of what constitutes exempt property (assets that don't have to be forfeited). Therefore, **the rules regarding bankruptcy cannot be generalized across America**; *you must look to your state's laws as well.*

Six types of bankruptcy exist under the **Federal Bankruptcy Code**. For the purposes of this book, *three of them will be mentioned – but only the most popular two used by the average consumer will be discussed at length.* The **legal categories of bankruptcies are identified as numbered chapters**, according to how they are listed in the code.

The Differences Between the Bankruptcy Chapters:

★ Chapter 7

A **Chapter 7** bankruptcy is also known as a *"liquidation"* and can be used by **individuals or businesses**. **A trustee is assigned by the court to "administer" the debtor's estate by selling non-exempt assets** (those that are not legally protected) *over a minimum amount* **and use the proceeds to satisfy creditor claims based on a priority schedule**. The net proceeds from the sale of assets are divided up *pro rata* among the creditors, and the remaining debt is forgiven. If the debtor has no unprotected assets, which is often the situation, the bankruptcy is often referred to as a *"no asset"* case. Once an account is discharged, creditors are forever barred from trying to collect the debt again. You can't include *alimony, child support, student loans, taxes* and *debt incurred to pay taxes* in a **Chapter 7 bankruptcy.**

<u>Note:</u> It has become **more difficult to file** for **Chapter 7** bankruptcy **since the implementation of the new rules** under the **Bankruptcy Abuse Prevention and Consumer Protection Act of 2005**. **Two of the main purposes** behind this act are to *(a) prevent folks from going bankrupt if they make too much money and are likely not budgeting it properly* (often having too much credit card debt and/or fast-cash-type of personal loans); and to *(b) remind consumers that there are other ways to deal with their debt that they may not have already thought of* – namely, **consumer credit counseling** (again, because **most of the time a person's financial turmoil is caused by the overuse of credit cards**).

 ## Chapter 11

Chapter 11 is a form of bankruptcy that *can be categorized as a "rehabilitation."* This chapter of the code is *primarily used by corporations and businesses in order to be afforded time to reorganize their situation* and eventually repay their creditors. **Sometimes, individuals use this chapter if they have substantial debts and assets.** To qualify, the secured debts must total more than $922,000 and the unsecured debts more than $307,000.

 ## Chapter 13

Chapter 13 is a form of *rehabilitation for individuals* who want to keep their assets and who have a regular source of income, because you will be *entering into a court-ordered repayment plan* that lasts **between three and five years**, and is based on several factors, including how you fit into a consumer financial index provided by the IRS. If, at anytime, you fail to comply with the court-ordered repayment plan, you risk losing the right to protect your assets under a Chapter 13 bankruptcy.

If you cannot qualify for approval under Chapter 7, you may be able to qualify under Chapter 13. *The benefit here is that you can usually keep your assets, including vehicles and, in some instances, your home.* **However, again, you must devote a portion of your future income to repay creditors** (and usually for between three and five years depending on the amount of disposable income available). Sometimes, a **Chapter 13** plan **may not require the repayment of general unsecured debt,** such as credit cards or medical bills.

Bankruptcy attorneys may not appreciate this, but **if you are on the fence about whether to file, you don't have to rush the issue,** at least at first. *You can file for bankruptcy at the eleventh hour (the last minute) if you need to.* Of course, there's a chance you'll be looking at higher attorneys' fees to accomplish a priority filing, but it can be done.

Hiring a Bankruptcy Attorney

The first step to filing bankruptcy is to hire an attorney – **one who concentrates in bankruptcy filings**. **The best way to find an attorney is through personal references,** which is not easy when you're not advertising to your friends that you are contemplating bankruptcy. **Other sources include your county or state bar association.**

Even before you decide to meet with an attorney, **prepare a list of all your creditors and accounts, and make copies of your last statements and collection letters**. **Your attorney may require more physical documentation from you, but this should get you started**. And, while this may seem obvious, you should set aside some money to cover your legal fees (not just for your attorney, but also for your court filing fees). Even though an attorney usually prefers to discuss his or her fees in person, you should at least ask ahead of time for a ballpark figure.

How Bankruptcy Affects Your Credit Report

After your bankruptcy case is finalized, your credit file should eventually be updated to report the bankruptcy outcome as one of the following...

The Three Possible Outcomes of Bankruptcy:

 **Discharged**

This is what unsecured creditors don't want to hear. **A "discharge" is a court order finalizing the bankruptcy** – forgiving all debts in a Chapter 7 and rescheduling those in a Chapter 13. Since *debts for alimony, child support, student loans and taxes are not forgiven,* they may still be pursued by collecting authorities. *A discharged bankruptcy can remain on your credit report for up to 10 years.*

★ Dismissed

This is when **the court dismisses your case because you did not qualify for bankruptcy protection.** In this instance, you remain responsible for the debts you tried to include and can be subject to the collection efforts of your creditors. And if that isn't bad enough, **a dismissed bankruptcy can stay on your report for up to seven years** (similar to your revolving or contract debts).

★ Withdrawn

Plain and simple – **you changed your mind and no longer want to file for bankruptcy protection.** *The problem is that even though you changed your mind, the filing still occurred, so this remark will continue to stay on your credit report for seven years* instead of the maximum 10 years allowed for discharged bankruptcies.

If you do decide that bankruptcy is the best option for you, **keep in mind that a bankruptcy can affect your credit score by as much as 200 points,** *and its last reported status can stay on your report for seven to ten years.* Fortunately, like any other adverse information, the more time that goes by, the less it will actually affect your score. And **as far as future credit goes, don't worry, you'll start receiving all kinds of credit offers in the mail before you know it** (they may not initially be the most favorable ones, but they'll eventually be there as well).

Chapter 12

Raising Your Credit Score in 10 Days:
Fast Fixes When Applying for a Mortgage

This Chapter Discusses:

★ **The Rapid Re-Score**
★ **Determining the Factors That Are Affecting Your Score**
★ **Assembling Your Evidence**
★ **Fast Fixes That Do Not Require Money**
★ **Fast Fixes That Require Money**

This chapter is serious. If you have just applied for a mortgage or haven't just yet, but need to and are in a mad rush, *this chapter will give you the fastest technique available for raising your credit score by as much as 100 points or more and in as few as 5 days* (but more realistically in fewer than 10). **The amount of the boost will vary based upon your personal situation, but these guerrilla tactics work and can actually be used when you are not applying for a mortgage. You would just have to wait a little longer to see the results** (usually 30 to 60 days).

Yes, these tactics are legal maneuvers, but are often unused by inexperienced (or unmotivated) loan officers. But don't worry; *now you'll know exactly what the last resort is and how you can take matters into your own hands.*

The Rapid Re-Score

This credit phenomenon is widely known in the mortgage industry as the **"rapid re-score."** However, the manner in which this technique must be used is unique to this *American Credit Repair* volume and it's EUNTK series counterpart, *American Mortgage.* This is because **most loan officers lack the extensive experience required to know how to legally manipulate your credit score.**

A *re-score* is *when you have evidence that data on your credit report has changed, and you present it to the credit reporting agencies (CRAs) to request an update with the goal of obtaining a recalculation of your credit score.* **The evidence is given directly to the CRAs by either the mortgage company or its third-party reseller**, from whom it obtains its credit reports.

All mortgage companies (e.g., bankers, brokers, lenders) have the ability to request a re-score. *The catch is that they have to pay for it at a cost of about $30 per item, per credit report. Since the chances are that all three credit reports will be used, it may cost $90 or so to request the re-score of just one item*, such as a credit card. But don't worry about your loan officer being deterred by the cost; **the fee will likely be passed on to you.** *So as long as you (or the lender) are willing to pay the re-score fee, you have a good shot at raising your score.*

Now, **this method is not as easy as simply saying I want a re-score** – *you are going to need to assemble your evidence of how the data on your report is incorrect and why it needs to be updated.* **This just takes some effort on your part and usually some money, which is well spent.** However, *there are a few techniques where no money is required to achieve positive results,* as you will soon discover…

This approach to raising your credit score will be broken down by the top items on your credit report – the ones that are most likely affecting your score. *Please read each one carefully and don't hesitate to throw in your own creativity and ingenuity, because no one knows your personal situation better than you.*

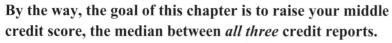

Determining the Factors That Are Affecting Your Score

Most loan officers should be willing to help you. After all, **they get paid only when the loan is funded,** so you shouldn't have to go at it alone. But just in case you do, *you'll know exactly how to proceed from this chapter.*

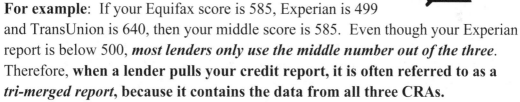

By the way, the goal of this chapter is to raise your middle credit score, the median between *all three* credit reports. For example: If your Equifax score is 585, Experian is 499 and TransUnion is 640, then your middle score is 585. Even though your Experian report is below 500, *most lenders only use the middle number out of the three*. Therefore, **when a lender pulls your credit report, it is often referred to as a *tri-merged report*, because it contains the data from all three CRAs.**

The important step here is to determine *why your score is low.* Fortunately, the *FACT Act requires the score factors* (those elements that make up your credit score) *be disclosed to you when applying for a mortgage.*

The most common types of factors that can affect your score are actually the obvious ones you may already be aware of…

☆ The Most Common Factors That Affect a Credit Score

- ♦ *Excessive Inquiries*

- ♦ *Credit Card Balances*

- ♦ *Late Payments*

- ♦ *Collection Accounts*

- ♦ *Public Records* (e.g., a bankruptcy, civil judgment or tax lien)

For the purposes of this chapter, public records will not be discussed – (although, if you are creative enough and have the time, you could try employing some of the same tactics to any civil judgment filings). Unfortunately, **the two other types of public records (bankruptcies and tax liens) cannot be addressed in a timely manner and are nearly impossible to do anything about days before a closing.** *But the other four score factors are quite manageable, so pay close attention to the remedies at hand.*

Assembling Your Evidence

Every tactic discussed in this chapter will require proof in order to get your credit file updated quickly – *and the only proof accepted is a letter or statement that has been issued by the creditor appearing on your credit report.*

In order to convince a CRA to rapidly update or correct erroneously reported information, a letter from the creditor should contain the following information...

☆ CRAs Usually Require the Following of Letters from Creditors:

- ♦ *Dated within the past 30 days*

- ♦ *Written on letterhead of creditor* with contact information

- ♦ *Accountholder's name and address*

- ♦ *Account number*

- ♦ *A specific and clearly stated reference to what information is to be updated on the credit report* (e.g. balance amount is $0)

- ♦ *Signature from the creditor's representative*

☆ CRAs Will Not Accept:

- *Copies of canceled checks or money order receipts*

- *Hand-written letters*

- *Letters without contact information or a date*

- *Divorce decree*

- *Paid receipts*

- *Third-party documentation*

By the way, **since time is of the essence, you will need to do your best to request the creditor to fax you.** If necessary, *try your best to get to the right person who will listen (and buy) your sob story* so your fax can be appropriately expedited through any internal red tape that may exist within the creditor's organization. We're talking an Oscar-caliber performance here; ya don't wanna come across as a "B" movie!

Fast Fixes That Do Not Require Money

Aside from the re-score fee itself (discussed in the first section of this chapter), *the tactics in this section will not require any additional money to be spent to raise your score.* However, these tactics may or may not give you the kind of boost you need. Nonetheless, *use everything at your disposal and don't get discouraged.* Each tactic has been broken down for you and should be *carefully* considered…

Options for Raising Your Credit Score Without Spending Money:

★ Excessive Inquiries

Any time your credit report is pulled because you allegedly applied for some extension of credit, your score will drop by as much as 5 points. So if you have 5 inquiries on file from various creditors, this could possibly be affecting your score by 25 points. **In order to help raise your score, you need to determine if any of these inquiries were legitimate –** *perhaps you didn't authorize some of them.*

The most efficient approach is to contact each of the companies that pulled your report and find out what reason they had for doing so. *In order to raise your credit score, you'll need to get a letter from someone within the company to attest to the fact that the inquiry was made in error and needs to be removed.* If you put up enough of a fuss, you may even be able to coax the creditor into helping you out even when the inquiry appears to be legitimate, but you were unaware at the time you were *granting* permission to pull your report. **Even if it's just one inquiry, every point in the right direction helps.**

★ Credit Card Balances

Credit card balances have a staggering impact on your credit score. **Even just a single dollar being reported – as opposed to a zero balance – can affect your creditworthiness.** So, here's the deal. Credit reports are usually behind by 30, 60 or even 90 days when reporting balances. *So if you know for a fact that your credit card balance is much lower than what is being reported on your credit report, you need to call your credit card company and get a letter faxed to you stating exactly what your balance is as of that day.* **You'd be surprised how much this could raise your score.**

★ Late Payments

You should contact any creditor that has reported your making a late payment. **A** *single* **30-day late payment on any account can have a serious negative impact on your score.** Now, it's a given you would automatically be hounding your creditor if an erroneous late payment was reported and you were never late. However, ***it's more likely that you did make a late payment and that's okay, because you still may be able to get it removed.*** **This tactic is especially effective when you've had a long relationship with your creditor** *and have not been late more than once or twice.*

Contact your creditor and admit your mistake by faxing a letter. If possible, ***call first*** and get the name of the person in charge of the finance or credit reporting department so you can personalize it. ***When drafting your letter,*** **be honest, direct and make yourself look as important as possible by printing it on letterhead with a professional title appearing under your name. You want to be sure to convey your continued pledge of customer loyalty in exchange for the company's assistance.** *While this tactic is not guaranteed to work, it has – many times before.*

In an effort to provide you with some encouragement, a **copy of an actual letter has been provided on the next page** – it was sent by facsimile to one of the largest automobile financing companies in America, requesting the removal of a late payment. ***On the page immediately following there is a copy of the creditor's actual response.***

A Copy of an Actual Letter Requesting the Removal of a Late Payment

SAMPLE

Date: August 1, 2007

Re: Account # 800-036-

Delivered by Facsimile to:

Attn:

Ms.

I recently discovered a 30-day late payment on my credit file for January 2007 being reported from ▉▉▉ Financial Services.

This may have been an oversight on my part to make a timely payment for that month. As you'll notice I have never been late at any other time for as long as I have had a relationship with your organization. If you check your records, you'll see that this is my second vehicle lease from ▉▉▉ and I plan to lease another one as soon as the current one expires. However, at this time, I am concerned that the January 2007 late payment may have a negative impact on my credit worthiness which could preclude me from receiving favorable financing offers in the future.

If you could kindly remove this derogatory remark, it would be a distinct pleasure for me to continue my commitment to your organization for many years to come.

Sincerely,

VP Marketing & Media Relations

A Copy of the Creditor's Response Agreeing to Remove the Late Payment

8/4/2007 8:07:39 AM   PAGE   2/002

08/04/07

   FL

Re: 800-036-

Dear

We recently received your correspondence regarding what you believe is incorrect or incomplete information on your credit report.

We have researched our records and have taken the following action with respect to how we report to the credit reporting agencies listed below:

An update has been sent to remove the delinquency indicator for January 2007. This account is now reporting closed as of June 2007, with a zero balance and the payment history as 0x30, 0x60 and 0x90.

We have updated our information with:

- TransUnion Corporation, P.O. Box 2000, 2 Baldwin Place, Chester, PA 19022 (800) 888-4213

- Equifax Credit Information Services, P.O.Box 740256, Atlanta, GA 30374 (800) 685-1111

- Experian, P.O. Box 2104, Allen, TX 75013 (888) 397-3742

- Innovis Consumer Assistance, P.O. Box 1358, Columbus, OH 43216-1358 (800) 540-2505

Should you have any additional questions or concerns, please contact us in writing at the above address.

Sincerely,

 Financial Services

DMS 308-01 (09/06)

★ Collection Accounts

The *only* **way to remove a collection account without paying them off first is to have evidence to present to the collection agency that the original creditor was paid.** Medical collections are probably the easiest to deal with if you can prove your insurance paid the claim. *Just be sure to take a firm but friendly approach when dealing with a collection agency.* Even though you may have the evidence and every law on your side, **the problem is that you can't afford to wait for the agency to update your report using its normal reporting methods** – which could take 30 to 60 days. *Your goal is to get the collection agency to fax you a letter as quickly as possible*, so you're going to have to work 'em a little bit again and try to win yourself another Oscar!

Fast Fixes That Require Money

If you have a little money to spend, the results attainable in this section far outweigh those that require no money. It's been said a million times before – cash is king. *You can buy your way out of almost anything.* Now, **this book does not suggest bribery** *(a little negotiating, perhaps, but nothing illegal!).* **Pay close attention and see for yourself** – *the end result is truly amazing!*

Options for Raising Your Credit Score When You Have Money to Spend:

★ Credit Card Balances

If you have anything but zero balances on your credit report, you need to pay them off – *and if your funds are limited, then you must allocate them accordingly:*

Pay off the smaller card balances first and then whatever is left, apply it to the larger balances. *Be sure you overnight your* *payment, make it over the phone or visit a local branch – do not use first class mail.* **If possible, it's best to visit a local branch** *and ask for an updated statement as soon as the payment is made* (or at least ask for a letter from one of the account representatives or assistant managers stating that the account now has a zero balance).

Don't let your credit card company stand behind some company policy excuse as to why it can't issue a letter or an updated statement. Just be sure to say that it is the only one holding up your mortgage from closing and that your four children, two dogs and goldfish won't have a place to live. **Any creditor can fulfill your request –** *just keep trying until you get hold of the right person.*

★ Collection Agencies

Here is where your money will really work for you. *Don't jump the gun, though* **– this is not as simple as you think.** *Not only do you want to pay the collection account off, but you also want the collection agency to remove the file completely as if it never existed.* That's because **having a zero balance on a collection account is nothing compared to having no collection account at all.**

*Don't worry***; the agency is hungry for money and will honor such a request the majority of the time.** So **for those of you who thought paying a collection account was a good step in the right direction, you were only** *half* **right – you** *need* **to get the agency to agree to remove any and all derogatory information in exchange for complete satisfaction of the outstanding debt.**

No collection agency will usually discuss or confirm such a request over the phone, so *you must contact it* **and ask for its fax number, so you can submit a written offer. A sample of such an offer appears on the following page, and** *a copy has also been provided on the enclosed CD-ROM.*

Lump Sum Payoff in Exchange for Removing Account from Credit Report

Your Name
Your Address

Today's Date

Creditor or Collection Agency Name
Address

Re: *My/Our* Name: *(include both spouses if appropriate)*
Your Reference Number: *(try not to provide your social security number)*
Original Creditor:
Original Account Number:

Dear Sir/Madam,

Thank you for agreeing to settle the above-referenced account and to remove any and all derogatory information from all of the major credit bureaus including, but not limited to, Experian, Equifax and TransUnion. To that end, enclosed find *my/our check/money order* number _____ in the amount of $ _____ , as the total amount we agreed on to settle and finalize this account. As we discussed, and you agreed, this payment is to be received in your office no later than ___date___ .

(Try to get the creditor or collection agency to send/fax you a letter of settlement first.)
For your reference, enclosed please find a copy of your letter dated ___date___ further reflecting this arrangement.

If this particular payment and/or terms cannot be accepted as part of our settlement arrangement, for any reason (including, but not limited to, information on the check is inaccurate and/or unacceptable, you did not receive this payment in accordance with our arrangement, or you received this check in error), please return the un-endorsed check to *me/us* as soon as possible. If the check is negotiated by you, and/or you do not return the check to *me/us* within 2 weeks of your receipt, *I/we* will presume this settlement arrangement is confirmed and further agreed to by you.

I/We anticipate this payment is accurate, and look forward to finalizing this arrangement.

Also, within the next 21 days, please send *me/us* a release on your letterhead confirming this account now has a zero balance and that the credit bureaus have been updated.

Sincerely yours,

Signature

_____
Printed Name

★ Late Payments

You can't buy your way out of previous late payments. **But if you are currently behind, contact the creditor to ask if it would agree to remove the most recent late payments – and re-age your account –** *in exchange for a large percentage of your outstanding balance*. At this point, it's always a good idea to hint about your thoughts of filing bankruptcy instead.

Unfortunately, the reality may be that if you were unable to pay the creditor in the first place, you probably wouldn't have the money now – but this tactic does work if you can afford to come up with the cash…

As mentioned earlier, public records are pretty much there to stay unless you have the time to fight them. So, *keep your focus on your creditors and collection accounts.* It will usually take only a couple of days to get a response (sometimes a few days longer) **to receive everything you need to have your loan officer submit all of the necessary documents for a re-score –** *which takes three to five days for the CRAs to respond to.* **Unfortunately, the rapid re-score service is usually offered** *only in connection with applying for a mortgage.* However, each of these tactics can still be used for raising your credit score. You just have to wait 30 to 60 days for the update to occur naturally.

Chapter 13

Marriage, Divorce and Credit:
Being Prepared

This Chapter Discusses:

★ **Before You Get Married**

★ **During the Marriage**

★ **Planning for the Divorce**

★ **How to Handle Your Accounts and Creditors**

As discussed earlier, **your credit score is based purely on data – *and nothing about your personal life should affect your score.*** Factors such as race, religion or nationality do not come into play. **Neither does your gender or marital status.** Nor does the divorce from a spouse directly change your credit score. However, *due to the nature of the loss of a spouse because of divorce or even death, there's a 90% chance that such a life-changing event will eventually negatively affect your consumer credit file!*

Many articles about debt issues discuss the "unlikely" event of divorce and how it can affect your credit. Well, the last we looked, divorce has not been an "unlikely" event for many years: **there's about a 50% chance that if you get married, you will get "un-married"** – *and adding in the untimely death of a spouse brings the unplanned separation statistic up to a staggering level.*

It's imprudent not to plan for one of these two occurrences; only the truly superstitious will avoid such planning, in the hope that ignoring it will mean that it will not happen.

Before You Get Married

Before you get married, while you are still in a blissful marriage engagement stage, **ask your loved one to sit down with you and review all of your current financial situations (including both of your credit reports) and to discuss your future expectations.**

If you have individual credit accounts or loans before you get married, consider keeping them in your own name. ***Don't cancel them and don't add your spouse's name to them; especially if you are working hard through your own efforts to maintain them*** (keeping them current). **If you ultimately divorce or lose a spouse, some day you may have to face some unexpected changes in your life such as having to obtain a new job, a new home or insurance soon after the event –** *and your individual credit rating is essential.* And remarkably, in today's credit-based society, you are regarded more highly in the eyes of a creditor when you have a lot of credit (even if some of it's bad), than someone who has no credit at all.

If you do add your spouse to an existing account, **he or she becomes an authorized user.** Although this is not a true joint account, *your spouse will benefit from the account as if the account were opened using both of your social security numbers.* And, although you should be able to just as easily remove your spouse's name from your account, it may take a few attempts from you.

Before you get married, you should give some thought to how you and your spouse will handle credit issues – *and a good place to start is with your current credit situations.* Look carefully at both your own and your prospective spouse's current credit ratings, and consider how best to preserve a good rating or fix a bad one. And **don't rule out postponing your marriage vows until a credit rating is improved;** *this may not be the romantic ideal, but it can be prudent.* **The best goal**

to have is for both spouses to have excellent ratings, *and the best way to achieve that is to be smart and to plan ahead*. A good tool for this purpose is a **prenuptial** or **antenuptial** agreement.

When most people think of a **prenuptial agreement** – after they get beyond the belief that it is anti-romantic – **they think about the preservation of assets and the limitation of alimony.** *Those are the traditional purposes of prenuptial agreements, but they are not the only benefits.*

Credit issues are fair game, and these days it is prudent to spell out how the couple will handle debt and credit during and at the conclusion of the marriage. Besides, *one's credit rating is an asset to be guarded and treasured just like any other.* A neglectful or malicious spouse can squander the asset of a good credit rating just as easily as a bank account, so **credit should be a principal concern of premarital planning and/or a prenuptial agreement.**

If you can't get past the unromantic nature of a formal prenuptial agreement, **at the very least, you should plan your use of credit in a manner that will preserve it as an asset of your own.** *The beauty of a credit rating as an asset is that it can't be distributed in a divorce.* It can thus be considered a *non-marital asset* that will always be yours, for better or worse. **So protect it, nurture it, and don't ever lose sight of the fact that it is yours now and forever.** If you intermingle your credit with your spouse's by opening joint accounts, you do so at your own peril, especially when his or her credit rating is below par. On the flipside, **if your spouse has an excellent score, then take advantage of it by opening joint accounts,** but keep a close eye on those accounts – because if finances begin to backslide, then your credit rating may suffer, and so will you. Creditors are not a party to your marriage or your divorce decree. *Once an account is joint, you cannot legally restrict one party from using it or require one party to become solely responsible for it.*

During the Marriage

Many spouses *(statistically, it's usually the women)* **don't think about getting involved in the family finances until it's too late.** While this may not be at the forefront of your mind when you are walking down the aisle, **the reality is that a divorce can cost you less in time, emotion and legal fees, if you are up-to-date on all of your family's debt and credit issues.** Therefore, *you should carefully and scrupulously involve yourself in your family's finances, or at the very least keep yourself informed.* This is especially true with volatile credit card accounts and their usage and payment patterns.

It is important to keep tabs on what accounts are out there – and which ones you are tied to as either a joint account holder or a person with signatory rights (authorized user). Keep an eye on the mail and ask questions of your spouse about the various account statements that come in. **Make sure that you know whether you have signatory or joint rights to any accounts, and if so, keep a close eye on the use of those accounts.** These days, the Internet has made it easier to follow accounts online, without tipping off or offending your spouse that you are doing so, so use that resource, especially when your spouse is secretive or reserved.

In fact, *an uncommunicative spouse should be a tip-off that something is up.* If your spouse suddenly becomes secretive, or otherwise will not keep you informed about finances, then your antenna should go up even higher. **That would be the time to gather information, and if secrecy is the order of the day, then the Internet can be a strong and powerful tool.**

So what should you be looking for? Don't immediately assume that your spouse is using a credit account to support a secret life or a paramour. Although that certainly is something that you might want to know about, with regard to your credit rating, the thing to be looking for is *increases in credit limits, slow payment history* or *non-payments*. Also **watch for the use of one credit card to pay off others**, as this is often a sign of financial difficulties. *Your spouse may not be doing something* *malicious.* **It may just be his or her embarrassment from losing a job or being involved in some other type of financial disaster that's keeping your spouse silent.** And it's in circumstances such as these that a marriage, through action or inaction, can be either broken or strengthened.

Mental or physical incapacity during a marriage can bring about the same financial nightmares that can test the strength of a relationship as surely as infidelity or fiscal irresponsibility. If you discover something that is being kept from you or threatens one or both of your credit ratings, *protecting your credit even in the worst of times can and should be done.* Just be careful on how you decide to approach your spouse about the situation. The last thing you want is to make matters worse by acting thoughtlessly.

Planning for the Divorce

Once you have determined that you are going to end your marriage, it's time to start planning. *The planning should begin immediately, because there's generally no benefit to waiting.* Even if you did not see the divorce coming and are blind-sided when the process server shows up at your door, **your first thought should be planning**.

This chapter focuses on the **credit-related aspects of planning your divorce,** with sincerest apologies to those of you seeking more advice on what to do when divorce looms. Obviously there are many other aspects of your divorce to concern yourself with, some of which – such as your children – are more important in the short run than your credit. You can read more about the process of divorce in the *American Divorce* volume.

There are **two professionals that you should contact immediately for advice** on planning your divorce, **an attorney** and a **Certified Divorce Financial Planner (CDFP).** The role of the attorney should be obvious. The role of the **CDFP** may be less known, as the CDFP is a relatively new profession recently gaining in popularity. *A CDFP is basically an accountant or financial planner who has decided to*

concentrate on the specific financial issues surrounding divorce. The expertise of the CDFP lies in being able to help individuals plan financially for the divorce and post-divorce periods. **A CDFP helps the spouse who has no prior knowledge of the family's finances become knowledgeable,** and also **helps the sophisticated spouse organize and better plan budgets and decide on appropriate divisions.**

A typical dilemma facing a divorcing person is **how to divide up all of the "stuff" – the tangible and intangible assets and debts**. A common scenario involves a family with two major assets, a home and a retirement account with roughly the same net value. Which one should you take? Should you sell the home? Refinance? Split the retirement account equally? A **CDFP** is **a good resource for these questions**, as he or she can help you determine what makes the most sense. **It may seem obvious that one spouse should take the home and the other the retirement account, but that's not always the case.** *Can the person taking the home afford to keep it up?* **Is there a difference in the values of the two investments beyond their dollar worth?** *Get the tools to answer these and similar questions from the proper professionals.*

How to Handle Your Accounts and Creditors

When it comes to credit in divorce planning, *knowledge is king.* This is the time to **familiarize yourself with the various credit accounts that you have opened as a family**. *You should determine what accounts exist and in whose name the accounts are held.* If you have signature privileges on an account owned by your spouse, you may already be liable on the debt as far as the creditor is concerned, so you should consider that account to be *joint*. Therefore, **it's wise to close all joint accounts and remove the other spouse from accounts in your name.** *This will eliminate the ability of the other spouse to incur additional debt for which you may be liable.* **The period of time from when the decision to get a divorce is made and the actual filing of the paperwork is a critical time for credit,** *because debt is often being accumulated as a spouse is planning an escape.* The spouse will purchase new clothes, furniture, cars, etc., and his or her *attorney's fees can be paid with joint accounts, too.* **Proper planning can prevent those situations from affecting you.**

An important step in preparing for a divorce is to pull up your credit report as soon as you can, and certainly before your divorce is finalized. *If your creditors and the reporting agencies are doing what they are supposed to be doing, your credit report should properly indicate how accounts are held.* For example, whether they are held by you alone, jointly with your ex or whether you are just an authorized user. **Your credit report will not indicate whether there is an authorized user on your own accounts.** So if your memory is not perfectly clear, *you should contact each creditor directly over the phone and say that you no longer authorize any other users* (especially "so-and-so") on such account – *and follow it up in writing.*

If the account is a loan, or if the creditor refuses to close the account because it has a balance, then demand the creditor "freeze" the account. *Once an account is labeled as "frozen," nobody should be able to charge more or increase the debt on it.* **Unfortunately, there is no way to prevent anyone else from attempting to re-open or re-activate an existing or previous account** – *so it's important to put your directives to the creditor in writing.* And, remember, **you should be reviewing your credit reports often**, as frequently as every six months.

As a general rule, **all debt incurred during the marriage, regardless of the reason or who actually benefited, is a marital liability** – *and the significance of that is the assumption that the spouses are equally liable.* **Creditors work this way, as well, when both spouses are associated with an account.** Strong consideration should be given as to how you will – as a couple – deal with joint debts. **A good plan involves one spouse taking a particular debt and paying it alone.** *A better plan would involve paying off the debt using marital assets.* **The best plans result in closing the account so that there is no possibility of incurring additional debt** – and you want to close the account after it's completely paid off.

On the other hand, **if an account, such as a credit card, is already *joint*, remember, it's possible your ex can continue to charge on it.** *If there is absolutely no way to completely split up the debt, then you are taking a risk that your ex will not make any timely payments toward the purchases.* **Make sure your divorce decree at least allows you to take your ex back to court to reimburse you for bringing such accounts up to date.** It's important to keep in mind, *the judge cannot order the*

credit reporting agencies (CRAs) to erase the negative marks on your credit reports. Another plan, instead, is to **ask your attorney's advice about agreeing to a larger property settlement in exchange for you taking over certain credit card and loan accounts so you can rely on yourself, not your ex, to make the future monthly payments on time.**

When there are assets, like a home, and significant debt, it's quite often prudent to sell the assets so that the joint debts can be paid and the accounts closed. Forget the emotional attachment that people can form with homes – you are going through one of the most devastating changes in life as can occur, and it's foolish to believe that your life will continue the same way as it has in the past minus the extra baggage. **Change is coming, and the sooner you make the transition from joint to separate lives, the better off you'll be in the long run.** That is what this advice is really about – *plan long range, not short. Expect a difficult short run, and plan your way through it.*

Most important in all of this is to have a realistic budget for during and after the divorce. The input of professionals in this exercise is critical, as you may not know what future funds you may have coming to you after the divorce, such as alimony or child support. **Your budget should include paying debt you incur**, *because you don't want to have the divorce result in damaging your creditworthiness.* It's for this reason that **it's often better to pay the debt in full using the proceeds from the sale of the home** than to live in the home that takes the bulk of your income to maintain and leaves you incapable of sustaining your credit.

When going through a divorce, an ideal outcome would be to completely separate out all of your finances, as opposed to keeping joint debt or assets and attempting to manage them post-divorce. If you are required to have a judge determine things for you, this a possible outcome. *Judges are often confined by the law to doing things in a certain way, and those ways may not benefit you.* **It's always more prudent to settle your dispute among yourselves and enter a "marital settlement agreement" that deals with all of the issues, spelling them out so that they make sense to you and anyone reading them.**

A settlement agreement can go into as much detail as your state allows and your attorney can draft. You can spell out the specifics regarding dividing up your debt and try to cover all contingencies. However, while this is all fine and good for you, *credit card companies and lenders are not party to (a part of) the divorce*, nor do they care. In other words, **it doesn't make any difference to them what the judge may or may not have ordered** – *they don't legally have to abide by any divorce arrangements*, no matter how good your attorney was.

If your agreement or divorce decree says that your spouse is to be liable for a particular debt, do not assume that the creditor won't come after you if the spouse defaults; *the creditor will, and your decree will not protect you.* As mentioned, if your name or social security number was used to open a loan or credit card, or you are listed as an authorized user, **even if you "turn over" such an account to your ex-spouse, if he or she does not keep up on the payments, guess whose credit report may be affected, even many, many years later:** *Yours!*

When it comes to mortgages, other secured debt (such as car loans) and personal loans, the ideal, again, is to divide the debt up cleanly. In other words, *liquidate or re-finance all of it so that only one person's name is associated with the ownership and the related debt.* Again, even if you have the world's best family law attorney who advises you of the true realities of post-divorce credit issues, **the simple truth may be that you can't afford to do what is "best for you."** Both spouses may have to "get back on their two feet" before certain financial arrangements can be finalized, such as re-financing a several-hundred-thousand-dollar mortgage. *If you can't sell the house now, provide in writing that it will be sold before a certain date or upon a contingency, such as when all the children living there reach the age of 18.*

Many of those who go through a divorce are often – and understandably – so caught up in the emotional and outward financial aspects of their breakup that the last thing on their minds is which spouse opened that MasterCard or gasoline credit card six years ago. And **while such credit issues may not be a priority during such a difficult time, they can (and often do) come back to bite you later.** *The simple truth is that they are a priority and you should make them so.* **Clearly they are not as critical as some divorce issues, but they should never, ever, be ignored.**

Chapter 14

You've Been Served:
What to Do When a Creditor Sues You

This Chapter Discusses:

★ The Makeup of a Lawsuit
★ Service of Process
★ Your First Reaction
★ The Type of Court
★ Attorneys' Fees

When working to improve your credit, there are tons of issues to consider. **If you are currently past due or have already defaulted on your bills, one of the more essential facts to face is that creditors or collection agencies may sue you to try to collect their money.** *It's imperative here that you understand this chapter is not written to give you legal advice.*

Absolutely the contrary – *If you get sued, or think you're going to be sued, it's necessary you contact a real live attorney in person to directly discuss your individual situation.* **Once you actually get served with a lawsuit, you should contact an attorney immediately,** because you have only a matter of days or weeks within which to submit a legal response to the suit, if you want to protect your rights. Time is certainly of the essence.

The Makeup of a Lawsuit

The party who brings a lawsuit (e.g., a creditor/collection agency) is known as the *Plaintiff, Complainant, or Petitioner.* The party who is being sued (e.g., the consumer/alleged debtor) is called the *Defendant or Respondent*.

A lawsuit is initially made up of **three basis parts**: the *Summons*, the *Complaint* (which is sometimes called the *Petition or Statement of Claim*), and the *Service of Process*. Each of the three have been explained below...

The Three Basic Parts of a Lawsuit:

☆ Summons

A *Summons* is *the initial document a Defendant-debtor receives* from the Plaintiff (creditor). This document **provides a Defendant with necessary information including the name and address of the Plaintiff and the court's address where the action is being brought.** This document **also provides either (1) a description of the time period within which the Defendant must answer the Complaint** or **(2) a scheduled date and time the Defendant** (as well as the Plaintiff) **must appear in court.**

☆ Complaint

A *Complaint* is **an account of the Plaintiff's (creditor's) side of what happened – including an enumerated explanation of why the Plaintiff should win the lawsuit and the damages** (amount of money) the Plaintiff is entitled to be awarded by the court.

☆ Service of Process

The *Service of Process* refers to the delivery of the Summons and Complaint. For practical purposes, *this equates to a receipt, showing that the two previous items* have been delivered as of a specified date, triggering the deadlines described in the Summons.

Most state statutes require that a Summons and Complaint be served upon the Defendant within a certain number of days after they are filed with the court, *usually 90–120 days.* If the Defendant is not properly served within this period of time, a new fee must be paid, and in some jurisdictions, the Complaint must be re-filed by the Plaintiff.

Service of Process

Depending on several factors, including the state where you reside, and the amount of debt you allegedly owe, initial lawsuit documents can be properly delivered to you in one or more of several ways.

The Three Common Ways Lawsuit Documents Can Be Delivered:

☆ Sheriff

A sheriff can serenade you at your front (or back) door – and if you're not home, he or she may be able to leave the documents with a household member above a certain age, while you're out working at one of your three jobs.

☆ Process Server

A process server (kind of like a private investigator) **is a person who is paid to research your whereabouts and trot after you pretty much anywhere** – including the grocery store and your place of employment.

★ Postal Carrier

Lawsuit documents can be delivered by mail (usually certified) using a postal carrier (along with your other mail, including the overdue bills from the 20+ other creditors you can't afford to pay).

Depending on your state's requirements, it may be possible for you to "hide" and actually avoid service for several days or weeks. However, *even if you are able to hide for a while,* **there are usually laws available in all court jurisdictions that can help the Plaintiff if the servers can't locate you in person.** The Plaintiff can ask the judge for permission to proceed with the lawsuit without serving you by *demonstrating (proving) to the court that you are intentionally avoiding service and that you are likely aware that you are being sued.* The court may then require the Plaintiff to make a few more reasonable efforts to put you on notice such as by publishing a notice in your local newspaper.

Once all reasonable attempts have been made to locate you, a judge can grant the Plaintiff's request and write an *"Order"* **for the court file, reflecting permission for the Plaintiff to proceed with the case against you.** *So if you choose to ignore the "issue,"* **it's possible the Plaintiff can prevail against you without your direct involvement –** *in which case, the Plaintiff can be awarded the full amount asked for in the lawsuit.* So, if you discover someone is trying to serve you, you may want to consider accepting the "news" as quickly and as quietly as possible.

Your First Reaction

Even if you think you've been considerate about keeping in contact with your creditors, you shouldn't be completely surprised if you get sued. Going back in time, you may see that **most of the collection letters you received said something to the effect that** *if you don't pay what you owe, the creditor will have no choice but to protect their legal rights.*

The reality is, even when a collection agency or a law firm sends you a letter directly claiming that the next step will be to sue you, it's really a gamble to try and guess ahead of time whether such a creditor will *actually* take you to court. And it's understandable to be baffled when you get sued by a creditor for an account with a relatively small balance compared to other, substantially larger accounts on which you may have also defaulted. When you have a smorgasbord of creditors to deal with, this is where an experienced attorney can give you a better idea of where your situation stands and help you weigh all your options.

It's rare, but possible that you can be sued and not even know about it. If you do find a lawsuit or judgment on your credit report that you didn't know about, *the first thing you should do is research the case that was filed against you.* **If the case was filed locally, go down to the courthouse and ask the clerk's office how you can get a copy of the case.** You may be able to go **online** to your **local clerk of courts** department and search under your name or the creditor's name. Once you've located the case, you should be able to view all the documents related to the suit, either on the courthouse computer or at the clerk's office where they store such hard files. *The lawsuit papers must provide you with the Plaintiff's information, including the name and number of the lawyer who brought the case.*

If you believe you were not properly served, you can attempt to argue inadequate service through the court system. *This is a tough area to understand on your own without the help of legal counsel.* The fact of the matter is that once you show up to court before the final hearing to contest the service of process, the judge or magistrate will likely look at you and try not to be sarcastic when he or she explains that since you are standing in front of the bench at that moment – **the court *is* going to recognize your awareness of the proceedings and indicate so in the court file.**

Although, the institution of a lawsuit, entry of a final judgment and procedures to collect a judgment are similar in most states, if a creditor sues you, it's important to understand that your rights and responsibilities are dependent upon your state and local laws.

A letter from a creditor's attorney does *not* necessarily mean you will be sued. *One recent trend is for creditors to use their attorneys to send form letters on legal letterhead to consumers who are only a few months past due on their accounts.* **This maneuver is used to encourage you not to get further behind on their payments.** Finance companies use this tactic regularly.

Now, if you were actually served with a lawsuit, the first thing you should do is *absolutely nothing* – for at least five minutes anyway. *Keep calm, and try not to panic – it's not the end of the world.*

The second thing you should do is sit down under good lighting and *actually read the documents you received.* In an effort to make you feel a little less confused, you must understand that the papers are written in *"legal-ese"* and are almost intended to be confusing to any person – even to some seasoned professionals. (***It's rumored that this is actually how attorneys have very cleverly ensured their own indispensability.)*** **It's not unusual for legal documents to need some interpretation or clarification – if you don't have an attorney, you should be able to ask the court for help.**

Even if you decide to hire an attorney to assist you with the lawsuit, whether to defend you (litigate) or to handle out-of-court negotiations (settle the case for you), **you should still try to learn and understand the basic contents of the lawsuit against you.** *Oftentimes, a lawsuit will be delivered to you already in duplicate with an exact copy (or two originals)* for you to have. **Read both sets very carefully to make sure the documents are identical** *(as opposed to two different accounts),* **and keep one copy for your records**.

As is the case with most consumers, **if you're delinquent or in default with one credit card or loan, you're likely delinquent or in default with others as well.** *The creditors around the country and their attorneys know of the law firms in your geographical area who concentrate in collection law* (and **most of them already have such firms on retainer or service contracts** to file suit against consumers in your county). So *there's a small, but possible, chance you may be sued by the same* *firm on behalf of two or more separate creditors or accounts with the same creditor.* If you receive more than several sets of papers (a bundle of papers stapled together), **be sure to read all sets of papers carefully!**

If you don't have an extra copy, make a copy of all the documents – *especially if you plan to leave the originals with someone else* (i.e., your attorney). Or ask the staff at your attorney's office to make you a copy before your conference so you can read along with anything the attorney may want to point out to you. **Of course it's up to you whether you just want to let the attorney handle all aspects of the case,** *but there are some vital parts of the lawsuit you should review either on your own or with an attorney.*

Another reason to read through all of the boring pages of a lawsuit is to look for something that may list any bank accounts or assets in your name. This a definite Red, White and Blue **flag indicating that** *someone is already doing an asset search on you to scare you into thinking you are already in jeopardy of losing your possessions.*

You may be looking at what's called an *Attachment to the lawsuit* – **its title will usually read something like** *"A Writ of Attachment,"* **that provides a list of your bank accounts, as well as a statement of the real property (homes, land) you may own.** This should be of concern to you if you live in one of a few states whose statutes allow for this type of procedure. *This is a powerful remedy that a creditor can use if and when it applies.*

A few states, such as **Connecticut, Massachusetts** and **New Hampshire,** allow and currently have on the books a **General Attachment Statute.** *When filed properly, this procedure allows a creditor to attach to the lawsuit* (literally staple to the back of) *a "Writ of Attachment" that lists property and bank accounts the creditor has supposedly discovered as belonging to the debtor.* **Once a copy is filed with the court, the transfer of any property listed is prohibited by the Defendant.** *The only way to have the property released is for the Defendant to* post a bond as security *for any judgment the Plaintiff-Creditor may be awarded.*

The Type of Court

When a creditor sues you, the case will fall into one of two main court venues or jurisdictions:

♦ *Civil Court* (which is equivalent to a *potential full litigation experience* and can involve *attorneys, judges, witnesses and even juries)* or

♦ *Small Claims Court* (which is designed to give consumers without an attorney a forum they can understand).

Civil Courts are reserved for cases in the court system that are considered **more serious and in need of a judge's and/or jury's professional devotion. Cases that belong in this court arena include** matters such as *spousal support (alimony) issues, child custody rights, criminal* and *felony cases (those* that may result in *serious fines, jail time and even imprisonment)* – and *cases involving the repayment of debt worth a certain minimal threshold of monetary damages* (money), typically more than $15,000.

Small Claims Court is just that: *a state court that hears civil (non-criminal) cases that protect private rights or recover monetary damages for wrongs suffered or money owed for what is categorized by your state as a comparatively "smaller amount."* Small Claims Court is the venue **for cases that involve a payment of money or services such as landlord/tenant disputes, personal injury and property damage claims**, or **claims for unpaid bills that do not exceed a certain amount.**

How you should respond or react to a lawsuit will depend on whether the case is filed in *Small Claims Court* **or not.** *If the case is a Small Claims matter, then the court papers will likely instruct you on what you need to do.* They may simply tell you to show up at a court hearing commonly referred to as a *Pre-Trial Conference* or *Pre-Trial Hearing.* **This is usually a large cattle-call scheduled** at a date and time when **the judge has a courtroom full of consumers in similar situations**, and each is called to the bench one case at a time.

The judge will ask for a short explanation of the case. The Plaintiff's lawyer who brought the case will usually speak first *and summarize the alleged situation for the judge* – after which, the judge will then ask you for your side of the story. *Presumably, you will have a defense – or else, you wouldn't be in a courtroom to begin with.* This is not a formal argument but rather a way for the judge to generally understand the issues.

The judge will likely ask both parties if they can come to an agreement and somehow settle the issue between them. *If you do not agree to a settlement amount or to make a certain number of monthly payments, the judge might then require both parties to go to a room down the hall where a mediator is waiting to "assist" the judge – by acting as an independent third-party who will help both parties come to a satisfactory resolution*.

Attorneys' Fees

Attorneys will usually charge fees in one or a combination of three ways: a *flat fee*, an *hourly fee* or a *contingency fee*.

The Three Ways Attorneys Charge for Their Services:

☆ Flat Fee

A **flat fee** is just that, **an established amount that is supposed to cover the entire representation for a designated issue.** (If the fee is relatively large, some attorneys may let you pay in installments – so long as the full amount is paid before the case is finalized.)

☆ Hourly Fee

An **hourly fee** is **a set amount that is earned by the attorney for each hour (or increments thereof) that work is performed.** In this fee arrangement, *the attorney will likely ask you for a payment up*

front to cover costs and for initial work commenced on your matter. This up-front payment **may be called a "deposit" retainer** – in which case, *the funds are put toward your final bill.*

If the payment is described as *"non-refundable,"* then the attorney will tell you whether it goes toward the final bill. **An important note:** Any fee labeled as **non-refundable** means *you don't get your money back even if you or the attorney decides not to proceed with the matter.*

★ Contingency

A *contingency fee* is *based on (contingent upon) the monetary outcome of a case.* **If you are the Plaintiff (the party bringing the lawsuit) and you are awarded money damages from the other side, the attorney will earn a portion of the award (30% to 40%).** Defendants are not given this fee arrangement because there is no monetary reward for defending a case (other than the reimbursement of the prevailing party's attorney fees).

<u>**An Important Reminder:**</u> The emphasis of *American Credit Repair* is designed to help you handle the majority of credit situations that affect your credit report, and if you are in default, many of your creditors will not take the time or expense to sue you. However, if you are wrongfully sued or if you **believe your rights as a consumer are being infringed upon in any way** – but *especially if you have just been served with a lawsuit* – **you should consider contacting an attorney immediately.**

Chapter 15

How to Establish or Re-Establish Credit: The Building Blocks

This Chapter Discusses:

★ Gasoline and Department Store Cards

★ Visiting Your Neighborhood Banker

★ Secured Credit Cards

★ Using a Co-Signer

★ Becoming an Authorized User

★ Maintaining Your Credit

Whether you didn't have much credit to begin with or had a lot and lost it, **it's actually not that difficult of a task to** *establish* **or** *re-establish* **yourself as a creditworthy consumer.** However, there is **one prerequisite** to this final chapter: *You must first make every attempt possible to remove the negative items from your credit file.* Otherwise, **if you apply for new credit prematurely, you could make your situation worse** by damaging your credit rating with excessive inquiries.

Now, **this doesn't mean that** *all* **derogatory items need to be removed** – this simply means that you should use the techniques in this book to the best of your ability. So, if you've done some preliminary work and most of the dust has settled, **here's how to build (or rebuild) your credit...**

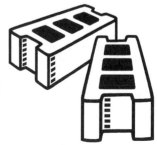

Gasoline and Department Store Cards

It's easy to apply and to be approved for these establishment cards – because they offer relatively small credit limits, plus they want you to buy their products. And **since you can only charge at their stations or stores (and sometimes their affiliates),** *the benefits outweigh the risks for the company.*

Oftentimes, you can **get approved immediately right at the checkout counter** – and it will seem that **the information you provide regarding your income and employment is not actually being verified at that moment** (that's because it's not). *As long as you have marginal credit, they should approve you.* If you apply for a gasoline card, **make sure it's not co-branded with a VISA or MasterCard logo** – those approval requirements are much more stringent than the ones intended just for gasoline and snack purchases.

Visiting Your Neighborhood Banker

Local banks and credit unions are more likely to grant you a small line of credit to build a relationship with them as compared to major national banks. Even if your credit isn't up to their standards, **they will often consider relaxing their scoring guidelines in exchange for receiving some type of security** – such as a *certificate of deposit* or a *secured savings account,* to ensure you make your payments on time. And, as you pay off the account, *you can then request a larger credit limit or further loans.* True relationship bankers are still out there – you just have to place a few calls to find them.

Secured Credit Cards

These accounts **work similarly to unsecured cards**, but are intended for those who have such a poor credit rating that no one will grant them an unsecured card.

Caution! *Secured credit cards are very expensive to maintain* (i.e., annual fees, high interest rates and stiff penalty fees if you're ever late or over your available credit limit). Therefore, *it's best that you don't plan on using a secured card as a means for regular spending.* **This type of account should only be used as a tool to establish credit.** Otherwise, you may end up creating more credit problems for yourself, should the fees and limits get out of hand.

The finance company or bank granting the credit will usually secure the card by asking you to **open a** *certificate of deposit (CD)* **for an amount equal to the credit line extended to you** (usually a few hundred dollars). For example, if you open a CD with $250, the credit line will most likely be $250 – minus whatever application or initial fees are charged by the credit card company (upwards of $75).

Just make sure the credit card company reports to the major credit reporting agencies (CRAs) so you can reap the full benefit of the account. By the way – **don't confuse this type of credit card with a prepaid one found at grocery stores, pharmacies and the like.** *Prepaid cards do not report to the CRAs.*

Once your credit is re-established in a year or two, **you can then ask the creditor if they will convert the account into a non-secured one.** *Whatever you do, don't close the account until you have unsecured ones to replace it.* Otherwise, **discipline yourself not to use it.**

As long as you keep a zero balance, it will help your credit score tremendously. Just be sure you limit yourself to *no more than 5 credit cards.* Mortgage lenders (those who would most likely offer the highest amount of credit you would ever need) **usually require only a minimum of three open accounts on your credit file to use as a basis for underwriting a loan.** Therefore, five accounts is more than adequate to meet any lender's requirements – **so long as you continue to keep your balances low and paid on time.**

Using a Co-Signer

While this book would admittedly never recommend you to act as a "*co-signer*" for anyone, **if you can get someone to assist you, then that's great!** *You are definitely more likely to get approved for certain cards and loans when there is a co-signer with good credit involved.*

But, just as you shouldn't be lending out your good name and credit score on a whim, you shouldn't expect others to risk that for you either. And, as stated, **there are other ways to improve your creditworthiness.** So try not to wear out your welcome – **consider using a co-signer only when** *absolutely* **necessary,** (i.e., when you need help financing a car). **You can always re-build your credit, but** *not* **necessarily lost friendships.**

Becoming an Authorized User

This is **similar to having a co-signer** – *except that there is no application process required.* All it takes is to have a friend, spouse or family member add you to an existing credit card account and – **Bam!** You've got instant credit. The responsibility falls on your primary account holder, because giving you the authority to sign on his or her account is potentially risky business.

However, you can ease the pain and protect your relationship by **telling friends and family you don't need your own card.** *Just adding your name to their account over the phone will put their account history onto your credit report.* Just hope that they continue to make their payments on time. Otherwise, **your credit could then be negatively affected by this maneuver.** Fortunately, the primary account holder (or you) **could request that you be removed as an authorized user at any time.**

Maintaining Your Credit

The importance of this brief chapter is not only about providing methods on how to establish or re-establish your credit, but also to show you **how to *maintain* it.** Otherwise, what's the point? **Here are some tips on how to preserve your good name as a consumer...**

Tips for Maintaining Your Credit:

☆ Pay Your Bills on Time

While it seems obvious that you should **make your payments each and every month**, *it's also important to know the grace period for each loan and credit card.* **Look at your statements!** In addition to saving your credit report score, *this will also save you on finance charges* that are often calculated from the day you use a revolving account, such as a credit card.

☆ Monitor Your Credit Report

Remember – you can monitor your credit reports once a year for free. You could even consider paying for more frequent copies (i.e., twice a year, every quarter or once a month). **You may be able to get more frequent intervals at no cost if you convince the CRA that you have concerns about your file.** But *don't wait around a month or so if something concerns you* – pay the minimal fee to order your reports right away.

☆ Balance Transfers – Read the Fine Print

There are many, many things you'll discover **if you just read your agreements.** The latest promotion is **balance transfers – *every company is offering them.*** And when interest rates on some of your accounts are much higher than others, it may seem like a good idea to

play the **balance transfer game** – *especially* **when you are being pushed by credit card competitors** all promising the grass is greener on the other side.

You must read the agreement carefully. The **low interest rate is often only good for a brief period of time** and **only pertains to the balances you transferred.** In most cases, *once you use the card for purchases, you blow the rate sky high.* Plus, there are still some **advantages for being a loyal customer to your original credit card.** *The longer you have been dealing with a creditor, the better it is for your credit report.* And, once you've proved your worthy again, **you can ask your current creditors for lower interest rates and other deals in exchange for keeping your business.**

★ Curb Your Credit Card Use

Try restricting the use of your credit cards. *Credit cards are not intended for regular daily use – that's what debit/check cards are intended for.* **Save your credit cards for emergencies or special occasions** (e.g., medical procedures, car repairs and vacations).

★ Use a Fraud Alert or Credit Freeze When Necessary

Because of identity theft, all three major CRAs can provide you with some extra protection for your reports – and *they don't cost you any money*: just **some time** on your part.

A "fraud alert" is a notation that is placed on your credit file that says you are – or you believe you are – a victim of fraud. Your phone number gets included with the notation. The idea here is that if someone should pretend to be you and apply for credit, *the potential creditor will see the fraud alert on your report along with an instruction to call you directly to confirm that it is really you who is submitting the application.*

A **credit "freeze"** allows a **further level of protection** – *preventing anyone from opening an account using your information.* If you choose to use a "freeze," then just **be prepared that *even you* won't be able to use or access your report immediately** should you suddenly decide to do so. **Some states even restrict their use altogether.** The CRA can give you more information on freezing your credit report and the necessary steps involved.

In addition to identity theft resolution and prevention, you may be able to use a fraud alert or credit freeze when you have other issues – *such as a messy divorce or an ex whom you don't trust...*

Conclusion

When being diligent about your credit file, there is certainly a lot to consider. The **FCRA, FACT Act** and **FDCPA** are *over 150 pages* of mind-numbing text, so don't worry or dwell on the fact that you may not have entirely grasped all the laws that govern your past and future credit. **It's okay to feel a little bewildered at this point –** *even the staff at the FTC has disclosed conflicting interpretations on many of the laws they govern.* The purpose of *American Credit Repair* is **to show you how to raise and maintain your credit score,** not to decode all the ramblings of the United States Congress. Consequently, the **more important and relevant sections of the three main credit report laws are cited and explained throughout the book** with **unabridged versions** (for those who are interested) **provided in their respective appendices,** at the back of the book.

And remember – **a perfect credit score is nearly impossible to attain.** Consumers who start with relatively good scores can be greatly affected by a credit reporting error – more so than a consumer whose credit score has already taken a few hits. *One late payment can knock down a good score dramatically.* On the flip side, the worse your credit score is, the less it is affected by one more late payment. **In either case, it can take as little as 10 days to 12 months to get your credit score back to a number to be taken seriously by future creditors, employers and insurers.** *Start today!*

★ Here Are a Few Friendly Reminders and Words of Caution:

- ♦ Monitor your **credit reports at least once a year**
- ♦ Send a **few dispute letters**
- ♦ **Start paying original creditors on time from this day forward** (ask them to help you catch up – they would rather do that than have you default)
- ♦ **Negotiate with any collection agencies** *(get it all in writing)*

- Look into using a **consumer credit counseling service** *only if* your interest rates are outrageously high, you can still afford the regular monthly payment, you are willing to close your accounts and you are not planning on applying for a mortgage with a local bank in the near future
- **Never use a credit repair organization**
- **Contact an attorney if you are contemplating filing for bankruptcy** (you don't have to follow through with the bankruptcy filing until you and your attorney are sure it's the best solution for you)
- **Contact a tax specialist if you feel a tax problem becomes too serious for you to handle**
- **Protect your identity the best that you can**
- **Under certain circumstances, you may have to just ignore your collection accounts as long as your property and wages are not jeopardized** – they will affect your score *less and less as each month goes by*, especially if you have other accounts you can keep open and current. **And, if necessary, instruct the collectors in writing to stop bothering you...**

The FCRA:
Fair Credit Reporting Act

THE FAIR CREDIT REPORTING ACT

As a public service, the staff of the Federal Trade Commission (FTC) has prepared the following complete text of the Fair Credit Reporting Act (FCRA), 15 U.S.C. § 1681 et seq. Although staff generally followed the format of the U.S. Code as published by the Government Printing Office, the format of this text does differ in minor ways from the Code (and from West's U.S. Code Annotated). For example, this version uses FCRA section numbers (§§ 601-625) in the headings. (The relevant U.S. Code citation is included with each section heading and each reference to the FCRA in the text.) Although the staff has made every effort to transcribe the statutory material accurately, this compendium is intended only as a convenience for the public and not a subtitute for the text in the U. S. Code. The Commission's website (www.ftc.gov) posted this document on December 31, 2007.

This version of the FCRA includes the amendments to the FCRA set forth in the Consumer Credit Reporting Reform Act of 1996 (Public Law 104-208, the Omnibus Consolidated Appropriations Act for Fiscal Year 1997, Title II, Subtitle D, Chapter 1), Section 311 of the Intelligence Authorization for Fiscal Year 1998 (Public Law 105-107), the Consumer Reporting Employment Clarification Act of 1998 (Public Law 105-347), Section 506 of the Gramm-Leach-Bliley Act (Public Law 106-102), Sections 358(g) and 505(c) of the Uniting and Strengthening America by Providing Appropriate Tools Required to Intercept and Obstruct Terrorism Act of 2001 (USA PATRIOT Act) (Public Law 107-56), the Fair and Accurate Credit Transactions Act of 2003 (FACT Act) (Public Law 108-159), and Section 719 of the Financial Services Regulatory Relief Act of 2006 (Public Law 109-351).

The provisions added to the FCRA by the FACT Act became effective at different times. In some cases, the provision includes its own effective date. In other cases, the FACT Act provides that the effective dates be prescribed by the FTC and Federal Reserve Board. See 16 CFR Part 602. (69 Fed. Reg. 6526; February 11, 2004) (69 Fed. Reg. 29061; May 20, 2004).

TABLE OF CONTENTS

§ 601. Short title

This title may be cited as the "Fair Credit Reporting Act".

§ 602. Congressional findings and statement of purpose [15 U.S.C. § 1681]

(a) *Accuracy and fairness of credit reporting.* The Congress makes the following findings:

    (1) The banking system is dependent upon fair and accurate credit reporting. Inaccurate credit reports directly impair the efficiency of the banking system, and unfair credit reporting methods undermine the public confidence which is essential to the continued functioning of the banking system.

    (2) An elaborate mechanism has been developed for investigating and evaluating the credit worthiness, credit standing, credit capacity, character, and general reputation of consumers.

    (3) Consumer reporting agencies have assumed a vital role in assembling and evaluating consumer credit and other information on consumers.

    (4) There is a need to insure that consumer reporting agencies exercise their grave responsibilities with fairness, impartiality, and a respect for the consumer's right to privacy.

(b) *Reasonable procedures.* It is the purpose of this title to require that consumer reporting agencies adopt reasonable procedures for meeting the needs of commerce for consumer credit, personnel, insurance, and other information in a manner which is fair and equitable to the consumer, with regard to the confidentiality, accuracy, relevancy, and proper utilization of such information in accordance with the requirements of this title.

§ 603. Definitions; rules of construction [15 U.S.C. § 1681a]

(a) Definitions and rules of construction set forth in this section are applicable for the purposes of this title.

(b) The term "person" means any individual, partnership, corporation, trust, estate, cooperative, association, government or governmental subdivision or agency, or other entity.

(c) The term "consumer" means an individual.

(d) Consumer Report

    (1) *In general.* The term "consumer report" means any written, oral, or other communication of any information by a consumer reporting agency bearing on a consumer's credit worthiness, credit standing, credit capacity, character, general reputation, personal characteristics, or mode of living which is used or expected to be used or collected in whole or in part for the purpose of serving as a factor in establishing the consumer's eligibility for

(A)   credit or insurance to be used primarily for personal, family, or household purposes;

(B)   employment purposes; or

(C)   any other purpose authorized under section 604 [§ 1681b].

(2) *Exclusions.* Except as provided in paragraph (3), the term "consumer report" does not include

(A)   subject to section 624, any

(i)   report containing information solely as to transactions or experiences between the consumer and the person making the report;

(ii)   communication of that information among persons related by common ownership or affiliated by corporate control; or

(iii)   communication of other information among persons related by common ownership or affiliated by corporate control, if it is clearly and conspicuously disclosed to the consumer that the information may be communicated among such persons and the consumer is given the opportunity, before the time that the information is initially communicated, to direct that such information not be communicated among such persons;

(B)   any authorization or approval of a specific extension of credit directly or indirectly by the issuer of a credit card or similar device;

(C)   any report in which a person who has been requested by a third party to make a specific extension of credit directly or indirectly to a consumer conveys his or her decision with respect to such request, if the third party advises the consumer of the name and address of the person to whom the request was made, and such person makes the disclosures to the consumer required under section 615 [§ 1681m]; or

(D)   a communication described in subsection (o) or (x).

(3) *Restriction on sharing of medical information.* Except for information or any communication of information disclosed as provided in section 604(g)(3), the exclusions in paragraph (2) shall not apply with respect to information disclosed to any person related by common ownership or affiliated by corporate control, if the information is--

(A)   medical information;

(B)   an individualized list or description based on the payment transactions of the consumer for medical products or services; or

4

(C) an aggregate list of identified consumers based on payment transactions for medical products or services.

(e) The term "investigative consumer report" means a consumer report or portion thereof in which information on a consumer's character, general reputation, personal characteristics, or mode of living is obtained through personal interviews with neighbors, friends, or associates of the consumer reported on or with others with whom he is acquainted or who may have knowledge concerning any such items of information. However, such information shall not include specific factual information on a consumer's credit record obtained directly from a creditor of the consumer or from a consumer reporting agency when such information was obtained directly from a creditor of the consumer or from the consumer.

(f) The term "consumer reporting agency" means any person which, for monetary fees, dues, or on a cooperative nonprofit basis, regularly engages in whole or in part in the practice of assembling or evaluating consumer credit information or other information on consumers for the purpose of furnishing consumer reports to third parties, and which uses any means or facility of interstate commerce for the purpose of preparing or furnishing consumer reports.

(g) The term "file," when used in connection with information on any consumer, means all of the information on that consumer recorded and retained by a consumer reporting agency regardless of how the information is stored.

(h) The term "employment purposes" when used in connection with a consumer report means a report used for the purpose of evaluating a consumer for employment, promotion, reassignment or retention as an employee.

(i) The term "medical information" --

(1) means information or data, whether oral or recorded, in any form or medium, created by or derived from a health care provider or the consumer, that relates to--

(A) the past, present, or future physical, mental, or behavioral health or condition of an individual;

(B) the provision of health care to an individual; or

(C) the payment for the provision of health care to an individual.

(2) does not include the age or gender of a consumer, demographic information about the consumer, including a consumer's residence address or e-mail address, or any other information about a consumer that does not relate to the physical, mental, or behavioral health or condition of a consumer, including the existence or value of any insurance policy.

(j) Definitions Relating to Child Support Obligations

    (1) The "overdue support" has the meaning given to such term in section 666(e) of title 42 [Social Security Act, 42 U.S.C. § 666(e)].

    (2) The term "State or local child support enforcement agency" means a State or local agency which administers a State or local program for establishing and enforcing child support obligations.

(k) Adverse Action

    (1) *Actions included.* The term "adverse action"

        (A)   has the same meaning as in section 701(d)(6) of the Equal Credit Opportunity Act; and

        (B)   means

            (i)   a denial or cancellation of, an increase in any charge for, or a reduction or other adverse or unfavorable change in the terms of coverage or amount of, any insurance, existing or applied for, in connection with the underwriting of insurance;

            (ii)   a denial of employment or any other decision for employment purposes that adversely affects any current or prospective employee;

            (iii)   a denial or cancellation of, an increase in any charge for, or any other adverse or unfavorable change in the terms of, any license or benefit described in section 604(a)(3)(D) [§ 1681b]; and

            (iv)   an action taken or determination that is

                (I)   made in connection with an application that was made by, or a transaction that was initiated by, any consumer, or in connection with a review of an account under section 604(a)(3)(F)(ii)[§ 1681b]; and

                (II)   adverse to the interests of the consumer.

    (2) *Applicable findings, decisions, commentary, and orders.* For purposes of any determination of whether an action is an adverse action under paragraph (1)(A), all appropriate final findings, decisions, commentary, and orders issued under section 701(d)(6) of the Equal Credit Opportunity Act by the Board of Governors of the Federal Reserve System or any court shall apply.

(*l*) The term "firm offer of credit or insurance" means any offer of credit or insurance to a consumer that will be honored if the consumer is determined, based on information in a consumer report on the consumer, to meet the specific criteria used to select the

6

consumer for the offer, except that the offer may be further conditioned on one or more of the following:

(1) The consumer being determined, based on information in the consumer's application for the credit or insurance, to meet specific criteria bearing on credit worthiness or insurability, as applicable, that are established

    (A)   before selection of the consumer for the offer; and

    (B)   for the purpose of determining whether to extend credit or insurance pursuant to the offer.

(2) Verification

    (A)   that the consumer continues to meet the specific criteria used to select the consumer for the offer, by using information in a consumer report on the consumer, information in the consumer's application for the credit or insurance, or other information bearing on the credit worthiness or insurability of the consumer; or

    (B)   of the information in the consumer's application for the credit or insurance, to determine that the consumer meets the specific criteria bearing on credit worthiness or insurability.

(3) The consumer furnishing any collateral that is a requirement for the extension of the credit or insurance that was

    (A)   established before selection of the consumer for the offer of credit or insurance; and

    (B)   disclosed to the consumer in the offer of credit or insurance.

(m) The term "credit or insurance transaction that is not initiated by the consumer" does not include the use of a consumer report by a person with which the consumer has an account or insurance policy, for purposes of

(1) reviewing the account or insurance policy; or

(2) collecting the account.

(n) The term "State" means any State, the Commonwealth of Puerto Rico, the District of Columbia, and any territory or possession of the United States.

(o) *Excluded communications.* A communication is described in this subsection if it is a communication

(1) that, but for subsection (d)(2)(D), would be an investigative consumer report;

(2) that is made to a prospective employer for the purpose of

    (A)   procuring an employee for the employer; or

    (B)   procuring an opportunity for a natural person to work for the employer;

(3) that is made by a person who regularly performs such procurement;

(4) that is not used by any person for any purpose other than a purpose described in subparagraph (A) or (B) of paragraph (2); and

(5) with respect to which

    (A)   the consumer who is the subject of the communication

        (i)   consents orally or in writing to the nature and scope of the communication, before the collection of any information for the purpose of making the communication;

        (ii)   consents orally or in writing to the making of the communication to a prospective employer, before the making of the communication; and

        (iii)   in the case of consent under clause (i) or (ii) given orally, is provided written confirmation of that consent by the person making the communication, not later than 3 business days after the receipt of the consent by that person;

    (B)   the person who makes the communication does not, for the purpose of making the communication, make any inquiry that if made by a prospective employer of the consumer who is the subject of the communication would violate any applicable Federal or State equal employment opportunity law or regulation; and

    (C)   the person who makes the communication

        (i)   discloses in writing to the consumer who is the subject of the communication, not later than 5 business days after receiving any request from the consumer for such disclosure, the nature and substance of all information in the consumer's file at the time of the request, except that the sources of any information that is acquired solely for use in making the communication and is actually used for no other purpose, need not be disclosed other than under appropriate discovery procedures in any court of competent jurisdiction in which an action is brought; and

        (ii)   notifies the consumer who is the subject of the communication, in writing, of the consumer's right to request the information described in clause (i).

(p) The term "consumer reporting agency that compiles and maintains files on consumers on a nationwide basis" means a consumer reporting agency that regularly engages in the practice of assembling or evaluating, and maintaining, for the purpose of furnishing consumer reports to third parties bearing on a consumer's credit worthiness, credit standing, or credit capacity, each of the following regarding consumers residing nationwide:

(1) Public record information.

(2) Credit account information from persons who furnish that information regularly and in the ordinary course of business.

(q) Definitions relating to fraud alerts.

(1) The term "active duty military consumer" means a consumer in military service who--

(A) is on active duty (as defined in section 101(d)(1) of title 10, United States Code) or is a reservist performing duty under a call or order to active duty under a provision of law referred to in section 101(a)(13) of title 10, United States Code; and

(B) is assigned to service away from the usual duty station of the consumer.

(2) The terms "fraud alert" and "active duty alert" mean a statement in the file of a consumer that--

(A) notifies all prospective users of a consumer report relating to the consumer that the consumer may be a victim of fraud, including identity theft, or is an active duty military consumer, as applicable; and

(B) is presented in a manner that facilitates a clear and conspicuous view of the statement described in subparagraph (A) by any person requesting such consumer report.

(3) The term "identity theft" means a fraud committed using the identifying information of another person, subject to such further definition as the Commission may prescribe, by regulation.   ***See also 16 CFR Part 603.2***
69 Fed. Reg. 63922 (11/03/04)

(4) The term "identity theft report" has the meaning given that term by rule of the Commission, and means, at a minimum, a report--

(A) that alleges an identity theft;

(B) that is a copy of an official, valid report filed by a consumer with an appropriate Federal, State, or local law enforcement agency, including the United States Postal Inspection Service, or such other government agency deemed appropriate by the Commission; and

(C)   the filing of which subjects the person filing the report to criminal penalties relating to the filing of false information if, in fact, the information in the report is false.   ***See also 16 CFR Part 603.3***
69 Fed. Reg. 63922 (11/03/04)

(5) The term "new credit plan" means a new account under an open end credit plan (as defined in section 103(i) of the Truth in Lending Act) or a new credit transaction not under an open end credit plan.

(r) Credit and Debit Related Terms

(1) The term "card issuer" means--

(A)   a credit card issuer, in the case of a credit card; and

(B)   a debit card issuer, in the case of a debit card.

(2) The term "credit card" has the same meaning as in section 103 of the Truth in Lending Act.

(3) The term "debit card" means any card issued by a financial institution to a consumer for use in initiating an electronic fund transfer from the account of the consumer at such financial institution, for the purpose of transferring money between accounts or obtaining money, property, labor, or services.

(4) The terms "account" and "electronic fund transfer" have the same meanings as in section 903 of the Electronic Fund Transfer Act.

(5) The terms "credit" and "creditor" have the same meanings as in section 702 of the Equal Credit Opportunity Act.

(s) The term "Federal banking agency" has the same meaning as in section 3 of the Federal Deposit Insurance Act.

(t) The term "financial institution" means a State or National bank, a State or Federal savings and loan association, a mutual savings bank, a State or Federal credit union, or any other person that, directly or indirectly, holds a transaction account (as defined in section 19(b) of the Federal Reserve Act) belonging to a consumer.

(u) The term "reseller" means a consumer reporting agency that--

(1) assembles and merges information contained in the database of another consumer reporting agency or multiple consumer reporting agencies concerning any consumer for purposes of furnishing such information to any third party, to the extent of such activities; and

(2) does not maintain a database of the assembled or merged information from which new consumer reports are produced.

(v) The term "Commission" means the Federal Trade Commission.

(w) The term "nationwide specialty consumer reporting agency" means a consumer reporting agency that compiles and maintains files on consumers on a nationwide basis relating to--

(1) medical records or payments;

(2) residential or tenant history;

(3) check writing history;

(4) employment history; or

(5) insurance claims.

(x) Exclusion of Certain Communications for Employee Investigations

(1) A communication is described in this subsection if--

    (A)   but for subsection (d)(2)(D), the communication would be a consumer report;

    (B)   the communication is made to an employer in connection with an investigation of–

        (i)   suspected misconduct relating to employment; or

        (ii)   compliance with Federal, State, or local laws and regulations, the rules of a self-regulatory organization, or any preexisting written policies of the employer;

    (C)   the communication is not made for the purpose of investigating a consumer's credit worthiness, credit standing, or credit capacity; and

    (D)   the communication is not provided to any person except--

        (i)   to the employer or an agent of the employer;

        (ii)   to any Federal or State officer, agency, or department, or any officer, agency, or department of a unit of general local government;

        (iii)   to any self-regulatory organization with regulatory authority over the activities of the employer or employee;

        (iv)   as otherwise required by law; or

        (v)   pursuant to section 608.

(2) *Subsequent disclosure.* After taking any adverse action based in whole or in part on a communication described in paragraph (1), the employer shall disclose to the

consumer a summary containing the nature and substance of the communication upon which the adverse action is based, except that the sources of information acquired solely for use in preparing what would be but for subsection (d)(2)(D) an investigative consumer report need not be disclosed.

(3) For purposes of this subsection, the term "self-regulatory organization" includes any self-regulatory organization (as defined in section 3(a)(26) of the Securities Exchange Act of 1934), any entity established under title I of the Sarbanes-Oxley Act of 2002, any board of trade designated by the Commodity Futures Trading Commission, and any futures association registered with such Commission.

§ 604. **Permissible purposes of consumer reports** [15 U.S.C. § 1681b]

(a) *In general.* Subject to subsection (c), any consumer reporting agency may furnish a consumer report under the following circumstances and no other:

(1) In response to the order of a court having jurisdiction to issue such an order, or a subpoena issued in connection with proceedings before a Federal grand jury.

(2) In accordance with the written instructions of the consumer to whom it relates.

(3) To a person which it has reason to believe

    (A)   intends to use the information in connection with a credit transaction involving the consumer on whom the information is to be furnished and involving the extension of credit to, or review or collection of an account of, the consumer; or

    (B)   intends to use the information for employment purposes; or

    (C)   intends to use the information in connection with the underwriting of insurance involving the consumer; or

    (D)   intends to use the information in connection with a determination of the consumer's eligibility for a license or other benefit granted by a governmental instrumentality required by law to consider an applicant's financial responsibility or status; or

    (E)   intends to use the information, as a potential investor or servicer, or current insurer, in connection with a valuation of, or an assessment of the credit or prepayment risks associated with, an existing credit obligation; or

    (F)   otherwise has a legitimate business need for the information

        (i)   in connection with a business transaction that is initiated by the consumer; or

        (ii)   to review an account to determine whether the consumer continues to meet the terms of the account.

(4) In response to a request by the head of a State or local child support enforcement agency (or a State or local government official authorized by the head of such an agency), if the person making the request certifies to the consumer reporting agency that

    (A)   the consumer report is needed for the purpose of establishing an individual's capacity to make child support payments or determining the appropriate level of such payments;

    (B)   the paternity of the consumer for the child to which the obligation relates has been established or acknowledged by the consumer in accordance with State laws under which the obligation arises (if required by those laws);

    (C)   the person has provided at least 10 days' prior notice to the consumer whose report is requested, by certified or registered mail to the last known address of the consumer, that the report will be requested; and

    (D)   the consumer report will be kept confidential, will be used solely for a purpose described in subparagraph (A), and will not be used in connection with any other civil, administrative, or criminal proceeding, or for any other purpose.

(5) To an agency administering a State plan under Section 454 of the Social Security Act (42 U.S.C. § 654) for use to set an initial or modified child support award.

(6) To the Federal Deposit Insurance Corporation or the National Credit Union Administration as part of its preparation for its appointment or as part of its exercise of powers, as conservator, receiver, or liquidating agent for an insured depository institution or insured credit union under the Federal Deposit Insurance Act or the Federal Credit Union Act, or other applicable Federal or State law, or in connection with the resolution or liquidation of a failed or failing insured depository institution or insured credit union, as applicable.

(b) Conditions for Furnishing and Using Consumer Reports for Employment Purposes.

    (1) *Certification from user.* A consumer reporting agency may furnish a consumer report for employment purposes only if

        (A)   the person who obtains such report from the agency certifies to the agency that

            (i)   the person has complied with paragraph (2) with respect to the consumer report, and the person will comply with paragraph (3) with respect to the consumer report if paragraph (3) becomes applicable; and

            (ii)   information from the consumer report will not be used in violation of any applicable Federal or State equal employment opportunity law or regulation; and

(B)   the consumer reporting agency provides with the report, or has previously provided, a summary of the consumer's rights under this title, as prescribed by the Federal Trade Commission under section 609(c)(3) [§ 1681g].

(2) Disclosure to Consumer.

(A)   *In general.* Except as provided in subparagraph (B), a person may not procure a consumer report, or cause a consumer report to be procured, for employment purposes with respect to any consumer, unless--

    (i)   a clear and conspicuous disclosure has been made in writing to the consumer at any time before the report is procured or caused to be procured, in a document that consists solely of the disclosure, that a consumer report may be obtained for employment purposes; and

    (ii)   the consumer has authorized in writing (which authorization may be made on the document referred to in clause (i)) the procurement of the report by that person.

(B)   *Application by mail, telephone, computer, or other similar means.* If a consumer described in subparagraph (C) applies for employment by mail, telephone, computer, or other similar means, at any time before a consumer report is procured or caused to be procured in connection with that application--

    (i)   the person who procures the consumer report on the consumer for employment purposes shall provide to the consumer, by oral, written, or electronic means, notice that a consumer report may be obtained for employment purposes, and a summary of the consumer's rights under section 615(a)(3); and

    (ii)   the consumer shall have consented, orally, in writing, or electronically to the procurement of the report by that person.

(C)   *Scope.* Subparagraph (B) shall apply to a person procuring a consumer report on a consumer in connection with the consumer's application for employment only if--

    (i)   the consumer is applying for a position over which the Secretary of Transportation has the power to establish qualifications and maximum hours of service pursuant to the provisions of section 31502 of title 49, or a position subject to safety regulation by a State transportation agency; and

    (ii)   as of the time at which the person procures the report or causes the report to be procured the only interaction between the consumer and the person in connection with that employment application has been by mail, telephone, computer, or other similar means.

(3) Conditions on use for adverse actions.

    (A)   *In general.* Except as provided in subparagraph (B), in using a consumer report for employment purposes, before taking any adverse action based in whole or in part on the report, the person intending to take such adverse action shall provide to the consumer to whom the report relates--

        (i)   a copy of the report; and

        (ii)   a description in writing of the rights of the consumer under this title, as prescribed by the Federal Trade Commission under section 609(c)(3).[1]

    (B)   Application by mail, telephone, computer, or other similar means.

        (i)   If a consumer described in subparagraph (C) applies for employment by mail, telephone, computer, or other similar means, and if a person who has procured a consumer report on the consumer for employment purposes takes adverse action on the employment application based in whole or in part on the report, then the person must provide to the consumer to whom the report relates, in lieu of the notices required under subparagraph (A) of this section and under section 615(a), within 3 business days of taking such action, an oral, written or electronic notification--

            (I)   that adverse action has been taken based in whole or in part on a consumer report received from a consumer reporting agency;

            (II)   of the name, address and telephone number of the consumer reporting agency that furnished the consumer report (including a toll-free telephone number established by the agency if the agency compiles and maintains files on consumers on a nationwide basis);

            (III)   that the consumer reporting agency did not make the decision to take the adverse action and is unable to provide to the consumer the specific reasons why the adverse action was taken; and

            (IV)   that the consumer may, upon providing proper identification, request a free copy of a report and may dispute with the consumer reporting agency the accuracy or completeness of any information in a report.

        (ii)   If, under clause (B)(i)(IV), the consumer requests a copy of a consumer report from the person who procured the report, then, within 3 business days of receiving the consumer's request, together with proper identification, the person must send or provide to the consumer a copy of a report and a copy of the consumer's rights as prescribed by the Federal Trade Commission under section 609(c)(3).

---

[1] The references in Sections 604(b)(3)(A) and 604(b)(3)(B) should be to Section 609(c)(**1**), not (c)(3) that no longer exists as the result of Congress' re-organization of Section 609(c) in 2003 (FACT Act).

(C) *Scope.* Subparagraph (B) shall apply to a person procuring a consumer report on a consumer in connection with the consumer's application for employment only if--

    (i) the consumer is applying for a position over which the Secretary of Transportation has the power to establish qualifications and maximum hours of service pursuant to the provisions of section 31502 of title 49, or a position subject to safety regulation by a State transportation agency; and

    (ii) as of the time at which the person procures the report or causes the report to be procured the only interaction between the consumer and the person in connection with that employment application has been by mail, telephone, computer, or other similar means.

(4) Exception for national security investigations.

    (A) *In general.* In the case of an agency or department of the United States Government which seeks to obtain and use a consumer report for employment purposes, paragraph (3) shall not apply to any adverse action by such agency or department which is based in part on such consumer report, if the head of such agency or department makes a written finding that–

        (i) the consumer report is relevant to a national security investigation of such agency or department;

        (ii) the investigation is within the jurisdiction of such agency or department;

        (iii) there is reason to believe that compliance with paragraph (3) will–

            (I) endanger the life or physical safety of any person;

            (II) result in flight from prosecution;

            (III) result in the destruction of, or tampering with, evidence relevant to the investigation;

            (IV) result in the intimidation of a potential witness relevant to the investigation;

            (V) result in the compromise of classified information; or

            (VI) otherwise seriously jeopardize or unduly delay the investigation or another official proceeding.

    (B) *Notification of consumer upon conclusion of investigation.* Upon the conclusion of a national security investigation described in subparagraph (A), or upon the determination that the exception under subparagraph (A) is no longer required for the reasons set forth in such subparagraph, the official exercising the authority in such subparagraph shall provide to the consumer

who is the subject of the consumer report with regard to which such finding was made--

   (i)   a copy of such consumer report with any classified information redacted as necessary;

   (ii) notice of any adverse action which is based, in part, on the consumer report; and

   (iii) the identification with reasonable specificity of the nature of the investigation for which the consumer report was sought.

(C)   *Delegation by head of agency or department.* For purposes of subparagraphs (A) and (B), the head of any agency or department of the United States Government may delegate his or her authorities under this paragraph to an official of such agency or department who has personnel security responsibilities and is a member of the Senior Executive Service or equivalent civilian or military rank.

(D)   *Report to the Congress.* Not later than January 31 of each year, the head of each agency and department of the United States Government that exercised authority under this paragraph during the preceding year shall submit a report to the Congress on the number of times the department or agency exercised such authority during the year.

(E)   *Definitions.* For purposes of this paragraph, the following definitions shall apply:

   (i)   The term "classified information" means information that is protected from unauthorized disclosure under Executive Order No. 12958 or successor orders.

   (ii) The term "national security investigation" means any official inquiry by an agency or department of the United States Government to determine the eligibility of a consumer to receive access or continued access to classified information or to determine whether classified information has been lost or compromised.

(c) Furnishing reports in connection with credit or insurance transactions that are not initiated by the consumer.

   (1) *In general.* A consumer reporting agency may furnish a consumer report relating to any consumer pursuant to subparagraph (A) or (C) of subsection (a)(3) in connection with any credit or insurance transaction that is not initiated by the consumer only if

      (A)   the consumer authorizes the agency to provide such report to such person; or

      (B) (i)   the transaction consists of a firm offer of credit or insurance;

          (ii) the consumer reporting agency has complied with subsection (e); and

(iii)   there is not in effect an election by the consumer, made in accordance with subsection (e), to have the consumer's name and address excluded from lists of names provided by the agency pursuant to this paragraph.

(2) *Limits on information received under paragraph (1)(B).* A person may receive pursuant to paragraph (1)(B) only

    (A)   the name and address of a consumer;

    (B)   an identifier that is not unique to the consumer and that is used by the person solely for the purpose of verifying the identity of the consumer; and

    (C)   other information pertaining to a consumer that does not identify the relationship or experience of the consumer with respect to a particular creditor or other entity.

(3) *Information regarding inquiries.* Except as provided in section 609(a)(5) [§1681g], a consumer reporting agency shall not furnish to any person a record of inquiries in connection with a credit or insurance transaction that is not initiated by a consumer.

(d) Reserved.

(e) Election of consumer to be excluded from lists.

(1) *In general.* A consumer may elect to have the consumer's name and address excluded from any list provided by a consumer reporting agency under subsection (c)(1)(B) in connection with a credit or insurance transaction that is not initiated by the consumer, by notifying the agency in accordance with paragraph (2) that the consumer does not consent to any use of a consumer report relating to the consumer in connection with any credit or insurance transaction that is not initiated by the consumer.

(2) *Manner of notification.* A consumer shall notify a consumer reporting agency under paragraph (1)

    (A)   through the notification system maintained by the agency under paragraph (5); or

    (B)   by submitting to the agency a signed notice of election form issued by the agency for purposes of this subparagraph.

(3) *Response of agency after notification through system.* Upon receipt of notification of the election of a consumer under paragraph (1) through the notification system maintained by the agency under paragraph (5), a consumer reporting agency shall

    (A)   inform the consumer that the election is effective only for the 5-year period following the election if the consumer does not submit to the agency a signed notice of election form issued by the agency for purposes of paragraph (2)(B); and

(B)   provide to the consumer a notice of election form, if requested by the consumer, not later than 5 business days after receipt of the notification of the election through the system established under paragraph (5), in the case of a request made at the time the consumer provides notification through the system.

(4) *Effectiveness of election.* An election of a consumer under paragraph (1)

    (A)   shall be effective with respect to a consumer reporting agency beginning 5 business days after the date on which the consumer notifies the agency in accordance with paragraph (2);

    (B)   shall be effective with respect to a consumer reporting agency

        (i)   subject to subparagraph (C), during the 5-year period beginning 5 business days after the date on which the consumer notifies the agency of the election, in the case of an election for which a consumer notifies the agency only in accordance with paragraph (2)(A); or

        (ii)   until the consumer notifies the agency under subparagraph (C), in the case of an election for which a consumer notifies the agency in accordance with paragraph (2)(B);

    (C)   shall not be effective after the date on which the consumer notifies the agency, through the notification system established by the agency under paragraph (5), that the election is no longer effective; and

    (D)   shall be effective with respect to each affiliate of the agency.

(5) Notification System

    (A)   *In general.* Each consumer reporting agency that, under subsection (c)(1)(B), furnishes a consumer report in connection with a credit or insurance transaction that is not initiated by a consumer, shall

        (i)   establish and maintain a notification system, including a toll-free telephone number, which permits any consumer whose consumer report is maintained by the agency to notify the agency, with appropriate identification, of the consumer's election to have the consumer's name and address excluded from any such list of names and addresses provided by the agency for such a transaction; and

        (ii)   publish by not later than 365 days after the date of enactment of the Consumer Credit Reporting Reform Act of 1996, and not less than annually thereafter, in a publication of general circulation in the area served by the agency

            (I)   a notification that information in consumer files maintained by the agency may be used in connection with such transactions; and

(II)   the address and toll-free telephone number for consumers to use to notify the agency of the consumer's election under clause (I).

(B)   *Establishment and maintenance as compliance.* Establishment and maintenance of a notification system (including a toll-free telephone number) and publication by a consumer reporting agency on the agency's own behalf and on behalf of any of its affiliates in accordance with this paragraph is deemed to be compliance with this paragraph by each of those affiliates.

(6) *Notification system by agencies that operate nationwide.* Each consumer reporting agency that compiles and maintains files on consumers on a nationwide basis shall establish and maintain a notification system for purposes of paragraph (5) jointly with other such consumer reporting agencies.

(f) *Certain use or obtaining of information prohibited.* A person shall not use or obtain a consumer report for any purpose unless

(1) the consumer report is obtained for a purpose for which the consumer report is authorized to be furnished under this section; and

(2) the purpose is certified in accordance with section 607 [§ 1681e] by a prospective user of the report through a general or specific certification.

(g) Protection of Medical Information

(1) *Limitation on consumer reporting agencies.* A consumer reporting agency shall not furnish for employment purposes, or in connection with a credit or insurance transaction, a consumer report that contains medical information (other than medical contact information treated in the manner required under section 605(a)(6)) about a consumer, unless--

(A)   if furnished in connection with an insurance transaction, the consumer affirmatively consents to the furnishing of the report;

(B)   if furnished for employment purposes or in connection with a credit transaction--

(i)   the information to be furnished is relevant to process or effect the employment or credit transaction; and

(ii)   the consumer provides specific written consent for the furnishing of the report that describes in clear and conspicuous language the use for which the information will be furnished; or

(C)   the information to be furnished pertains solely to transactions, accounts, or balances relating to debts arising from the receipt of medical services, products, or devises, where such information, other than account status or amounts, is restricted or reported using codes that do not identify, or do not

provide information sufficient to infer, the specific provider or the nature of such services, products, or devices, as provided in section 605(a)(6).

(2) *Limitation on creditors.* Except as permitted pursuant to paragraph (3)(C) or regulations prescribed under paragraph (5)(A), a creditor shall not obtain or use medical information (other than medical contact information treated in the manner required under section 605(a)(6)) pertaining to a consumer in connection with any determination of the consumer's eligibility, or continued eligibility, for credit.

(3) *Actions authorized by federal law, insurance activities and regulatory determinations.* Section 603(d)(3) shall not be construed so as to treat information or any communication of information as a consumer report if the information or communication is disclosed--

(A)   in connection with the business of insurance or annuities, including the activities described in section 18B of the model Privacy of Consumer Financial and Health Information Regulation issued by the National Association of Insurance Commissioners (as in effect on January 1, 2003);

(B)   for any purpose permitted without authorization under the Standards for Individually Identifiable Health Information promulgated by the Department of Health and Human Services pursuant to the Health Insurance Portability and Accountability Act of 1996, or referred to under section 1179 of such Act, or described in section 502(e) of Public Law 106-102; or

(C)   as otherwise determined to be necessary and appropriate, by regulation or order and subject to paragraph (6), by the Commission, any Federal banking agency or the National Credit Union Administration (with respect to any financial institution subject to the jurisdiction of such agency or Administration under paragraph (1), (2), or (3) of section 621(b), or the applicable State insurance authority (with respect to any person engaged in providing insurance or annuities).

(4)   *Limitation on redisclosure of medical information.* Any person that receives medical information pursuant to paragraph (1) or (3) shall not disclose such information to any other person, except as necessary to carry out the purpose for which the information was initially disclosed, or as otherwise permitted by statute, regulation, or order.

(5)   Regulations and Effective Date for Paragraph (2)

(A)   *Regulations required.* Each Federal banking agency and the National Credit Union Administration shall, subject to paragraph (6) and after notice and opportunity for comment, prescribe regulations that permit transactions under paragraph (2) that are determined to be necessary and appropriate to protect legitimate operational, transactional, risk, consumer, and other needs (and which shall include permitting actions necessary for administrative verification purposes), consistent with the intent of paragraph (2) to restrict the use of medical information for inappropriate purposes.

(B)   *Final regulations required.* The Federal banking agencies and the National Credit Union Administration shall issue the regulations required under sub-paragraph (A) in final form before the end of the 6-month period beginning on the date of enactment of the Fair and Accurate Credit Transactions Act of 2003.   ***See also 12 CFR Parts 41/222/232/334/571/717***
70 Fed. Reg. 70664 (11/22/05)

(6) *Coordination with other laws.* No provision of this subsection shall be construed as altering, affecting, or superseding the applicability of any other provision of Federal law relating to medical confidentiality.

§ 605. Requirements relating to information contained in consumer reports   [15 U.S.C. §1681c]

(a) *Information excluded from consumer reports.* Except as authorized under subsection (b) of this section, no consumer reporting agency may make any consumer report containing any of the following items of information:

(1) Cases under title 11 [United States Code] or under the Bankruptcy Act that, from the date of entry of the order for relief or the date of adjudication, as the case may be, antedate the report by more than 10 years.

(2) Civil suits, civil judgments, and records of arrest that from date of entry, antedate the report by more than seven years or until the governing statute of limitations has expired, whichever is the longer period.

(3) Paid tax liens which, from date of payment, antedate the report by more than seven years.

(4) Accounts placed for collection or charged to profit and loss which antedate the report by more than seven years.[2]

(5) Any other adverse item of information, other than records of convictions of crimes which antedates the report by more than seven years.[2]

(6) The name, address, and telephone number of any medical information furnisher that has notified the agency of its status, unless--

(A) such name, address, and telephone number are restricted or reported using codes that do not identify, or provide information sufficient to infer, the specific provider or the nature of such services, products, or devices to a person other than the consumer; or

(B) the report is being provided to an insurance company for a purpose relating to engaging in the business of insurance other than property and casualty insurance.

---

[2] The reporting periods have been lengthened for certain adverse information pertaining to U.S. Government insured or guaranteed student loans, or pertaining to national direct student loans. See sections 430A(f) and 463(c)(3) of the Higher Education Act of 1965, 20 U.S.C. 1080a(f) and 20 U.S.C. 1087cc(c)(3), respectively.

(b) *Exempted cases.* The provisions of paragraphs (1) through (5) of subsection (a) of this section are not applicable in the case of any consumer credit report to be used in connection with

(1) a credit transaction involving, or which may reasonably be expected to involve, a principal amount of $150,000 or more;

(2) the underwriting of life insurance involving, or which may reasonably be expected to involve, a face amount of $150,000 or more; or

(3) the employment of any individual at an annual salary which equals, or which may reasonably be expected to equal $75,000, or more.

(c) Running of Reporting Period

(1) *In general.* The 7-year period referred to in paragraphs (4) and (6) [3] of subsection (a) shall begin, with respect to any delinquent account that is placed for collection (internally or by referral to a third party, whichever is earlier), charged to profit and loss, or subjected to any similar action, upon the expiration of the 180-day period beginning on the date of the commencement of the delinquency which immediately preceded the collection activity, charge to profit and loss, or similar action.

(2) *Effective date.* Paragraph (1) shall apply only to items of information added to the file of a consumer on or after the date that is 455 days after the date of enactment of the Consumer Credit Reporting Reform Act of 1996.

(d) Information Required to be Disclosed

(1) *Title 11 information.* Any consumer reporting agency that furnishes a consumer report that contains information regarding any case involving the consumer that arises under title 11, United States Code, shall include in the report an identification of the chapter of such title 11 under which such case arises if provided by the source of the information. If any case arising or filed under title 11, United States Code, is withdrawn by the consumer before a final judgment, the consumer reporting agency shall include in the report that such case or filing was withdrawn upon receipt of documentation certifying such withdrawal.

(2) *Key factor in credit score information.* Any consumer reporting agency that furnishes a consumer report that contains any credit score or any other risk score or predictor on any consumer shall include in the report a clear and conspicuous statement that a key factor (as defined in section 609(f)(2)(B)) that adversely affected such score or predictor was the number of enquiries, if such a predictor was in fact a key factor that adversely affected such score. This paragraph shall not apply to a check services company, acting as such, which issues authorizations for the purpose of approving or processing negotiable instruments, electronic fund transfers, or similar methods of payments, but only to the extent that such company is engaged in such activities.

---

[3] This provision, added in September 1996, should read "paragraphs (4) and *(5)*...." Prior Section 605(a)(6) was amended and re-designated as Section 605(a)(5) in November 1998. The current Section 605(a)(6), added in December 2003 and now containing no reference to any 7-year period, is obviously inapplicable.

(e) *Indication of closure of account by consumer.* If a consumer reporting agency is notified pursuant to section 623(a)(4) [§ 1681s-2] that a credit account of a consumer was voluntarily closed by the consumer, the agency shall indicate that fact in any consumer report that includes information related to the account.

(f) *Indication of dispute by consumer.* If a consumer reporting agency is notified pursuant to section 623(a)(3) [§ 1681s-2] that information regarding a consumer who was furnished to the agency is disputed by the consumer, the agency shall indicate that fact in each consumer report that includes the disputed information.

(g) Truncation of Credit Card and Debit Card Numbers

    (1) In *general.* Except as otherwise provided in this subsection, no person that accepts credit cards or debit cards for the transaction of business shall print more than the last 5 digits of the card number or the expiration date upon any receipt provided to the cardholder at the point of the sale or transaction.

    (2) *Limitation.* This subsection shall apply only to receipts that are electronically printed, and shall not apply to transactions in which the sole means of recording a credit card or debit card account number is by handwriting or by an imprint or copy of the card.

    (3) *Effective date.* This subsection shall become effective--

        (A)   3 years after the date of enactment of this subsection, with respect to any cash register or other machine or device that electronically prints receipts for credit card or debit card transactions that is in use before January 1, 2005; and

        (B)   1 year after the date of enactment of this subsection, with respect to any cash register or other machine or device that electronically prints receipts for credit card or debit card transactions that is first put into use on or after January 1, 2005.

(h) Notice of Discrepancy in Address

    (1) *In general.* If a person has requested a consumer report relating to a consumer from a consumer reporting agency described in section 603(p), the request includes an address for the consumer that substantially differs from the addresses in the file of the consumer, and the agency provides a consumer report in response to the request, the consumer reporting agency shall notify the requester of the existence of the discrepancy.

                                                             See also 16 CFR Part 681.1

    (2) Regulations   ***72 Fed. Reg. 63771-72 (11/09/07)***

        (A)   *Regulations required.* The Federal banking agencies, the National Credit Union Administration, and the Commission shall jointly, with respect to the entities that are subject to their respective enforcement authority under section 621, prescribe regulations providing guidance regarding reasonable policies and procedures that a user of a consumer report should employ when such user has received a notice of discrepancy under paragraph (1).

(B)   *Policies and procedures to be included.* The regulations prescribed under subparagraph (A) shall describe reasonable policies and procedures for use by a user of a consumer report--

   (i)   to form a reasonable belief that the user knows the identity of the person to whom the consumer report pertains; and

   (ii)   if the user establishes a continuing relationship with the consumer, and the user regularly and in the ordinary course of business furnishes information to the consumer reporting agency from which the notice of discrepancy pertaining to the consumer was obtained, to reconcile the address of the consumer with the consumer reporting agency by furnishing such address to such consumer reporting agency as part of information regularly furnished by the user for the period in which the relationship is established.

§ 605A. Identity theft prevention; fraud alerts and active duty alerts [15 U.S.C. §1681c-1]

(a) One-call Fraud Alerts

(1) *Initial alerts.* Upon the direct request of a consumer, or an individual acting on behalf of or as a personal representative of a consumer, who asserts in good faith a suspicion that the consumer has been or is about to become a victim of fraud or related crime, including identity theft, a consumer reporting agency described in section 603(p) that maintains a file on the consumer and has received appropriate proof of the identity of the requester shall--

   (A)   include a fraud alert in the file of that consumer, and also provide that alert along with any credit score generated in using that file, for a period of not less than 90 days, beginning on the date of such request, unless the consumer or such representative requests that such fraud alert be removed before the end of such period, and the agency has received appropriate proof of the identity of the requester for such purpose; and

   (B)   refer the information regarding the fraud alert under this paragraph to each of the other consumer reporting agencies described in section 603(p), in accordance with procedures developed under section 621(f).

(2) *Access to free reports.* In any case in which a consumer reporting agency includes a fraud alert in the file of a consumer pursuant to this subsection, the consumer reporting agency shall--

   (A)   disclose to the consumer that the consumer may request a free copy of the file of the consumer pursuant to section 612(d); and

   (B)   provide to the consumer all disclosures required to be made under section 609, without charge to the consumer, not later than 3 business days after any request described in subparagraph (A).

(b) Extended Alerts

(1) *In general.* Upon the direct request of a consumer, or an individual acting on behalf of or as a personal representative of a consumer, who submits an identity theft report to a consumer reporting agency described in section 603(p) that maintains a file on the consumer, if the agency has received appropriate proof of the identity of the requester, the agency shall--

(A)   include a fraud alert in the file of that consumer, and also provide that alert along with any credit score generated in using that file, during the 7-year period beginning on the date of such request, unless the consumer or such representative requests that such fraud alert be removed before the end of such period and the agency has received appropriate proof of the identity of the requester for such purpose;

(B)   during the 5-year period beginning on the date of such request, exclude the consumer from any list of consumers prepared by the consumer reporting agency and provided to any third party to offer credit or insurance to the consumer as part of a transaction that was not initiated by the consumer, unless the consumer or such representative requests that such exclusion be rescinded before the end of such period; and

(C)   refer the information regarding the extended fraud alert under this paragraph to each of the other consumer reporting agencies described in section 603(p), in accordance with procedures developed under section 621(f).

(2) *Access to free reports.* In any case in which a consumer reporting agency includes a fraud alert in the file of a consumer pursuant to this subsection, the consumer reporting agency shall--

(A)   disclose to the consumer that the consumer may request 2 free copies of the file of the consumer pursuant to section 612(d) during the 12-month period beginning on the date on which the fraud alert was included in the file; and

(B)   provide to the consumer all disclosures required to be made under section 609, without charge to the consumer, not later than 3 business days after any request described in subparagraph (A).

(c) *Active duty alerts.* Upon the direct request of an active duty military consumer, or an individual acting on behalf of or as a personal representative of an active duty military consumer, a consumer reporting agency described in section 603(p) that maintains a file on the active duty military consumer and has received appropriate proof of the identity of the requester shall--

(1) include an active duty alert in the file of that active duty military consumer, and also provide that alert along with any credit score generated in using that file, during a period of not less than 12 months, or such longer period as the Commission shall determine, by regulation, beginning on the date of the request, unless the active duty

military consumer or such representative requests that such fraud alert be removed before the end of such period, and the agency has received appropriate proof of the identity of the requester for such purpose;

(2) during the 2-year period beginning on the date of such request, exclude the active duty military consumer from any list of consumers prepared by the consumer reporting agency and provided to any third party to offer credit or insurance to the consumer as part of a transaction that was not initiated by the consumer, unless the consumer requests that such exclusion be rescinded before the end of such period; and

(3) refer the information regarding the active duty alert to each of the other consumer reporting agencies described in section 603(p), in accordance with procedures developed under section 621(f).   ***See also 16 CFR Part 613.1***
69 Fed. Reg. 63922 (11/03/04)

(d) *Procedures.* Each consumer reporting agency described in section 603(p) shall establish policies and procedures to comply with this section, including procedures that inform consumers of the availability of initial, extended, and active duty alerts and procedures that allow consumers and active duty military consumers to request initial, extended, or active duty alerts (as applicable) in a simple and easy manner, including by telephone.

(e) *Referrals of alerts.* Each consumer reporting agency described in section 603(p) that receives a referral of a fraud alert or active duty alert from another consumer reporting agency pursuant to this section shall, as though the agency received the request from the consumer directly, follow the procedures required under--

(1) paragraphs (1)(A) and (2) of subsection (a), in the case of a referral under subsection (a)(1)(B);

(2) paragraphs (1)(A), (1)(B), and (2) of subsection (b), in the case of a referral under subsection (b)(1)(C); and

(3) paragraphs (1) and (2) of subsection (c), in the case of a referral under subsection (c)(3).

(f) *Duty of reseller to reconvey alert.* A reseller shall include in its report any fraud alert or active duty alert placed in the file of a consumer pursuant to this section by another consumer reporting agency.

(g) *Duty of other consumer reporting agencies to provide contact information.* If a consumer contacts any consumer reporting agency that is not described in section 603(p) to communicate a suspicion that the consumer has been or is about to become a victim of fraud or related crime, including identity theft, the agency shall provide information to the consumer on how to contact the Commission and the consumer reporting agencies described in section 603(p) to obtain more detailed information and request alerts under this section.

(h) Limitations on Use of Information for Credit Extensions

(1) Requirements for initial and active duty alerts-

(A) *Notification.* Each initial fraud alert and active duty alert under this section shall include information that notifies all prospective users of a consumer report on the consumer to which the alert relates that the consumer does not authorize the establishment of any new credit plan or extension of credit, other than under an open-end credit plan (as defined in section 103(i)), in the name of the consumer, or issuance of an additional card on an existing credit account requested by a consumer, or any increase in credit limit on an existing credit account requested by a consumer, except in accordance with subparagraph (B).

(B) Limitation on Users

(i) *In general.* No prospective user of a consumer report that includes an initial fraud alert or an active duty alert in accordance with this section may establish a new credit plan or extension of credit, other than under an open-end credit plan (as defined in section 103(i)), in the name of the consumer, or issue an additional card on an existing credit account requested by a consumer, or grant any increase in credit limit on an existing credit account requested by a consumer, unless the user utilizes reasonable policies and procedures to form a reasonable belief that the user knows the identity of the person making the request.

(ii) *Verification.* If a consumer requesting the alert has specified a telephone number to be used for identity verification purposes, before authorizing any new credit plan or extension described in clause (i) in the name of such consumer, a user of such consumer report shall contact the consumer using that telephone number or take reasonable steps to verify the consumer's identity and confirm that the application for a new credit plan is not the result of identity theft.

(2) Requirements for Extended Alerts

(A) *Notification.* Each extended alert under this section shall include information that provides all prospective users of a consumer report relating to a consumer with–

(i) notification that the consumer does not authorize the establishment of any new credit plan or extension of credit described in clause (i), other than under an open-end credit plan (as defined in section 103(i)), in the name of the consumer, or issuance of an additional card on an existing credit account requested by a consumer, or any increase in credit limit on an existing credit account requested by a consumer, except in accordance with subparagraph (B); and

(ii) a telephone number or other reasonable contact method designated by the consumer.

(B) *Limitation on users.* No prospective user of a consumer report or of a credit score generated using the information in the file of a consumer that includes an extended fraud alert in accordance with this section may establish a new credit plan or extension of credit, other than under an open-end credit plan (as defined in section 103(i)), in the name of the consumer, or issue an additional card on an existing credit account requested by a consumer, or any increase in credit limit on an existing credit account requested by a consumer, unless the user contacts the consumer in person or using the contact method described in subparagraph (A)(ii) to confirm that the application for a new credit plan or increase in credit limit, or request for an additional card is not the result of identity theft.

§ 605B. Block of information resulting from identity theft [15 U.S.C. §1681c-2]

(a) *Block.* Except as otherwise provided in this section, a consumer reporting agency shall block the reporting of any information in the file of a consumer that the consumer identifies as information that resulted from an alleged identity theft, not later than 4 business days after the date of receipt by such agency of–

(1) appropriate proof of the identity of the consumer;

(2) a copy of an identity theft report;

(3) the identification of such information by the consumer; and

(4) a statement by the consumer that the information is not information relating to any transaction by the consumer.

(b) *Notification.* A consumer reporting agency shall promptly notify the furnisher of information identified by the consumer under subsection (a)--

(1) that the information may be a result of identity theft;

(2) that an identity theft report has been filed;

(3) that a block has been requested under this section; and

(4) of the effective dates of the block.

(c) Authority to Decline or Rescind

(1) *In general.* A consumer reporting agency may decline to block, or may rescind any block, of information relating to a consumer under this section, if the consumer reporting agency reasonably determines that--

(A) the information was blocked in error or a block was requested by the consumer in error;

(B)   the information was blocked, or a block was requested by the consumer, on the basis of a material misrepresentation of fact by the consumer relevant to the request to block; or

(C)   the consumer obtained possession of goods, services, or money as a result of the blocked transaction or transactions.

(2) *Notification to consumer.* If a block of information is declined or rescinded under this subsection, the affected consumer shall be notified promptly, in the same manner as consumers are notified of the reinsertion of information under section 611(a)(5)(B).

(3) *Significance of block.* For purposes of this subsection, if a consumer reporting agency rescinds a block, the presence of information in the file of a consumer prior to the blocking of such information is not evidence of whether the consumer knew or should have known that the consumer obtained possession of any goods, services, or money as a result of the block.

(d) Exception for Resellers

(1) *No reseller file.* This section shall not apply to a consumer reporting agency, if the consumer reporting agency--

(A)   is a reseller;

(B)   is not, at the time of the request of the consumer under subsection (a), otherwise furnishing or reselling a consumer report concerning the information identified by the consumer; and

(C)   informs the consumer, by any means, that the consumer may report the identity theft to the Commission to obtain consumer information regarding identity theft.

(2) *Reseller with file.* The sole obligation of the consumer reporting agency under this section, with regard to any request of a consumer under this section, shall be to block the consumer report maintained by the consumer reporting agency from any subsequent use, if--

(A)   the consumer, in accordance with the provisions of subsection (a), identifies, to a consumer reporting agency, information in the file of the consumer that resulted from identity theft; and

(B)   the consumer reporting agency is a reseller of the identified information.

(3) *Notice.* In carrying out its obligation under paragraph (2), the reseller shall promptly provide a notice to the consumer of the decision to block the file. Such notice shall contain the name, address, and telephone number of each consumer reporting agency from which the consumer information was obtained for resale.

(e) *Exception for verification companies.* The provisions of this section do not apply to a check services company, acting as such, which issues authorizations for the purpose of approving

or processing negotiable instruments, electronic fund transfers, or similar methods of payments, except that, beginning 4 business days after receipt of information described in paragraphs (1) through (3) of subsection (a), a check services company shall not report to a national consumer reporting agency described in section 603(p), any information identified in the subject identity theft report as resulting from identity theft.

(f) *Access to blocked information by law enforcement agencies.* No provision of this section shall be construed as requiring a consumer reporting agency to prevent a Federal, State, or local law enforcement agency from accessing blocked information in a consumer file to which the agency could otherwise obtain access under this title.

§ **606. Disclosure of investigative consumer reports** [15 U.S.C. § 1681d]

(a) *Disclosure of fact of preparation.* A person may not procure or cause to be prepared an investigative consumer report on any consumer unless

(1) it is clearly and accurately disclosed to the consumer that an investigative consumer report including information as to his character, general reputation, personal characteristics and mode of living, whichever are applicable, may be made, and such disclosure

(A) is made in a writing mailed, or otherwise delivered, to the consumer, not later than three days after the date on which the report was first requested, and

(B) includes a statement informing the consumer of his right to request the additional disclosures provided for under subsection (b) of this section and the written summary of the rights of the consumer prepared pursuant to section 609(c) [§ 1681g]; and

(2) the person certifies or has certified to the consumer reporting agency that

(A) the person has made the disclosures to the consumer required by paragraph (1); and

(B) the person will comply with subsection (b).

(b) *Disclosure on request of nature and scope of investigation.* Any person who procures or causes to be prepared an investigative consumer report on any consumer shall, upon written request made by the consumer within a reasonable period of time after the receipt by him of the disclosure required by subsection (a)(1) of this section, make a complete and accurate disclosure of the nature and scope of the investigation requested. This disclosure shall be made in a writing mailed, or otherwise delivered, to the consumer not later than five days after the date on which the request for such disclosure was received from the consumer or such report was first requested, whichever is the later.

(c) *Limitation on liability upon showing of reasonable procedures for compliance with provisions.* No person may be held liable for any violation of subsection (a) or (b) of this section if he shows by a preponderance of the evidence that at the time of the violation he maintained reasonable procedures to assure compliance with subsection (a) or (b) of this section.

(d) Prohibitions

(1) *Certification.* A consumer reporting agency shall not prepare or furnish investigative consumer report unless the agency has received a certification under subsection (a)(2) from the person who requested the report.

(2) *Inquiries.* A consumer reporting agency shall not make an inquiry for the purpose of preparing an investigative consumer report on a consumer for employment purposes if the making of the inquiry by an employer or prospective employer of the consumer would violate any applicable Federal or State equal employment opportunity law or regulation.

(3) *Certain public record information.* Except as otherwise provided in section 613 [§ 1681k], a consumer reporting agency shall not furnish an investigative consumer report that includes information that is a matter of public record and that relates to an arrest, indictment, conviction, civil judicial action, tax lien, or outstanding judgment, unless the agency has verified the accuracy of the information during the 30-day period ending on the date on which the report is furnished.

(4) *Certain adverse information.* A consumer reporting agency shall not prepare or furnish an investigative consumer report on a consumer that contains information that is adverse to the interest of the consumer and that is obtained through a personal interview with a neighbor, friend, or associate of the consumer or with another person with whom the consumer is acquainted or who has knowledge of such item of information, unless

(A)   the agency has followed reasonable procedures to obtain confirmation of the information, from an additional source that has independent and direct knowledge of the information; or

(B)   the person interviewed is the best possible source of the information.

§ 607. Compliance procedures [15 U.S.C. § 1681e]

(a) *Identity and purposes of credit users.* Every consumer reporting agency shall maintain reasonable procedures designed to avoid violations of section 605 [§ 1681c] and to limit the furnishing of consumer reports to the purposes listed under section 604 [§ 1681b] of this title. These procedures shall require that prospective users of the information identify themselves, certify the purposes for which the information is sought, and certify that the information will be used for no other purpose. Every consumer reporting agency shall make a reasonable effort to verify the identity of a new prospective user and the uses certified by such prospective user prior to furnishing such user a consumer report. No consumer reporting agency may furnish a consumer report to any person if it has reasonable grounds for believing that the consumer report will not be used for a purpose listed in section 604 [§ 1681b] of this title.

(b) *Accuracy of report.* Whenever a consumer reporting agency prepares a consumer report it shall follow reasonable procedures to assure maximum possible accuracy of the information concerning the individual about whom the report relates.

(c) *Disclosure of consumer reports by users allowed.* A consumer reporting agency may not prohibit a user of a consumer report furnished by the agency on a consumer from disclosing the contents of the report to the consumer, if adverse action against the consumer has been taken by the user based in whole or in part on the report.

(d) Notice to Users and Furnishers of Information

    (1) *Notice requirement.* A consumer reporting agency shall provide to any person

        (A)   who regularly and in the ordinary course of business furnishes information to the agency with respect to any consumer; or

        (B)   to whom a consumer report is provided by the agency;

    a notice of such person's responsibilities under this title.   ***See also 16 CFR 698, App G-H 69 Fed. Reg. 69776 (11/30/04)***

    (2) *Content of notice.* The Federal Trade Commission shall prescribe the content of notices under paragraph (1), and a consumer reporting agency shall be in compliance with this subsection if it provides a notice under paragraph (1) that is substantially similar to the Federal Trade Commission prescription under this paragraph.

(e) Procurement of Consumer Report for Resale

    (1) *Disclosure.* A person may not procure a consumer report for purposes of reselling the report (or any information in the report) unless the person discloses to the consumer reporting agency that originally furnishes the report

        (A)   the identity of the end-user of the report (or information); and

        (B)   each permissible purpose under section 604 [§ 1681b] for which the report is furnished to the end-user of the report (or information).

    (2) *Responsibilities of procurers for resale.* A person who procures a consumer report for purposes of reselling the report (or any information in the report) shall

        (A)   establish and comply with reasonable procedures designed to ensure that the report (or information) is resold by the person only for a purpose for which the report may be furnished under section 604 [§ 1681b], including by requiring that each person to which the report (or information) is resold and that resells or provides the report (or information) to any other person

            (i)   identifies each end user of the resold report (or information);

            (ii)   certifies each purpose for which the report (or information) will be used; and

            (iii)   certifies that the report (or information) will be used for no other purpose; and

(B)   before reselling the report, make reasonable efforts to verify the identifications and certifications made under subparagraph (A).

(3) *Resale of consumer report to a federal agency or department.* Notwithstanding paragraph (1) or (2), a person who procures a consumer report for purposes of reselling the report (or any information in the report) shall not disclose the identity of the end-user of the report under paragraph (1) or (2) if–

(A)   the end user is an agency or department of the United States Government which procures the report from the person for purposes of determining the eligibility of the consumer concerned to receive access or continued access to classified information (as defined in section 604(b)(4)(E)(i)); and

(B)   the agency or department certifies in writing to the person reselling the report that nondisclosure is necessary to protect classified information or the safety of persons employed by or contracting with, or undergoing investigation for work or contracting with the agency or department.

§ 608. Disclosures to governmental agencies [15 U.S.C. § 1681f]

Notwithstanding the provisions of section 604 [§ 1681b] of this title, a consumer reporting agency may furnish identifying information respecting any consumer, limited to his name, address, former addresses, places of employment, or former places of employment, to a governmental agency.

§ 609. Disclosures to consumers [15 U.S.C. § 1681g]

(a) *Information on file; sources; report recipients.* Every consumer reporting agency shall, upon request, and subject to 610(a)(1) [§ 1681h], clearly and accurately disclose to the consumer:

(1) All information in the consumer's file at the time of the request except that--

(A)   if the consumer to whom the file relates requests that the first 5 digits of the social security number (or similar identification number) of the consumer not be included in the disclosure and the consumer reporting agency has received appropriate proof of the identity of the requester, the consumer reporting agency shall so truncate such number in such disclosure; and

(B)   nothing in this paragraph shall be construed to require a consumer reporting agency to disclose to a consumer any information concerning credit scores or any other risk scores or predictors relating to the consumer.

(2) The sources of the information; except that the sources of information acquired solely for use in preparing an investigative consumer report and actually use for no other purpose need not be disclosed: Provided, That in the event an action is brought under this title, such sources shall be available to the plaintiff under appropriate discovery procedures in the court in which the action is brought.

(3) (A) Identification of each person (including each end-user identified under section 607(e)(1) [§ 1681e]) that procured a consumer report

    (i) for employment purposes, during the 2-year period preceding the date on which the request is made; or

    (ii) for any other purpose, during the 1-year period preceding the date on which the request is made.

(B) An identification of a person under subparagraph (A) shall include

    (i) the name of the person or, if applicable, the trade name (written in full) under which such person conducts business; and

    (ii) upon request of the consumer, the address and telephone number of the person.

(C) Subparagraph (A) does not apply if--

    (i) the end user is an agency or department of the United States Government that procures the report from the person for purposes of determining the eligibility of the consumer to whom the report relates to receive access or continued access to classified information (as defined in section 604(b)(4)(E)(i)); and

    (ii) the head of the agency or department makes a written finding as prescribed under section 604(b)(4)(A).

(4) The dates, original payees, and amounts of any checks upon which is based any adverse characterization of the consumer, included in the file at the time of the disclosure.

(5) A record of all inquiries received by the agency during the 1-year period preceding the request that identified the consumer in connection with a credit or insurance transaction that was not initiated by the consumer.

(6) If the consumer requests the credit file and not the credit score, a statement that the consumer may request and obtain a credit score.

(b) *Exempt information.* The requirements of subsection (a) of this section respecting the disclosure of sources of information and the recipients of consumer reports do not apply to information received or consumer reports furnished prior to the effective date of this title except to the extent that the matter involved is contained in the files of the consumer reporting agency on that date.

(c) Summary of Rights to Obtain and Dispute Information in Consumer Reports and to Obtain Credit Scores   *See also 16 CFR Part 698, App F*
                                                                   69 Fed. Reg. 69776 (11/30/04)

(1) Commission Summary of Rights Required

(A) *In general.* The Commission shall prepare a model summary of the rights of consumers under this title.

(B)   *Content of summary.* The summary of rights prepared under subparagraph (A) shall include a description of–

(i)   the right of a consumer to obtain a copy of a consumer report under subsection (a) from each consumer reporting agency;

(ii)   the frequency and circumstances under which a consumer is entitled to receive a consumer report without charge under section 612;

(iii) the right of a consumer to dispute information in the file of the consumer under section 611;

(iv)   the right of a consumer to obtain a credit score from a consumer reporting agency, and a description of how to obtain a credit score;

(v)   the method by which a consumer can contact, and obtain a consumer report from, a consumer reporting agency without charge, as provided in the regulations of the Commission prescribed under section 211(c) of the Fair and Accurate Credit Transactions Act of 2003; and

(vi)   the method by which a consumer can contact, and obtain a consumer report from, a consumer reporting agency described in section 603(w), as provided in the regulations of the Commission prescribed under section 612(a)(1)(C).

(C)   *Availability of summary of rights.* The Commission shall--

(i)   actively publicize the availability of the summary of rights prepared under this paragraph;

(ii)   conspicuously post on its Internet website the availability of such summary of rights; and

(iii) promptly make such summary of rights available to consumers, on request.

(2) *Summary of rights required to be included with agency disclosures.* A consumer reporting agency shall provide to a consumer, with each written disclosure by the agency to the consumer under this section--

(A)   the summary of rights prepared by the Commission under paragraph (1);

(B)   in the case of a consumer reporting agency described in section 603(p), a toll-free telephone number established by the agency, at which personnel are accessible to consumers during normal business hours;

(C)   a list of all Federal agencies responsible for enforcing any provision of this title, and the address and any appropriate phone number of each such agency, in a form that will assist the consumer in selecting the appropriate agency;

(D)   a statement that the consumer may have additional rights under State law, and that the consumer may wish to contact a State or local consumer protection agency or a State attorney general (or the equivalent thereof) to learn of those rights; and

(E)   a statement that a consumer reporting agency is not required to remove accurate derogatory information from the file of a consumer, unless the information is outdated under section 605 or cannot be verified.

(d) Summary of Rights of Identity Theft Victims   *See also 16 CFR Part 698, App E*
69 Fed. Reg. 69776 (11/30/04)

(1) *In general.* The Commission, in consultation with the Federal banking agencies and the National Credit Union Administration, shall prepare a model summary of the rights of consumers under this title with respect to the procedures for remedying the effects of fraud or identity theft involving credit, an electronic fund transfer, or an account or transaction at or with a financial institution or other creditor.

(2) *Summary of rights and contact information.* Beginning 60 days after the date on which the model summary of rights is prescribed in final form by the Commission pursuant to paragraph (1), if any consumer contacts a consumer reporting agency and expresses a belief that the consumer is a victim of fraud or identity theft involving credit, an electronic fund transfer, or an account or transaction at or with a financial institution or other creditor, the consumer reporting agency shall, in addition to any other action that the agency may take, provide the consumer with a summary of rights that contains all of the information required by the Commission under paragraph (1), and information on how to contact the Commission to obtain more detailed information.

(e) Information Available to Victims

(1) *In general.* For the purpose of documenting fraudulent transactions resulting from identity theft, not later than 30 days after the date of receipt of a request from a victim in accordance with paragraph (3), and subject to verification of the identity of the victim and the claim of identity theft in accordance with paragraph (2), a business entity that has provided credit to, provided for consideration products, goods, or services to, accepted payment from, or otherwise entered into a commercial transaction for consideration with, a person who has allegedly made unauthorized use of the means of identification of the victim, shall provide a copy of application and business transaction records in the control of the business entity, whether maintained by the business entity or by another person on behalf of the business entity, evidencing any transaction alleged to be a result of identity theft to--

(A)   the victim;

(B)   any Federal, State, or local government law enforcement agency or officer specified by the victim in such a request; or

(C)   any law enforcement agency investigating the identity theft and authorized by the victim to take receipt of records provided under this subsection.

(2) *Verification of identity and claim.* Before a business entity provides any information under paragraph (1), unless the business entity, at its discretion, otherwise has a high degree of confidence that it knows the identity of the victim making a request under paragraph (1), the victim shall provide to the business entity--

    (A)   as proof of positive identification of the victim, at the election of the business entity–

        (i)   the presentation of a government-issued identification card;

        (ii)   personally identifying information of the same type as was provided to the business entity by the unauthorized person; or

        (iii)   personally identifying information that the business entity typically requests from new applicants or for new transactions, at the time of the victim's request for information, including any documentation described in clauses (i) and (ii); and

    (B)   as proof of a claim of identity theft, at the election of the business entity--

        (i)   a copy of a police report evidencing the claim of the victim of identity theft; and

        (ii)   a properly completed--

            (I)   copy of a standardized affidavit of identity theft developed and made available by the Commission; or

            (II)   an affidavit of fact that is acceptable to the business entity for that purpose.

(3) *Procedures.* The request of a victim under paragraph (1) shall--

    (A)   be in writing;

    (B)   be mailed to an address specified by the business entity, if any; and

    (C)   if asked by the business entity, include relevant information about any transaction alleged to be a result of identity theft to facilitate compliance with this section including–

        (i)   if known by the victim (or if readily obtainable by the victim), the date of the application or transaction; and

        (ii)   if known by the victim (or if readily obtainable by the victim), any other identifying information such as an account or transaction number.

(4) *No charge to victim.* Information required to be provided under paragraph (1) shall be so provided without charge.

(5) *Authority to decline to provide information.* A business entity may decline to provide information under paragraph (1) if, in the exercise of good faith, the business entity determines that--

    (A)   this subsection does not require disclosure of the information;

    (B)   after reviewing the information provided pursuant to paragraph (2), the business entity does not have a high degree of confidence in knowing the true identity of the individual requesting the information;

    (C)   the request for the information is based on a misrepresentation of fact by the individual requesting the information relevant to the request for information; or

    (D)   the information requested is Internet navigational data or similar information about a person's visit to a website or online service.

(6) *Limitation on liability.* Except as provided in section 621, sections 616 and 617 do not apply to any violation of this subsection.

(7) *Limitation on civil liability.* No business entity may be held civilly liable under any provision of Federal, State, or other law for disclosure, made in good faith pursuant to this subsection.

(8) *No new recordkeeping obligation.* Nothing in this subsection creates an obligation on the part of a business entity to obtain, retain, or maintain information or records that are not otherwise required to be obtained, retained, or maintained in the ordinary course of its business or under other applicable law.

(9) Rule of Construction

    (A)   *In general.* No provision of subtitle A of title V of Public Law 106-102, prohibiting the disclosure of financial information by a business entity to third parties shall be used to deny disclosure of information to the victim under this subsection.

    (B)   *Limitation.* Except as provided in subparagraph (A), nothing in this subsection permits a business entity to disclose information, including information to law enforcement under subparagraphs (B) and (C) of paragraph (1), that the business entity is otherwise prohibited from disclosing under any other applicable provision of Federal or State law.

(10) *Affirmative defense.* In any civil action brought to enforce this subsection, it is an affirmative defense (which the defendant must establish by a preponderance of the evidence) for a business entity to file an affidavit or answer stating that–

    (A)   the business entity has made a reasonably diligent search of its available business records; and

    (B)   the records requested under this subsection do not exist or are not reasonably available.

(11) *Definition of victim.* For purposes of this subsection, the term "victim" means a consumer whose means of identification or financial information has been used or transferred (or has been alleged to have been used or transferred) without the authority of that consumer, with the intent to commit, or to aid or abet, an identity theft or a similar crime.

(12) *Effective date.* This subsection shall become effective 180 days after the date of enactment of this subsection.

(13) *Effectiveness study.* Not later than 18 months after the date of enactment of this subsection, the Comptroller General of the United States shall submit a report to Congress assessing the effectiveness of this provision.

(f) Disclosure of Credit Scores

(1) *In general.* Upon the request of a consumer for a credit score, a consumer reporting agency shall supply to the consumer a statement indicating that the information and credit scoring model may be different than the credit score that may be used by the lender, and a notice which shall include--

   (A)   the current credit score of the consumer or the most recent credit score of the consumer that was previously calculated by the credit reporting agency for a purpose related to the extension of credit;

   (B)   the range of possible credit scores under the model used;

   (C)   all of the key factors that adversely affected the credit score of the consumer in the model used, the total number of which shall not exceed 4, subject to paragraph (9);

   (D)   the date on which the credit score was created; and

   (E)   the name of the person or entity that provided the credit score or credit file upon which the credit score was created.

(2) *Definitions.* For purposes of this subsection, the following definitions shall apply:

   (A)   The term "credit score" --

      (i)   means a numerical value or a categorization derived from a statistical tool or modeling system used by a person who makes or arranges a loan to predict the likelihood of certain credit behaviors, including default (and the numerical value or the categorization derived from such analysis may also be referred to as a "risk predictor" or "risk score"); and

      (ii)   does not include--

         (I)   any mortgage score or rating of an automated underwriting system that considers one or more factors in addition to credit information,

including the loan to value ratio, the amount of down payment, or the financial assets of a consumer; or

(II) any other elements of the underwriting process or underwriting decision.

(B) The term "key factors" means all relevant elements or reasons adversely affecting the credit score for the particular individual, listed in the order of their importance based on their effect on the credit score.

(3) *Timeframe and manner of disclosure.* The information required by this subsection shall be provided in the same timeframe and manner as the information described in subsection (a).

(4) *Applicability to certain uses.* This subsection shall not be construed so as to compel a consumer reporting agency to develop or disclose a score if the agency does not--

(A) distribute scores that are used in connection with residential real property loans; or

(B) develop scores that assist credit providers in understanding the general credit behavior of a consumer and predicting the future credit behavior of the consumer.

(5) Applicability to credit scores developed by another person.

(A) *In general.* This subsection shall not be construed to require a consumer reporting agency that distributes credit scores developed by another person or entity to provide a further explanation of them, or to process a dispute arising pursuant to section 611, except that the consumer reporting agency shall provide the consumer with the name and address and website for contacting the person or entity who developed the score or developed the methodology of the score.

(B) *Exception.* This paragraph shall not apply to a consumer reporting agency that develops or modifies scores that are developed by another person or entity.

(6) *Maintenance of credit scores not required.* This subsection shall not be construed to require a consumer reporting agency to maintain credit scores in its files.

(7) *Compliance in certain cases.* In complying with this subsection, a consumer reporting agency shall--

(A) supply the consumer with a credit score that is derived from a credit scoring model that is widely distributed to users by that consumer reporting agency in connection with residential real property loans or with a credit score that assists the consumer in understanding the credit scoring assessment of the credit behavior of the consumer and predictions about the future credit behavior of the consumer; and

    (B)   a statement indicating that the information and credit scoring model may be different than that used by the lender.

  (8) *Fair and reasonable fee.* A consumer reporting agency may charge a fair and reasonable fee, as determined by the Commission, for providing the information required under this subsection.   **See also 69 Fed. Reg. 64698 (11/08/04)**

  (9) *Use of enquiries as a key factor.* If a key factor that adversely affects the credit score of a consumer consists of the number of enquiries made with respect to a consumer report, that factor shall be included in the disclosure pursuant to paragraph (1)(C) without regard to the numerical limitation in such paragraph.

(g) Disclosure of Credit Scores by Certain Mortgage Lenders

  (1) *In general.* Any person who makes or arranges loans and who uses a consumer credit score, as defined in subsection (f), in connection with an application initiated or sought by a consumer for a closed end loan or the establishment of an open end loan for a consumer purpose that is secured by 1 to 4 units of residential real property (hereafter in this subsection referred to as the "lender") shall provide the following to the consumer as soon as reasonably practicable:

    (A)   Information Required under Subsection (f)

        (i)   *In general.* A copy of the information identified in subsection (f) that was obtained from a consumer reporting agency or was developed and used by the user of the information.

        (ii)   *Notice under subparagraph (D).* In addition to the information provided to it by a third party that provided the credit score or scores, a lender is only required to provide the notice contained in subparagraph (D).

    (B)   Disclosures in Case of Automated Underwriting System

        (i)   *In general.* If a person that is subject to this subsection uses an automated underwriting system to underwrite a loan, that person may satisfy the obligation to provide a credit score by disclosing a credit score and associated key factors supplied by a consumer reporting agency.

        (ii)   *Numerical credit score.* However, if a numerical credit score is generated by an automated underwriting system used by an enterprise, and that score is disclosed to the person, the score shall be disclosed to the consumer consistent with subparagraph (C).

        (iii)   *Enterprise defined.* For purposes of this subparagraph, the term "enterprise" has the same meaning as in paragraph (6) of section 1303 of the Federal Housing Enterprises Financial Safety and Soundness Act of 1992.

    (C)   *Disclosures of credit scores not obtained from a consumer reporting agency.* A person that is subject to the provisions of this subsection and that uses a credit score, other than a credit score provided by a consumer reporting agency, may

satisfy the obligation to provide a credit score by disclosing a credit score and associated key factors supplied by a consumer reporting agency.

(D) *Notice to home loan applicants.* A copy of the following notice, which shall include the name, address, and telephone number of each consumer reporting agency providing a credit score that was used:

"Notice To The Home Loan Applicant

"In connection with your application for a home loan, the lender must disclose to you the score that a consumer reporting agency distributed to users and the lender used in connection with your home loan, and the key factors affecting your credit scores.

"The credit score is a computer generated summary calculated at the time of the request and based on information that a consumer reporting agency or lender has on file. The scores are based on data about your credit history and payment patterns. Credit scores are important because they are used to assist the lender in determining whether you will obtain a loan. They may also be used to determine what interest rate you may be offered on the mortgage. Credit scores can change over time, depending on your conduct, how your credit history and payment patterns change, and how credit scoring technologies change.

"Because the score is based on information in your credit history, it is very important that you review the credit-related information that is being furnished to make sure it is accurate. Credit records may vary from one company to another.

"If you have questions about your credit score or the credit information that is furnished to you, contact the consumer reporting agency at the address and telephone number provided with this notice, or contact the lender, if the lender developed or generated the credit score. The consumer reporting agency plays no part in the decision to take any action on the loan application and is unable to provide you with specific reasons for the decision on a loan application.

"If you have questions concerning the terms of the loan, contact the lender."

(E) *Actions not required under this subsection.* This subsection shall not require any person to–

    (i) explain the information provided pursuant to subsection (f);

    (ii) disclose any information other than a credit score or key factors, as defined in subsection (f);

    (iii) disclose any credit score or related information obtained by the user after a loan has closed;

    (iv) provide more than 1 disclosure per loan transaction; or

    (v) provide the disclosure required by this subsection when another person has made the disclosure to the consumer for that loan transaction.

(F)   No Obligation for Content

     (i)   *In general.* The obligation of any person pursuant to this subsection shall be limited solely to providing a copy of the information that was received from the consumer reporting agency.

     (ii)   *Limit on liability.* No person has liability under this subsection for the content of that information or for the omission of any information within the report provided by the consumer reporting agency.

(G)   *Person defined as excluding enterprise.* As used in this subsection, the term "person" does not include an enterprise (as defined in paragraph (6) of section 1303 of the Federal Housing Enterprises Financial Safety and Soundness Act of 1992).

(2) Prohibition on Disclosure Clauses Null and Void

(A)   *In general.* Any provision in a contract that prohibits the disclosure of a credit score by a person who makes or arranges loans or a consumer reporting agency is void.

(B)   *No liability for disclosure under this subsection-* A lender shall not have liability under any contractual provision for disclosure of a credit score pursuant to this subsection.

§ 610. Conditions and form of disclosure to consumers [15 U.S.C. § 1681h]

(a) In General

(1) *Proper identification.* A consumer reporting agency shall require, as a condition of making the disclosures required under section 609 [§ 1681g], that the consumer furnish proper identification.

(2) *Disclosure in writing.* Except as provided in subsection (b), the disclosures required to be made under section 609 [§ 1681g] shall be provided under that section in writing.

(b) Other Forms of Disclosure

(1) *In general.* If authorized by a consumer, a consumer reporting agency may make the disclosures required under 609 [§ 1681g]

     (A)   other than in writing; and

     (B)   in such form as may be

         (i)   specified by the consumer in accordance with paragraph (2); and

         (ii)   available from the agency.

(2) *Form.* A consumer may specify pursuant to paragraph (1) that disclosures under section 609 [§ 1681g] shall be made

    (A)   in person, upon the appearance of the consumer at the place of business of the consumer reporting agency where disclosures are regularly provided, during normal business hours, and on reasonable notice;

    (B)   by telephone, if the consumer has made a written request for disclosure by telephone;

    (C)   by electronic means, if available from the agency; or

    (D)   by any other reasonable means that is available from the agency.

(c) *Trained personnel.* Any consumer reporting agency shall provide trained personnel to explain to the consumer any information furnished to him pursuant to section 609 [§ 1681g] of this title.

(d) *Persons accompanying consumer.* The consumer shall be permitted to be accompanied by one other person of his choosing, who shall furnish reasonable identification. A consumer reporting agency may require the consumer to furnish a written statement granting permission to the consumer reporting agency to discuss the consumer's file in such person's presence.

(e) *Limitation of liability.* Except as provided in sections 616 and 617 [§§1681n and 1681o] of this title, no consumer may bring any action or proceeding in the nature of defamation, invasion of privacy, or negligence with respect to the reporting of information against any consumer reporting agency, any user of information, or any person who furnishes information to a consumer reporting agency, based on information disclosed pursuant to section 609, 610, or 615 [§§ 1681g, 1681h, or 1681m] of this title or based on information disclosed by a user of a consumer report to or for a consumer against whom the user has taken adverse action, based in whole or in part on the report, except as to false information furnished with malice or willful intent to injure such consumer.

§ 611. Procedure in case of disputed accuracy [15 U.S.C. § 1681i]

(a) Reinvestigations of Disputed Information

    (1) Reinvestigation Required

        (A)   *In general.* Subject to subsection (f), if the completeness or accuracy of any item of information contained in a consumer's file at a consumer reporting agency is disputed by the consumer and the consumer notifies the agency directly, or indirectly through a reseller, of such dispute, the agency shall, free of charge, conduct a reasonable reinvestigation to determine whether the disputed information is inaccurate and record the current status of the disputed information, or delete the item from the file in accordance with paragraph (5), before the end of the 30-day period beginning on the date on which the agency receives the notice of the dispute from the consumer or reseller.

(B)   *Extension of period to reinvestigate.* Except as provided in subparagraph (C), the 30-day period described in subparagraph (A) may be extended for not more than 15 additional days if the consumer reporting agency receives information from the consumer during that 30-day period that is relevant to the reinvestigation.

(C)   *Limitations on extension of period to reinvestigate.* Subparagraph (B) shall not apply to any reinvestigation in which, during the 30-day period described in subparagraph (A), the information that is the subject of the reinvestigation is found to be inaccurate or incomplete or the consumer reporting agency determines that the information cannot be verified.

(2) Prompt Notice of Dispute to Furnisher of Information

(A)   *In general.* Before the expiration of the 5-business-day period beginning on the date on which a consumer reporting agency receives notice of a dispute from any consumer or a reseller in accordance with paragraph (1), the agency shall provide notification of the dispute to any person who provided any item of information in dispute, at the address and in the manner established with the person. The notice shall include all relevant information regarding the dispute that the agency has received from the consumer or reseller.

(B)   *Provision of other information.* The consumer reporting agency shall promptly provide to the person who provided the information in dispute all relevant information regarding the dispute that is received by the agency from the consumer or the reseller after the period referred to in subparagraph (A) and before the end of the period referred to in paragraph (1)(A).

(3) Determination That Dispute Is Frivolous or Irrelevant

(A)   *In general.* Notwithstanding paragraph (1), a consumer reporting agency may terminate a reinvestigation of information disputed by a consumer under that paragraph if the agency reasonably determines that the dispute by the consumer is frivolous or irrelevant, including by reason of a failure by a consumer to provide sufficient information to investigate the disputed information.

(B)   *Notice of determination.* Upon making any determination in accordance with subparagraph (A) that a dispute is frivolous or irrelevant, a consumer reporting agency shall notify the consumer of such determination not later than 5 business days after making such determination, by mail or, if authorized by the consumer for that purpose, by any other means available to the agency.

(C)   *Contents of notice.* A notice under subparagraph (B) shall include

(i)   the reasons for the determination under subparagraph (A); and

(ii)   identification of any information required to investigate the disputed information, which may consist of a standardized form describing the general nature of such information.

46

(4) *Consideration of consumer information.* In conducting any reinvestigation under paragraph (1) with respect to disputed information in the file of any consumer, the consumer reporting agency shall review and consider all relevant information submitted by the consumer in the period described in paragraph (1)(A) with respect to such disputed information.

(5) Treatment of Inaccurate or Unverifiable Information

    (A)   *In general.* If, after any reinvestigation under paragraph (1) of any information disputed by a consumer, an item of the information is found to be inaccurate or incomplete or cannot be verified, the consumer reporting agency shall–

        (i)   promptly delete that item of information from the file of the consumer, or modify that item of information, as appropriate, based on the results of the reinvestigation; and

        (ii)   promptly notify the furnisher of that information that the information has been modified or deleted from the file of the consumer.

    (B)   Requirements Relating to Reinsertion of Previously Deleted Material

        (i)   *Certification of accuracy of information.* If any information is deleted from a consumer's file pursuant to subparagraph (A), the information may not be reinserted in the file by the consumer reporting agency unless the person who furnishes the information certifies that the information is complete and accurate.

        (ii)   *Notice to consumer.* If any information that has been deleted from a consumer's file pursuant to subparagraph (A) is reinserted in the file, the consumer reporting agency shall notify the consumer of the reinsertion in writing not later than 5 business days after the reinsertion or, if authorized by the consumer for that purpose, by any other means available to the agency.

        (iii)   *Additional information.* As part of, or in addition to, the notice under clause (ii), a consumer reporting agency shall provide to a consumer in writing not later than 5 business days after the date of the reinsertion

            (I)   a statement that the disputed information has been reinserted;

            (II)   the business name and address of any furnisher of information contacted and the telephone number of such furnisher, if reasonably available, or of any furnisher of information that contacted the consumer reporting agency, in connection with the reinsertion of such information; and

            (III)   a notice that the consumer has the right to add a statement to the consumer's file disputing the accuracy or completeness of the disputed information.

(C) *Procedures to prevent reappearance.* A consumer reporting agency shall maintain reasonable procedures designed to prevent the reappearance in a consumer's file, and in consumer reports on the consumer, of information that is deleted pursuant to this paragraph (other than information that is reinserted in accordance with subparagraph (B)(i)).

(D) *Automated reinvestigation system.* Any consumer reporting agency that compiles and maintains files on consumers on a nationwide basis shall implement an automated system through which furnishers of information to that consumer reporting agency may report the results of a reinvestigation that finds incomplete or inaccurate information in a consumer's file to other such consumer reporting agencies.

(6) Notice of Results of Reinvestigation

(A) *In general.* A consumer reporting agency shall provide written notice to a consumer of the results of a reinvestigation under this subsection not later than 5 business days after the completion of the reinvestigation, by mail or, if authorized by the consumer for that purpose, by other means available to the agency.

(B) *Contents.* As part of, or in addition to, the notice under subparagraph (A), a consumer reporting agency shall provide to a consumer in writing before the expiration of the 5-day period referred to in subparagraph (A)

(i) a statement that the reinvestigation is completed;

(ii) a consumer report that is based upon the consumer's file as that file is revised as a result of the reinvestigation;

(iii) a notice that, if requested by the consumer, a description of the procedure used to determine the accuracy and completeness of the information shall be provided to the consumer by the agency, including the business name and address of any furnisher of information contacted in connection with such information and the telephone number of such furnisher, if reasonably available;

(iv) a notice that the consumer has the right to add a statement to the consumer's file disputing the accuracy or completeness of the information; and

(v) a notice that the consumer has the right to request under subsection (d) that the consumer reporting agency furnish notifications under that subsection.

(7) *Description of reinvestigation procedure.* A consumer reporting agency shall provide to a consumer a description referred to in paragraph (6)(B)(iii) by not later than 15 days after receiving a request from the consumer for that description.

(8) *Expedited dispute resolution.* If a dispute regarding an item of information in a consumer's file at a consumer reporting agency is resolved in accordance with paragraph (5)(A) by the deletion of the disputed information by not later than 3 business days after the date on which the agency receives notice of the dispute from the consumer in accordance with paragraph (1)(A), then the agency shall not be required to comply with paragraphs (2), (6), and (7) with respect to that dispute if the agency

(A) provides prompt notice of the deletion to the consumer by telephone;

(B) includes in that notice, or in a written notice that accompanies a confirmation and consumer report provided in accordance with subparagraph (C), a statement of the consumer's right to request under subsection (d) that the agency furnish notifications under that subsection; and

(C) provides written confirmation of the deletion and a copy of a consumer report on the consumer that is based on the consumer's file after the deletion, not later than 5 business days after making the deletion.

(b) *Statement of dispute.* If the reinvestigation does not resolve the dispute, the consumer may file a brief statement setting forth the nature of the dispute. The consumer reporting agency may limit such statements to not more than one hundred words if it provides the consumer with assistance in writing a clear summary of the dispute.

(c) *Notification of consumer dispute in subsequent consumer reports.* Whenever a statement of a dispute is filed, unless there is reasonable grounds to believe that it is frivolous or irrelevant, the consumer reporting agency shall, in any subsequent report containing the information in question, clearly note that it is disputed by the consumer and provide either the consumer's statement or a clear and accurate codification or summary thereof.

(d) *Notification of deletion of disputed information.* Following any deletion of information which is found to be inaccurate or whose accuracy can no longer be verified or any notation as to disputed information, the consumer reporting agency shall, at the request of the consumer, furnish notification that the item has been deleted or the statement, codification or summary pursuant to subsection (b) or (c) of this section to any person specifically designated by the consumer who has within two years prior thereto received a consumer report for employment purposes, or within six months prior thereto received a consumer report for any other purpose, which contained the deleted or disputed information.

(e) Treatment of Complaints and Report to Congress

(1) *In general.* The Commission shall--

(A) compile all complaints that it receives that a file of a consumer that is maintained by a consumer reporting agency described in section 603(p) contains incomplete or inaccurate information, with respect to which, the consumer appears to have disputed the completeness or accuracy with the consumer reporting agency or otherwise utilized the procedures provided by subsection (a); and

(B)   transmit each such complaint to each consumer reporting agency involved.

(2) *Exclusion.* Complaints received or obtained by the Commission pursuant to its investigative authority under the Federal Trade Commission Act shall not be subject to paragraph (1).

(3) *Agency responsibilities.* Each consumer reporting agency described in section 603(p) that receives a complaint transmitted by the Commission pursuant to paragraph (1) shall--

(A)   review each such complaint to determine whether all legal obligations imposed on the consumer reporting agency under this title (including any obligation imposed by an applicable court or administrative order) have been met with respect to the subject matter of the complaint;

(B)   provide reports on a regular basis to the Commission regarding the determinations of and actions taken by the consumer reporting agency, if any, in connection with its review of such complaints; and

(C)   maintain, for a reasonable time period, records regarding the disposition of each such complaint that is sufficient to demonstrate compliance with this subsection.

(4) *Rulemaking authority.* The Commission may prescribe regulations, as appropriate to implement this subsection.

(5) *Annual report.* The Commission shall submit to the Committee on Banking, Housing, and Urban Affairs of the Senate and the Committee on Financial Services of the House of Representatives an annual report regarding information gathered by the Commission under this subsection.'.

(f) Reinvestigation Requirement Applicable to Resellers

(1) *Exemption from general reinvestigation requirement.* Except as provided in paragraph (2), a reseller shall be exempt from the requirements of this section.

(2) *Action required upon receiving notice of a dispute.* If a reseller receives a notice from a consumer of a dispute concerning the completeness or accuracy of any item of information contained in a consumer report on such consumer produced by the reseller, the reseller shall, within 5 business days of receiving the notice, and free of charge–

(A)   determine whether the item of information is incomplete or inaccurate as a result of an act or omission of the reseller; and

(B)   if (i)   the reseller determines that the item of information is incomplete or inaccurate as a result of an act or omission of the reseller, not later than 20 days after receiving the notice, correct the information in the consumer report or delete it; or

    (ii)   if the reseller determines that the item of information is not incomplete or inaccurate as a result of an act or omission of the reseller, convey the notice of the dispute, together with all relevant information provided by the consumer, to each consumer reporting agency that provided the reseller with the information that is the subject of the dispute, using an address or a notification mechanism specified by the consumer reporting agency for such notices.

(3) *Responsibility of consumer reporting agency to notify consumer through reseller.* Upon the completion of a reinvestigation under this section of a dispute concerning the completeness or accuracy of any information in the file of a consumer by a consumer reporting agency that received notice of the dispute from a reseller under paragraph (2)--

    (A)   the notice by the consumer reporting agency under paragraph (6), (7), or (8) of subsection (a) shall be provided to the reseller in lieu of the consumer; and

    (B)   the reseller shall immediately reconvey such notice to the consumer, including any notice of a deletion by telephone in the manner required under paragraph (8)(A).

(4) *Reseller reinvestigations.* No provision of this subsection shall be construed as prohibiting a reseller from conducting a reinvestigation of a consumer dispute directly.

§ 612. Charges for certain disclosures [15 U.S.C. § 1681j]   *See also 16 CFR Part 610*
69 Fed. Reg. 35467 (06/24/04)

(a) Free Annual Disclosure

(1) Nationwide Consumer Reporting Agencies

    (A)   *In general.* All consumer reporting agencies described in subsections (p) and (w) of section 603 shall make all disclosures pursuant to section 609 once during any 12-month period upon request of the consumer and without charge to the consumer.

    (B)   *Centralized source.* Subparagraph (A) shall apply with respect to a consumer reporting agency described in section 603(p) only if the request from the consumer is made using the centralized source established for such purpose in accordance with section 211(c) of the Fair and Accurate Credit Transactions Act of 2003.

    (C)   Nationwide Specialty Consumer Reporting Agency

        (i)   *In general.* The Commission shall prescribe regulations applicable to each consumer reporting agency described in section 603(w) to require the establishment of a streamlined process for consumers to request consumer reports under subparagraph (A), which shall include, at a minimum, the establishment by each such agency of a toll-free telephone number for such requests.

(ii)   *Considerations.* In prescribing regulations under clause (i), the Commission shall consider–

     (I)   the significant demands that may be placed on consumer reporting agencies in providing such consumer reports;

     (II)   appropriate means to ensure that consumer reporting agencies can satisfactorily meet those demands, including the efficacy of a system of staggering the availability to consumers of such consumer reports; and

     (III)   the ease by which consumers should be able to contact consumer reporting agencies with respect to access to such consumer reports.

(iii)   *Date of issuance.* The Commission shall issue the regulations required by this subparagraph in final form not later than 6 months after the date of enactment of the Fair and Accurate Credit Transactions Act of 2003.

(iv)   *Consideration of ability to comply.* The regulations of the Commission under this subparagraph shall establish an effective date by which each nationwide specialty consumer reporting agency (as defined in section 603(w)) shall be required to comply with subsection (a), which effective date--

     (I)   shall be established after consideration of the ability of each nationwide specialty consumer reporting agency to comply with subsection (a); and

     (II)   shall be not later than 6 months after the date on which such regulations are issued in final form (or such additional period not to exceed 3 months, as the Commission determines appropriate).

(2) *Timing.* A consumer reporting agency shall provide a consumer report under paragraph (1) not later than 15 days after the date on which the request is received under paragraph (1).

(3) *Reinvestigations.* Notwithstanding the time periods specified in section 611(a)(1), a reinvestigation under that section by a consumer reporting agency upon a request of a consumer that is made after receiving a consumer report under this subsection shall be completed not later than 45 days after the date on which the request is received.

(4) *Exception for first 12 months of operation.* This subsection shall not apply to a consumer reporting agency that has not been furnishing consumer reports to third parties on a continuing basis during the 12-month period preceding a request under paragraph (1), with respect to consumers residing nationwide.

(b) *Free disclosure after adverse notice to consumer.* Each consumer reporting agency that maintains a file on a consumer shall make all disclosures pursuant to section 609 [§ 1681g] without charge to the consumer if, not later than 60 days after receipt by such

consumer of a notification pursuant to section 615 [§ 1681m], or of a notification from a debt collection agency affiliated with that consumer reporting agency stating that the consumer's credit rating may be or has been adversely affected, the consumer makes a request under section 609 [§ 1681g].

(c) *Free disclosure under certain other circumstances.* Upon the request of the consumer, a consumer reporting agency shall make all disclosures pursuant to section 609 [§ 1681g] once during any 12-month period without charge to that consumer if the consumer certifies in writing that the consumer

  (1) is unemployed and intends to apply for employment in the 60-day period beginning on the date on which the certification is made;

  (2) is a recipient of public welfare assistance; or

  (3) has reason to believe that the file on the consumer at the agency contains inaccurate information due to fraud.

(d) *Free disclosures in connection with fraud alerts.* Upon the request of a consumer, a consumer reporting agency described in section 603(p) shall make all disclosures pursuant to section 609 without charge to the consumer, as provided in subsections (a)(2) and (b)(2) of section 605A, as applicable.

(e) *Other charges prohibited* A consumer reporting agency shall not impose any charge on a consumer for providing any notification required by this title or making any disclosure required by this title, except as authorized by subsection (f).

(f) Reasonable Charges Allowed for Certain Disclosures

  (1) *In general.* In the case of a request from a consumer other than a request that is covered by any of subsections (a) through (d), a consumer reporting agency may impose a reasonable charge on a consumer

    (A) for making a disclosure to the consumer pursuant to section 609 [§ 1681g], which charge

      (i) shall not exceed $8;[4] and

      (ii) shall be indicated to the consumer before making the disclosure; and

    (B) for furnishing, pursuant to 611(d) [§ 1681i], following a reinvestigation under section 611(a) [§ 1681i], a statement, codification, or summary to a person designated by the consumer under that section after the 30-day period beginning on the date of notification of the consumer under paragraph (6) or (8) of section 611(a) [§ 1681i] with respect to the reinvestigation, which charge

---

[4] Pursuant to Section 612(f)(2), the Federal Trade Commission increased the maximum allowable charge to $10.50, effective January 1, 2008. See 72 Fed. Reg. 71912 (Dec. 19, 2005).

(i)   shall not exceed the charge that the agency would impose on each
designated recipient for a consumer report; and

(ii)   shall be indicated to the consumer before furnishing such information.

(2) *Modification of amount.* The Federal Trade Commission shall increase the amount
referred to in paragraph (1)(A)(i) on January 1 of each year, based proportionally on
changes in the Consumer Price Index, with fractional changes rounded to the nearest
fifty cents.

§ 613. Public record information for employment purposes [15 U.S.C. § 1681k]

(a) *In general.* A consumer reporting agency which furnishes a consumer report for
employment purposes and which for that purpose compiles and reports items of
information on consumers which are matters of public record and are likely to have an
adverse effect upon a consumer's ability to obtain employment shall

(1) at the time such public record information is reported to the user of such consumer
report, notify the consumer of the fact that public record information is being
reported by the consumer reporting agency, together with the name and address of the
person to whom such information is being reported; or

(2) maintain strict procedures designed to insure that whenever public record information
which is likely to have an adverse effect on a consumer's ability to obtain
employment is reported it is complete and up to date. For purposes of this paragraph,
items of public record relating to arrests, indictments, convictions, suits, tax liens, and
outstanding judgments shall be considered up to date if the current public record
status of the item at the time of the report is reported.

(b) *Exemption for national security investigations.* Subsection (a) does not apply in the case
of an agency or department of the United States Government that seeks to obtain and use
a consumer report for employment purposes, if the head of the agency or department
makes a written finding as prescribed under section 604(b)(4)(A).

§ 614. Restrictions on investigative consumer reports [15 U.S.C. § 1681*l*]

Whenever a consumer reporting agency prepares an investigative consumer report, no
adverse information in the consumer report (other than information which is a matter of public
record) may be included in a subsequent consumer report unless such adverse information has
been verified in the process of making such subsequent consumer report, or the adverse
information was received within the three-month period preceding the date the subsequent report
is furnished.

§ 615. Requirements on users of consumer reports [15 U.S.C. § 1681m]

(a) *Duties of users taking adverse actions on the basis of information contained in consumer
reports.* If any person takes any adverse action with respect to any consumer that is
based in whole or in part on any information contained in a consumer report, the person
shall

(1) provide oral, written, or electronic notice of the adverse action to the consumer;

(2) provide to the consumer orally, in writing, or electronically

    (A)   the name, address, and telephone number of the consumer reporting agency (including a toll-free telephone number established by the agency if the agency compiles and maintains files on consumers on a nationwide basis) that furnished the report to the person; and

    (B)   a statement that the consumer reporting agency did not make the decision to take the adverse action and is unable to provide the consumer the specific reasons why the adverse action was taken; and

(3) provide to the consumer an oral, written, or electronic notice of the consumer's right

    (A)   to obtain, under section 612 [§ 1681j], a free copy of a consumer report on the consumer from the consumer reporting agency referred to in paragraph (2), which notice shall include an indication of the 60-day period under that section for obtaining such a copy; and

    (B)   to dispute, under section 611 [§ 1681i], with a consumer reporting agency the accuracy or completeness of any information in a consumer report furnished by the agency.

(b) Adverse Action Based on Information Obtained from Third Parties Other than Consumer Reporting Agencies

(1) *In general.* Whenever credit for personal, family, or household purposes involving a consumer is denied or the charge for such credit is increased either wholly or partly because of information obtained from a person other than a consumer reporting agency bearing upon the consumer's credit worthiness, credit standing, credit capacity, character, general reputation, personal characteristics, or mode of living, the user of such information shall, within a reasonable period of time, upon the consumer's written request for the reasons for such adverse action received within sixty days after learning of such adverse action, disclose the nature of the information to the consumer. The user of such information shall clearly and accurately disclose to the consumer his right to make such written request at the time such adverse action is communicated to the consumer.

(2) Duties of Person Taking Certain Actions Based on Information Provided by Affiliate

    (A)   *Duties, generally.* If a person takes an action described in subparagraph (B) with respect to a consumer, based in whole or in part on information described in subparagraph (C), the person shall

        (i)   notify the consumer of the action, including a statement that the consumer may obtain the information in accordance with clause (ii); and

        (ii)   upon a written request from the consumer received within 60 days after transmittal of the notice required by clause (i), disclose to the consumer the nature of the information upon which the action is based by not later than 30 days after receipt of the request.

(B) *Action described.* An action referred to in subparagraph (A) is an adverse action described in section 603(k)(1)(A) [§ 1681a], taken in connection with a transaction initiated by the consumer, or any adverse action described in clause (i) or (ii) of section 603(k)(1)(B) [§ 1681a].

(C) *Information described.* Information referred to in subparagraph (A)

(i) except as provided in clause (ii), is information that

(I) is furnished to the person taking the action by a person related by common ownership or affiliated by common corporate control to the person taking the action; and

(II) bears on the credit worthiness, credit standing, credit capacity, character, general reputation, personal characteristics, or mode of living of the consumer; and

(ii) does not include

(I) information solely as to transactions or experiences between the consumer and the person furnishing the information; or

(II) information in a consumer report.

(c) *Reasonable procedures to assure compliance.* No person shall be held liable for any violation of this section if he shows by a preponderance of the evidence that at the time of the alleged violation he maintained reasonable procedures to assure compliance with the provisions of this section.

(d) Duties of Users Making Written Credit or Insurance Solicitations on the Basis of Information Contained in Consumer Files

(1) *In general.* Any person who uses a consumer report on any consumer in connection with any credit or insurance transaction that is not initiated by the consumer, that is provided to that person under section 604(c)(1)(B) [§ 1681b], shall provide with each written solicitation made to the consumer regarding the transaction a clear and conspicuous statement that

(A) information contained in the consumer's consumer report was used in connection with the transaction;

(B) the consumer received the offer of credit or insurance because the consumer satisfied the criteria for credit worthiness or insurability under which the consumer was selected for the offer;

(C) if applicable, the credit or insurance may not be extended if, after the consumer responds to the offer, the consumer does not meet the criteria used

to select the consumer for the offer or any applicable criteria bearing on credit worthiness or insurability or does not furnish any required collateral;

(D)   the consumer has a right to prohibit information contained in the consumer's file with any consumer reporting agency from being used in connection with any credit or insurance transaction that is not initiated by the consumer; and

(E)   the consumer may exercise the right referred to in subparagraph (D) by notifying a notification system established under section 604(e) [§ 1681b].

(2) *Disclosure of address and telephone number; format.* A statement under paragraph (1) shall--

(A)   include the address and toll-free telephone number of the appropriate notification system established under section 604(e); and

(B)   be presented in such format and in such type size and manner as to be simple and easy to understand, as established by the Commission, by rule, in consultation with the Federal banking agencies and the National Credit Union Administration.

> *See also 16 CFR Part 642*
> *16 CFR Part 698 App A*
> *70 Fed. Reg. 5022 (01/31/05)*

(3) *Maintaining criteria on file.* A person who makes an offer of credit or insurance to a consumer under a credit or insurance transaction described in paragraph (1) shall maintain on file the criteria used to select the consumer to receive the offer, all criteria bearing on credit worthiness or insurability, as applicable, that are the basis for determining whether or not to extend credit or insurance pursuant to the offer, and any requirement for the furnishing of collateral as a condition of the extension of credit or insurance, until the expiration of the 3-year period beginning on the date on which the offer is made to the consumer.

(4) *Authority of federal agencies regarding unfair or deceptive acts or practices not affected.* This section is not intended to affect the authority of any Federal or State agency to enforce a prohibition against unfair or deceptive acts or practices, including the making of false or misleading statements in connection with a credit or insurance transaction that is not initiated by the consumer.

(e) Red Flag Guidelines and Regulations Required

> *See also 16 CFR Part 681.2-681.3*
> *72 Fed. Reg. 63772-74 (11/09/07)*

(1) *Guidelines.* The Federal banking agencies, the National Credit Union Administration, and the Commission shall jointly, with respect to the entities that are subject to their respective enforcement authority under section 621–

(A)   establish and maintain guidelines for use by each financial institution and each creditor regarding identity theft with respect to account holders at, or customers of, such entities, and update such guidelines as often as necessary;

(B)   prescribe regulations requiring each financial institution and each creditor to establish reasonable policies and procedures for implementing the guidelines established pursuant to subparagraph (A), to identify possible risks to account holders or customers or to the safety and soundness of the institution or customers; and

(C) prescribe regulations applicable to card issuers to ensure that, if a card issuer receives notification of a change of address for an existing account, and within a short period of time (during at least the first 30 days after such notification is received) receives a request for an additional or replacement card for the same account, the card issuer may not issue the additional or replacement card, unless the card issuer, in accordance with reasonable policies and procedures–

    (i) notifies the cardholder of the request at the former address of the cardholder and provides to the cardholder a means of promptly reporting incorrect address changes;

    (ii) notifies the cardholder of the request by such other means of communication as the cardholder and the card issuer previously agreed to; or

    (iii) uses other means of assessing the validity of the change of address, in accordance with reasonable policies and procedures established by the card issuer in accordance with the regulations prescribed under subparagraph (B).

(2) Criteria

(A) *In general.* In developing the guidelines required by paragraph (1)(A), the agencies described in paragraph (1) shall identify patterns, practices, and specific forms of activity that indicate the possible existence of identity theft.

(B) *Inactive accounts.* In developing the guidelines required by paragraph (1)(A), the agencies described in paragraph (1) shall consider including reasonable guidelines providing that when a transaction occurs with respect to a credit or deposit account that has been inactive for more than 2 years, the creditor or financial institution shall follow reasonable policies and procedures that provide for notice to be given to a consumer in a manner reasonably designed to reduce the likelihood of identity theft with respect to such account.

(3) *Consistency with verification requirements.* Guidelines established pursuant to paragraph (1) shall not be inconsistent with the policies and procedures required under section 5318(l) of title 31, United States Code.

(f) Prohibition on Sale or Transfer of Debt Caused by Identity Theft

(1) *In general.* No person shall sell, transfer for consideration, or place for collection a debt that such person has been notified under section 605B has resulted from identity theft.

(2) *Applicability.* The prohibitions of this subsection shall apply to all persons collecting a debt described in paragraph (1) after the date of a notification under paragraph (1).

(3) *Rule of construction.* Nothing in this subsection shall be construed to prohibit--

    (A)   the repurchase of a debt in any case in which the assignee of the debt requires such repurchase because the debt has resulted from identity theft;

    (B)   the securitization of a debt or the pledging of a portfolio of debt as collateral in connection with a borrowing; or

    (C)   the transfer of debt as a result of a merger, acquisition, purchase and assumption transaction, or transfer of substantially all of the assets of an entity.

(g) *Debt collector communications concerning identity theft.* If a person acting as a debt collector (as that term is defined in title VIII) on behalf of a third party that is a creditor or other user of a consumer report is notified that any information relating to a debt that the person is attempting to collect may be fraudulent or may be the result of identity theft, that person shall--

    (1) notify the third party that the information may be fraudulent or may be the result of identity theft; and

    (2) upon request of the consumer to whom the debt purportedly relates, provide to the consumer all information to which the consumer would otherwise be entitled if the consumer were not a victim of identity theft, but wished to dispute the debt under provisions of law applicable to that person.

(h) Duties of Users in Certain Credit Transactions

    (1) *In general.* Subject to rules prescribed as provided in paragraph (6), if any person uses a consumer report in connection with an application for, or a grant, extension, or other provision of, credit on material terms that are materially less favorable than the most favorable terms available to a substantial proportion of consumers from or through that person, based in whole or in part on a consumer report, the person shall provide an oral, written, or electronic notice to the consumer in the form and manner required by regulations prescribed in accordance with this subsection.

    (2) *Timing.* The notice required under paragraph (1) may be provided at the time of an application for, or a grant, extension, or other provision of, credit or the time of communication of an approval of an application for, or grant, extension, or other provision of, credit, except as provided in the regulations prescribed under paragraph (6).

    (3) *Exceptions.* No notice shall be required from a person under this subsection if–

    (A)   the consumer applied for specific material terms and was granted those terms, unless those terms were initially specified by the person after the transaction was initiated by the consumer and after the person obtained a consumer report; or

    (B)   the person has provided or will provide a notice to the consumer under subsection (a) in connection with the transaction.

(4) *Other notice not sufficient.* A person that is required to provide a notice under subsection (a) cannot meet that requirement by providing a notice under this subsection.

(5) *Content and delivery of notice.* A notice under this subsection shall, at a minimum–

    (A)   include a statement informing the consumer that the terms offered to the consumer are set based on information from a consumer report;

    (B)   identify the consumer reporting agency furnishing the report;

    (C)   include a statement informing the consumer that the consumer may obtain a copy of a consumer report from that consumer reporting agency without charge; and

    (D)   include the contact information specified by that consumer reporting agency for obtaining such consumer reports (including a toll-free telephone number established by the agency in the case of a consumer reporting agency described in section 603(p)).

(6) Rulemaking

    (A)   *Rules required.* The Commission and the Board shall jointly prescribe rules.

    (B)   *Content.* Rules required by subparagraph (A) shall address, but are not limited to–

        (i)   the form, content, time, and manner of delivery of any notice under this subsection;

        (ii)   clarification of the meaning of terms used in this subsection, including what credit terms are material, and when credit terms are materially less favorable;

        (iii)   exceptions to the notice requirement under this subsection for classes of persons or transactions regarding which the agencies determine that notice would not significantly benefit consumers;

        (iv)   a model notice that may be used to comply with this subsection; and

        (v)   the timing of the notice required under paragraph (1), including the circumstances under which the notice must be provided after the terms offered to the consumer were set based on information from a consumer report.

(7) *Compliance.* A person shall not be liable for failure to perform the duties required by this section if, at the time of the failure, the person maintained reasonable policies and procedures to comply with this section.

(8) Enforcement

    (A)   *No civil actions.* Sections 616 and 617 shall not apply to any failure by any person to comply with this section.

    (B)   *Administrative enforcement.* This section shall be enforced exclusively under section 621 by the Federal agencies and officials identified in that section.

§ 616. Civil liability for willful noncompliance [15 U.S.C. § 1681n]

(a) *In general.* Any person who willfully fails to comply with any requirement imposed under this title with respect to any consumer is liable to that consumer in an amount equal to the sum of

    (1) (A)   any actual damages sustained by the consumer as a result of the failure or damages of not less than $100 and not more than $1,000; or

        (B)   in the case of liability of a natural person for obtaining a consumer report under false pretenses or knowingly without a permissible purpose, actual damages sustained by the consumer as a result of the failure or $1,000, whichever is greater;

    (2) such amount of punitive damages as the court may allow; and

    (3) in the case of any successful action to enforce any liability under this section, the costs of the action together with reasonable attorney's fees as determined by the court.

(b) *Civil liability for knowing noncompliance.* Any person who obtains a consumer report from a consumer reporting agency under false pretenses or knowingly without a permissible purpose shall be liable to the consumer reporting agency for actual damages sustained by the consumer reporting agency or $1,000, whichever is greater.

(c) *Attorney's fees.* Upon a finding by the court that an unsuccessful pleading, motion, or other paper filed in connection with an action under this section was filed in bad faith or for purposes of harassment, the court shall award to the prevailing party attorney's fees reasonable in relation to the work expended in responding to the pleading, motion, or other paper.

§ 617. Civil liability for negligent noncompliance [15 U.S.C. § 1681o]

(a) *In general.* Any person who is negligent in failing to comply with any requirement imposed under this title with respect to any consumer is liable to that consumer in an amount equal to the sum of

    (1) any actual damages sustained by the consumer as a result of the failure; and

    (2) in the case of any successful action to enforce any liability under this section, the costs of the action together with reasonable attorney's fees as determined by the court.

(b) *Attorney's fees.* On a finding by the court that an unsuccessful pleading, motion, or other paper filed in connection with an action under this section was filed in bad faith or for purposes of harassment, the court shall award to the prevailing party attorney's fees reasonable in relation to the work expended in responding to the pleading, motion, or other paper.

§ 618. Jurisdiction of courts; limitation of actions [15 U.S.C. § 1681p]

An action to enforce any liability created under this title may be brought in any appropriate United States district court, without regard to the amount in controversy, or in any other court of competent jurisdiction, not later than the earlier of (1) 2 years after the date of discovery by the plaintiff of the violation that is the basis for such liability; or (2) 5 years after the date on which the violation that is the basis for such liability occurs.

§ 619. Obtaining information under false pretenses [15 U.S.C. § 1681q]

Any person who knowingly and willfully obtains information on a consumer from a consumer reporting agency under false pretenses shall be fined under title 18, United States Code, imprisoned for not more than 2 years, or both.

§ 620. Unauthorized disclosures by officers or employees [15 U.S.C. § 1681r]

Any officer or employee of a consumer reporting agency who knowingly and willfully provides information concerning an individual from the agency's files to a person not authorized to receive that information shall be fined under title 18, United States Code, imprisoned for not more than 2 years, or both.

§ 621. Administrative enforcement [15 U.S.C. § 1681s]

(a) (1) *Enforcement by Federal Trade Commission.* Compliance with the requirements imposed under this title shall be enforced under the Federal Trade Commission Act [15 U.S.C. §§ 41 et seq.] by the Federal Trade Commission with respect to consumer reporting agencies and all other persons subject thereto, except to the extent that enforcement of the requirements imposed under this title is specifically committed to some other government agency under subsection (b) hereof. For the purpose of the exercise by the Federal Trade Commission of its functions and powers under the Federal Trade Commission Act, a violation of any requirement or prohibition imposed under this title shall constitute an unfair or deceptive act or practice in commerce in violation of section 5(a) of the Federal Trade Commission Act [15 U.S.C. § 45(a)] and shall be subject to enforcement by the Federal Trade Commission under section 5(b) thereof [15 U.S.C. § 45(b)] with respect to any consumer reporting agency or person subject to enforcement by the Federal Trade Commission pursuant to this subsection, irrespective of whether that person is engaged in commerce or meets any other jurisdictional tests in the Federal Trade Commission Act. The Federal Trade Commission shall have such procedural, investigative, and enforcement powers, including the power to issue procedural rules in enforcing compliance with the requirements imposed under this title and to require the filing of reports, the production of documents, and the appearance of witnesses as though the applicable terms and conditions of the Federal Trade Commission Act were part of

this title. Any person violating any of the provisions of this title shall be subject to the penalties and entitled to the privileges and immunities provided in the Federal Trade Commission Act as though the applicable terms and provisions thereof were part of this title.

(2) (A)   In the event of a knowing violation, which constitutes a pattern or practice of violations of this title, the Commission may commence a civil action to recover a civil penalty in a district court of the United States against any person that violates this title. In such action, such person shall be liable for a civil penalty of not more than $2,500 per violation.

(B)   In determining the amount of a civil penalty under subparagraph (A), the court shall take into account the degree of culpability, any history of prior such conduct, ability to pay, effect on ability to continue to do business, and such other matters as justice may require.

(3) Notwithstanding paragraph (2), a court may not impose any civil penalty on a person for a violation of section 623(a)(1) [§ 1681s-2] unless the person has been enjoined from committing the violation, or ordered not to commit the violation, in an action or proceeding brought by or on behalf of the Federal Trade Commission, and has violated the injunction or order, and the court may not impose any civil penalty for any violation occurring before the date of the violation of the injunction or order.

(b) *Enforcement by other agencies.* Compliance with the requirements imposed under this title with respect to consumer reporting agencies, persons who use consumer reports from such agencies, persons who furnish information to such agencies, and users of information that are subject to subsection (d) of section 615 [§ 1681m] shall be enforced under

(1) section 8 of the Federal Deposit Insurance Act [12 U.S.C. § 1818], in the case of

(A)   national banks, and Federal branches and Federal agencies of foreign banks, by the Office of the Comptroller of the Currency;

(B)   member banks of the Federal Reserve System (other than national banks), branches and agencies of foreign banks (other than Federal branches, Federal agencies, and insured State branches of foreign banks), commercial lending companies owned or controlled by foreign banks, and organizations operating under section 25 or 25A of the Federal Reserve Act [12 U.S.C. §§ 601 et seq., §§ 611 et seq], by the Board of Governors of the Federal Reserve System; and

(C)   banks insured by the Federal Deposit Insurance Corporation (other than members of the Federal Reserve System) and insured State branches of foreign banks, by the Board of Directors of the Federal Deposit Insurance Corporation;

(2) section 8 of the Federal Deposit Insurance Act [12 U.S.C. § 1818], by the Director of the Office of Thrift Supervision, in the case of a savings association the deposits of which are insured by the Federal Deposit Insurance Corporation;

(3) the Federal Credit Union Act [12 U.S.C. §§ 1751 et seq.], by the Administrator of the National Credit Union Administration [National Credit Union Administration Board] with respect to any Federal credit union;

(4) subtitle IV of title 49 [49 U.S.C. §§ 10101 et seq.], by the Secretary of Transportation, with respect to all carriers subject to the jurisdiction of the Surface Transportation Board;

(5) the Federal Aviation Act of 1958 [49 U.S.C. Appx §§ 1301 et seq.], by the Secretary of Transportation with respect to any air carrier or foreign air carrier subject to that Act [49 U.S.C. Appx §§ 1301 et seq.]; and

(6) the Packers and Stockyards Act, 1921 [7 U.S.C. §§ 181 et seq.] (except as provided in section 406 of that Act [7 U.S.C. §§ 226 and 227]), by the Secretary of Agriculture with respect to any activities subject to that Act.

The terms used in paragraph (1) that are not defined in this title or otherwise defined in section 3(s) of the Federal Deposit Insurance Act (12 U.S.C. §1813(s)) shall have the meaning given to them in section 1(b) of the International Banking Act of 1978 (12 U.S.C. § 3101).

(c) State Action for Violations

(1) *Authority of states.* In addition to such other remedies as are provided under State law, if the chief law enforcement officer of a State, or an official or agency designated by a State, has reason to believe that any person has violated or is violating this title, the State

    (A)   may bring an action to enjoin such violation in any appropriate United States district court or in any other court of competent jurisdiction;

    (B)   subject to paragraph (5), may bring an action on behalf of the residents of the State to recover

        (i)   damages for which the person is liable to such residents under sections 616 and 617 [§§ 1681n and 1681o] as a result of the violation;

        (ii)   in the case of a violation described in any of paragraphs (1) through (3) of section 623(c) [§ 1681s-2], damages for which the person would, but for section 623(c), be liable to such residents as a result of the violation; or

        (iii)   damages of not more than $1,000 for each willful or negligent violation; and

    (C)   in the case of any successful action under subparagraph (A) or (B), shall be awarded the costs of the action and reasonable attorney fees as determined by the court.

(2) *Rights of federal regulators.* The State shall serve prior written notice of any action under paragraph (1) upon the Federal Trade Commission or the appropriate Federal

regulator determined under subsection (b) and provide the Commission or appropriate Federal regulator with a copy of its complaint, except in any case in which such prior notice is not feasible, in which case the State shall serve such notice immediately upon instituting such action. The Federal Trade Commission or appropriate Federal regulator shall have the right

(A)   to intervene in the action;

(B)   upon so intervening, to be heard on all matters arising therein;

(C)   to remove the action to the appropriate United States district court; and

(D)   to file petitions for appeal.

(3) *Investigatory powers.* For purposes of bringing any action under this subsection, nothing in this subsection shall prevent the chief law enforcement officer, or an official or agency designated by a State, from exercising the powers conferred on the chief law enforcement officer or such official by the laws of such State to conduct investigations or to administer oaths or affirmations or to compel the attendance of witnesses or the production of documentary and other evidence.

(4) *Limitation on state action while federal action pending.* If the Federal Trade Commission or the appropriate Federal regulator has instituted a civil action or an administrative action under section 8 of the Federal Deposit Insurance Act for a violation of this title, no State may, during the pendency of such action, bring an action under this section against any defendant named in the complaint of the Commission or the appropriate Federal regulator for any violation of this title that is alleged in that complaint.

(5) Limitations on State Actions for Certain Violations

(A)   *Violation of injunction required.* A State may not bring an action against a person under paragraph (1)(B) for a violation described in any of paragraphs (1) through (3) of section 623(c), unless

(i)   the person has been enjoined from committing the violation, in an action brought by the State under paragraph (1)(A); and

(ii)   the person has violated the injunction.

(B)   *Limitation on damages recoverable.* In an action against a person under paragraph (1)(B) for a violation described in any of paragraphs (1) through (3) of section 623(c), a State may not recover any damages incurred before the date of the violation of an injunction on which the action is based.

(d) *Enforcement under other authority.* For the purpose of the exercise by any agency referred to in subsection (b) of this section of its powers under any Act referred to in that subsection, a violation of any requirement imposed under this title shall be deemed to be a violation of a requirement imposed under that Act. In addition to its powers under any provision of law specifically referred to in subsection (b) of this section, each of the agencies referred to in that subsection may exercise, for the purpose of enforcing compliance with any requirement imposed under this title any other authority conferred on it by law.

(e) Regulatory authority

(1) The Federal banking agencies referred to in paragraphs (1) and (2) of subsection (b) shall jointly prescribe such regulations as necessary to carry out the purposes of this Act with respect to any persons identified under paragraphs (1) and (2) of subsection (b), and the Board of Governors of the Federal Reserve System shall have authority to prescribe regulations consistent with such joint regulations with respect to bank holding companies and affiliates (other than depository institutions and consumer reporting agencies) of such holding companies.

(2) The Board of the National Credit Union Administration shall prescribe such regulations as necessary to carry out the purposes of this Act with respect to any persons identified under paragraph (3) of subsection (b).

(f) Coordination of Consumer Complaint Investigations

(1) *In general.* Each consumer reporting agency described in section 603(p) shall develop and maintain procedures for the referral to each other such agency of any consumer complaint received by the agency alleging identity theft, or requesting a fraud alert under section 605A or a block under section 605B.

(2) *Model form and procedure for reporting identity theft.* The Commission, in consultation with the Federal banking agencies and the National Credit Union Administration, shall develop a model form and model procedures to be used by consumers who are victims of identity theft for contacting and informing creditors and consumer reporting agencies of the fraud. *See also 70 Fed.Reg. 21792 (04/27/05)*

(3) *Annual summary reports.* Each consumer reporting agency described in section 603(p) shall submit an annual summary report to the Commission on consumer complaints received by the agency on identity theft or fraud alerts.

(g) *FTC regulation of coding of trade names.* If the Commission determines that a person described in paragraph (9) of section 623(a) has not met the requirements of such paragraph, the Commission shall take action to ensure the person's compliance with such paragraph, which may include issuing model guidance or prescribing reasonable policies and procedures, as necessary to ensure that such person complies with such paragraph.

§ 622. Information on overdue child support obligations [15 U.S.C. § 1681s-1]

Notwithstanding any other provision of this title, a consumer reporting agency shall include in any consumer report furnished by the agency in accordance with section 604 [§ 1681b] of this title, any information on the failure of the consumer to pay overdue support which

(1) is provided

(A) to the consumer reporting agency by a State or local child support enforcement agency; or

    (B)   to the consumer reporting agency and verified by any local, State, or Federal government agency; and

(2) antedates the report by 7 years or less.

§ 623. Responsibilities of furnishers of information to consumer reporting agencies
[15 U.S.C. § 1681s-2]

  (a) Duty of Furnishers of Information to Provide Accurate Information

  (1) Prohibition

    (A)   *Reporting information with actual knowledge of errors.* A person shall not furnish any information relating to a consumer to any consumer reporting agency if the person knows or has reasonable cause to believe that the information is inaccurate.

    (B)   *Reporting information after notice and confirmation of errors.* A person shall not furnish information relating to a consumer to any consumer reporting agency if

      (i)   the person has been notified by the consumer, at the address specified by the person for such notices, that specific information is inaccurate; and

      (ii)   the information is, in fact, inaccurate.

    (C)   *No address requirement.* A person who clearly and conspicuously specifies to the consumer an address for notices referred to in subparagraph (B) shall not be subject to subparagraph (A); however, nothing in subparagraph (B) shall require a person to specify such an address.

    (D)   *Definition.* For purposes of subparagraph (A), the term "reasonable cause to believe that the information is inaccurate" means having specific knowledge, other than solely allegations by the consumer, that would cause a reasonable person to have substantial doubts about the accuracy of the information.

  (2) *Duty to correct and update information.* A person who

    (A)   regularly and in the ordinary course of business furnishes information to one or more consumer reporting agencies about the person's transactions or experiences with any consumer; and

    (B)   has furnished to a consumer reporting agency information that the person determines is not complete or accurate, shall promptly notify the consumer reporting agency of that determination and provide to the agency any corrections to that information, or any additional information, that is necessary to make the information provided by the person to the agency complete and accurate, and shall not thereafter furnish to the agency any of the information that remains not complete or accurate.

(3) *Duty to provide notice of dispute.* If the completeness or accuracy of any information furnished by any person to any consumer reporting agency is disputed to such person by a consumer, the person may not furnish the information to any consumer reporting agency without notice that such information is disputed by the consumer.

(4) *Duty to provide notice of closed accounts.* A person who regularly and in the ordinary course of business furnishes information to a consumer reporting agency regarding a consumer who has a credit account with that person shall notify the agency of the voluntary closure of the account by the consumer, in information regularly furnished for the period in which the account is closed.

(5) Duty to Provide Notice of Delinquency of Accounts

    (A)   *In general.* A person who furnishes information to a consumer reporting agency regarding a delinquent account being placed for collection, charged to profit or loss, or subjected to any similar action shall, not later than 90 days after furnishing the information, notify the agency of the date of delinquency on the account, which shall be the month and year of the commencement of the delinquency on the account that immediately preceded the action.

    (B)   *Rule of construction.* For purposes of this paragraph only, and provided that the consumer does not dispute the information, a person that furnishes information on a delinquent account that is placed for collection, charged for profit or loss, or subjected to any similar action, complies with this paragraph, if–

        (i)   the person reports the same date of delinquency as that provided by the creditor to which the account was owed at the time at which the commencement of the delinquency occurred, if the creditor previously reported that date of delinquency to a consumer reporting agency;

        (ii)   the creditor did not previously report the date of delinquency to a consumer reporting agency, and the person establishes and follows reasonable procedures to obtain the date of delinquency from the creditor or another reliable source and reports that date to a consumer reporting agency as the date of delinquency; or

        (iii)   the creditor did not previously report the date of delinquency to a consumer reporting agency and the date of delinquency cannot be reasonably obtained as provided in clause (ii), the person establishes and follows reasonable procedures to ensure the date reported as the date of delinquency precedes the date on which the account is placed for collection, charged to profit or loss, or subjected to any similar action, and reports such date to the credit reporting agency.

(6) Duties of Furnishers Upon Notice of Identity Theft-Related Information

    (A)   *Reasonable procedures.* A person that furnishes information to any consumer reporting agency shall have in place reasonable procedures to respond to any notification that it receives from a consumer reporting agency under section

605B relating to information resulting from identity theft, to prevent that person from refurnishing such blocked information.

(B)   *Information alleged to result from identity theft.* If a consumer submits an identity theft report to a person who furnishes information to a consumer reporting agency at the address specified by that person for receiving such reports stating that information maintained by such person that purports to relate to the consumer resulted from identity theft, the person may not furnish such information that purports to relate to the consumer to any consumer reporting agency, unless the person subsequently knows or is informed by the consumer that the information is correct.

(7) Negative Information

(A)   Notice to Consumer Required

(i)   *In general.* If any financial institution that extends credit and regularly and in the ordinary course of business furnishes information to a consumer reporting agency described in section 603(p) furnishes negative information to such an agency regarding credit extended to a customer, the financial institution shall provide a notice of such furnishing of negative information, in writing, to the customer.

(ii)   *Notice effective for subsequent submissions.* After providing such notice, the financial institution may submit additional negative information to a consumer reporting agency described in section 603(p) with respect to the same transaction, extension of credit, account, or customer without providing additional notice to the customer.

(B)   Time of Notice

(i)   *In general.* The notice required under subparagraph (A) shall be provided to the customer prior to, or no later than 30 days after, furnishing the negative information to a consumer reporting agency described in section 603(p).

(ii)   *Coordination with new account disclosures.* If the notice is provided to the customer prior to furnishing the negative information to a consumer reporting agency, the notice may not be included in the initial disclosures provided under section 127(a) of the Truth in Lending Act.

(C)   *Coordination with other disclosures*- The notice required under subparagraph (A)--

(i)   may be included on or with any notice of default, any billing statement, or any other materials provided to the customer; and

(ii)   must be clear and conspicuous.

(D) Model Disclosure

    (i) *Duty of board to prepare.* The Board shall prescribe a brief model disclosure a financial institution may use to comply with subparagraph (A), which shall not exceed 30 words. ***See also 12 CFR Part 222, App B 70 Fed. Reg. 33281 (06/15/04)***

    (ii) *Use of model not required.* No provision of this paragraph shall be construed as requiring a financial institution to use any such model form prescribed by the Board.

    (iii) *Compliance using model.* A financial institution shall be deemed to be in compliance with subparagraph (A) if the financial institution uses any such model form prescribed by the Board, or the financial institution uses any such model form and rearranges its format.

(E) *Use of notice without submitting negative information.* No provision of this paragraph shall be construed as requiring a financial institution that has provided a customer with a notice described in subparagraph (A) to furnish negative information about the customer to a consumer reporting agency.

(F) *Safe harbor.* A financial institution shall not be liable for failure to perform the duties required by this paragraph if, at the time of the failure, the financial institution maintained reasonable policies and procedures to comply with this paragraph or the financial institution reasonably believed that the institution is prohibited, by law, from contacting the consumer.

(G) *Definitions.* For purposes of this paragraph, the following definitions shall apply:

    (i) The term "negative information" means information concerning a customer's delinquencies, late payments, insolvency, or any form of default.

    (ii) The terms "customer" and "financial institution" have the same meanings as in section 509 Public Law 106-102.

(8) Ability of Consumer to Dispute Information Directly with Furnisher

(A) *In general.* The Federal banking agencies, the National Credit Union Administration, and the Commission shall jointly prescribe regulations that shall identify the circumstances under which a furnisher shall be required to reinvestigate a dispute concerning the accuracy of information contained in a consumer report on the consumer, based on a direct request of a consumer.

(B) *Considerations.* In prescribing regulations under subparagraph (A), the agencies shall weigh--

    (i) the benefits to consumers with the costs on furnishers and the credit reporting system;

(ii)   the impact on the overall accuracy and integrity of consumer reports of any such requirements;

(iii)   whether direct contact by the consumer with the furnisher would likely result in the most expeditious resolution of any such dispute; and

(iv)   the potential impact on the credit reporting process if credit repair organizations, as defined in section 403(3) [15 U.S.C. §1679a(3)], including entities that would be a credit repair organization, but for section 403(3)(B)(i), are able to circumvent the prohibition in subparagraph (G).

(C)   *Applicability.* Subparagraphs (D) through (G) shall apply in any circumstance identified under the regulations promulgated under subparagraph (A).

(D)   *Submitting a notice of dispute-* A consumer who seeks to dispute the accuracy of information shall provide a dispute notice directly to such person at the address specified by the person for such notices that--

(i)   identifies the specific information that is being disputed;

(ii)   explains the basis for the dispute; and

(iii)   includes all supporting documentation required by the furnisher to substantiate the basis of the dispute.

(E)   *Duty of person after receiving notice of dispute.* After receiving a notice of dispute from a consumer pursuant to subparagraph (D), the person that provided the information in dispute to a consumer reporting agency shall–

(i)   conduct an investigation with respect to the disputed information;

(ii)   review all relevant information provided by the consumer with the notice;

(iii)   complete such person's investigation of the dispute and report the results of the investigation to the consumer before the expiration of the period under section 611(a)(1) within which a consumer reporting agency would be required to complete its action if the consumer had elected to dispute the information under that section; and

(iv)   if the investigation finds that the information reported was inaccurate, promptly notify each consumer reporting agency to which the person furnished the inaccurate information of that determination and provide to the agency any correction to that information that is necessary to make the information provided by the person accurate.

71

(F)   Frivolous or Irrelevant Dispute

    (i)   *In general.* This paragraph shall not apply if the person receiving a notice of a dispute from a consumer reasonably determines that the dispute is frivolous or irrelevant, including--

        (I)   by reason of the failure of a consumer to provide sufficient information to investigate the disputed information; or

        (II)   the submission by a consumer of a dispute that is substantially the same as a dispute previously submitted by or for the consumer, either directly to the person or through a consumer reporting agency under subsection (b), with respect to which the person has already performed the person's duties under this paragraph or subsection (b), as applicable.

    (ii)   *Notice of determination.* Upon making any determination under clause (i) that a dispute is frivolous or irrelevant, the person shall notify the consumer of such determination not later than 5 business days after making such determination, by mail or, if authorized by the consumer for that purpose, by any other means available to the person.

    (iii)   *Contents of notice.* A notice under clause (ii) shall include--

        (I)   the reasons for the determination under clause (i); and

        (II)   identification of any information required to investigate the disputed information, which may consist of a standardized form describing the general nature of such information.

(G)   *Exclusion of credit repair organizations.* This paragraph shall not apply if the notice of the dispute is submitted by, is prepared on behalf of the consumer by, or is submitted on a form supplied to the consumer by, a credit repair organization, as defined in section 403(3), or an entity that would be a credit repair organization, but for section 403(3)(B)(i).

(9) *Duty to provide notice of status as medical information furnisher.* A person whose primary business is providing medical services, products, or devices, or the person's agent or assignee, who furnishes information to a consumer reporting agency on a consumer shall be considered a medical information furnisher for purposes of this title, and shall notify the agency of such status.

(b) Duties of Furnishers of Information upon Notice of Dispute

(1) *In general.* After receiving notice pursuant to section 611(a)(2) [§ 1681i] of a dispute with regard to the completeness or accuracy of any information provided by a person to a consumer reporting agency, the person shall

(A)   conduct an investigation with respect to the disputed information;

(B)   review all relevant information provided by the consumer reporting agency pursuant to section 611(a)(2) [§ 1681i];

(C)   report the results of the investigation to the consumer reporting agency;

(D)   if the investigation finds that the information is incomplete or inaccurate, report those results to all other consumer reporting agencies to which the person furnished the information and that compile and maintain files on consumers on a nationwide basis; and

(E)   if an item of information disputed by a consumer is found to be inaccurate or incomplete or cannot be verified after any reinvestigation under paragraph (1), for purposes of reporting to a consumer reporting agency only, as appropriate, based on the results of the reinvestigation promptly–

(i)   modify that item of information;

(ii)   delete that item of information; or

(iii)   permanently block the reporting of that item of information.

(2) *Deadline.* A person shall complete all investigations, reviews, and reports required under paragraph (1) regarding information provided by the person to a consumer reporting agency, before the expiration of the period under section 611(a)(1) [§ 1681i] within which the consumer reporting agency is required to complete actions required by that section regarding that information.

(c) *Limitation on liability.* Except as provided in section 621(c)(1)(B), sections 616 and 617 do not apply to any violation of--

(1) subsection (a) of this section, including any regulations issued thereunder;

(2) subsection (e) of this section, except that nothing in this paragraph shall limit, expand, or otherwise affect liability under section 616 or 617, as applicable, for violations of subsection (b) of this section; or

(3) subsection (e) of section 615.

(d) *Limitation on enforcement.* The provisions of law described in paragraphs (1) through (3) of subsection (c) (other than with respect to the exception described in paragraph (2) of subsection (c)) shall be enforced exclusively as provided under section 621 by the Federal agencies and officials and the State officials identified in section 621.

(e) Accuracy Guidelines and Regulations Required

(1) *Guidelines.* The Federal banking agencies, the National Credit Union Administration, and the Commission shall, with respect to the entities that are subject to their respective enforcement authority under section 621, and in coordination as described in paragraph (2)--

(A)   establish and maintain guidelines for use by each person that furnishes
        information to a consumer reporting agency regarding the accuracy and
        integrity of the information relating to consumers that such entities furnish to
        consumer reporting agencies, and update such guidelines as often as
        necessary; and

(B)   prescribe regulations requiring each person that furnishes information to a
        consumer reporting agency to establish reasonable policies and procedures for
        implementing the guidelines established pursuant to subparagraph (A).

(2) *Coordination.* Each agency required to prescribe regulations under paragraph (1)
shall consult and coordinate with each other such agency so that, to the extent
possible, the regulations prescribed by each such entity are consistent and comparable
with the regulations prescribed by each other such agency.

(3) *Criteria.* In developing the guidelines required by paragraph (1)(A), the agencies
described in paragraph (1) shall--

(A)   identify patterns, practices, and specific forms of activity that can compromise
        the accuracy and integrity of information furnished to consumer reporting
        agencies;

(B)   review the methods (including technological means) used to furnish
        information relating to consumers to consumer reporting agencies;

(C)   determine whether persons that furnish information to consumer reporting
        agencies maintain and enforce policies to assure the accuracy and integrity of
        information furnished to consumer reporting agencies; and

(D)   examine the policies and processes that persons that furnish information to
        consumer reporting agencies employ to conduct reinvestigations and correct
        inaccurate information relating to consumers that has been furnished to
        consumer reporting agencies.

§ 624. Affiliate sharing [15 U.S.C. § 1681s-3]   *See also 16 CFR Parts 680, 698 Appx C*
                                                             72 Fed. Reg. 61455-64 (10/30/07)

(a) Special Rule for Solicitation for Purposes of Marketing)

(1) *Notice.* Any person that receives from another person related to it by common
ownership or affiliated by corporate control a communication of information that
would be a consumer report, but for clauses (i), (ii), and (iii) of section 603(d)(2)(A),
may not use the information to make a solicitation for marketing purposes to a
consumer about its products or services, unless--

(A)   it is clearly and conspicuously disclosed to the consumer that the information
        may be communicated among such persons for purposes of making such
        solicitations to the consumer; and

(B)   the consumer is provided an opportunity and a simple method to prohibit the
        making of such solicitations to the consumer by such person.

(2) Consumer Choice

   (A)   *In general.* The notice required under paragraph (1) shall allow the consumer the opportunity to prohibit all solicitations referred to in such paragraph, and may allow the consumer to choose from different options when electing to prohibit the sending of such solicitations, including options regarding the types of entities and information covered, and which methods of delivering solicitations the consumer elects to prohibit.

   (B)   *Format.* Notwithstanding subparagraph (A), the notice required under paragraph (1) shall be clear, conspicuous, and concise, and any method provided under paragraph (1)(B) shall be simple. The regulations prescribed to implement this section shall provide specific guidance regarding how to comply with such standards.

(3) Duration

   (A)   *In general.* The election of a consumer pursuant to paragraph (1)(B) to prohibit the making of solicitations shall be effective for at least 5 years, beginning on the date on which the person receives the election of the consumer, unless the consumer requests that such election be revoked.

   (B)   *Notice upon expiration of effective period.* At such time as the election of a consumer pursuant to paragraph (1)(B) is no longer effective, a person may not use information that the person receives in the manner described in paragraph (1) to make any solicitation for marketing purposes to the consumer, unless the consumer receives a notice and an opportunity, using a simple method, to extend the opt-out for another period of at least 5 years, pursuant to the procedures described in paragraph (1).

(4) *Scope.* This section shall not apply to a person–

   (A)   using information to make a solicitation for marketing purposes to a consumer with whom the person has a pre-existing business relationship;

   (B)   using information to facilitate communications to an individual for whose benefit the person provides employee benefit or other services pursuant to a contract with an employer related to and arising out of the current employment relationship or status of the individual as a participant or beneficiary of an employee benefit plan;

   (C)   using information to perform services on behalf of another person related by common ownership or affiliated by corporate control, except that this subparagraph shall not be construed as permitting a person to send solicitations on behalf of another person, if such other person would not be permitted to send the solicitation on its own behalf as a result of the election of the consumer to prohibit solicitations under paragraph (1)(B);

(D)   using information in response to a communication initiated by the consumer;

(E)   using information in response to solicitations authorized or requested by the consumer; or

(F)   if compliance with this section by that person would prevent compliance by that person with any provision of State insurance laws pertaining to unfair discrimination in any State in which the person is lawfully doing business.

(5) *No retroactivity.* This subsection shall not prohibit the use of information to send a solicitation to a consumer if such information was received prior to the date on which persons are required to comply with regulations implementing this subsection.

(b) *Notice for other purposes permissible.* A notice or other disclosure under this section may be coordinated and consolidated with any other notice required to be issued under any other provision of law by a person that is subject to this section, and a notice or other disclosure that is equivalent to the notice required by subsection (a), and that is provided by a person described in subsection (a) to a consumer together with disclosures required by any other provision of law, shall satisfy the requirements of subsection (a).

(c) *User requirements.* Requirements with respect to the use by a person of information received from another person related to it by common ownership or affiliated by corporate control, such as the requirements of this section, constitute requirements with respect to the exchange of information among persons affiliated by common ownership or common corporate control, within the meaning of section 625(b)(2).

(d) *Definitions.* For purposes of this section, the following definitions shall apply:

(1) The term "pre-existing business relationship" means a relationship between a person, or a person's licensed agent, and a consumer, based on--

(A)   a financial contract between a person and a consumer which is in force;

(B)   the purchase, rental, or lease by the consumer of that person's goods or services, or a financial transaction (including holding an active account or a policy in force or having another continuing relationship) between the consumer and that person during the 18-month period immediately preceding the date on which the consumer is sent a solicitation covered by this section;

(C)   an inquiry or application by the consumer regarding a product or service offered by that person, during the 3-month period immediately preceding the date on which the consumer is sent a solicitation covered by this section; or

(D)   any other pre-existing customer relationship defined in the regulations implementing this section.

(2) The term "solicitation" means the marketing of a product or service initiated by a person to a particular consumer that is based on an exchange of information described

in subsection (a), and is intended to encourage the consumer to purchase such product or service, but does not include communications that are directed at the general public or determined not to be a solicitation by the regulations prescribed under this section.

§ 625. Relation to State laws [15 U.S.C. § 1681t]

(a) *In general.* Except as provided in subsections (b) and (c), this title does not annul, alter, affect, or exempt any person subject to the provisions of this title from complying with the laws of any State with respect to the collection, distribution, or use of any information on consumers, or for the prevention or mitigation of identity theft, except to the extent that those laws are inconsistent with any provision of this title, and then only to the extent of the inconsistency.

(b) *General exceptions.* No requirement or prohibition may be imposed under the laws of any State

(1) with respect to any subject matter regulated under

   (A)   subsection (c) or (e) of section 604 [§ 1681b], relating to the prescreening of consumer reports;

   (B)   section 611 [§ 1681i], relating to the time by which a consumer reporting agency must take any action, including the provision of notification to a consumer or other person, in any procedure related to the disputed accuracy of information in a consumer's file, except that this subparagraph shall not apply to any State law in effect on the date of enactment of the Consumer Credit Reporting Reform Act of 1996;

   (C)   subsections (a) and (b) of section 615 [§ 1681m], relating to the duties of a person who takes any adverse action with respect to a consumer;

   (D)   section 615(d) [§ 1681m], relating to the duties of persons who use a consumer report of a consumer in connection with any credit or insurance transaction that is not initiated by the consumer and that consists of a firm offer of credit or insurance;

   (E)   section 605 [§ 1681c], relating to information contained in consumer reports, except that this subparagraph shall not apply to any State law in effect on the date of enactment of the Consumer Credit Reporting Reform Act of 1996;

   (F)   section 623 [§ 1681s-2], relating to the responsibilities of persons who furnish information to consumer reporting agencies, except that this paragraph shall not apply

      (i)   with respect to section 54A(a) of chapter 93 of the Massachusetts Annotated Laws (as in effect on the date of enactment of the Consumer Credit Reporting Reform Act of 1996); or

(ii)   with respect to section 1785.25(a) of the California Civil Code (as in effect on the date of enactment of the Consumer Credit Reporting Reform Act of 1996);

(G)   section 609(e), relating to information available to victims under section 609(e);

(H)   section 624, relating to the exchange and use of information to make a solicitation for marketing purposes; or

(I)   section 615(h), relating to the duties of users of consumer reports to provide notice with respect to terms in certain credit transactions;

(2) with respect to the exchange of information among persons affiliated by common ownership or common corporate control, except that this paragraph shall not apply with respect to subsection (a) or (c)(1) of section 2480e of title 9, Vermont Statutes Annotated (as in effect on the date of enactment of the Consumer Credit Reporting Reform Act of 1996);

(3) with respect to the disclosures required to be made under subsection (c), (d), (e), or (g) of section 609, or subsection (f) of section 609 relating to the disclosure of credit scores for credit granting purposes, except that this paragraph--

(A)   shall not apply with respect to sections 1785.10, 1785.16, and 1785.20.2 of the California Civil Code (as in effect on the date of enactment of the Fair and Accurate Credit Transactions Act of 2003) and section 1785.15 through section 1785.15.2 of such Code (as in effect on such date);

(B)   shall not apply with respect to sections 5-3-106(2) and 212-14.3-104.3 of the Colorado Revised Statutes (as in effect on the date of enactment of the Fair and Accurate Credit Transactions Act of 2003); and

(C)   shall not be construed as limiting, annulling, affecting, or superseding any provision of the laws of any State regulating the use in an insurance activity, or regulating disclosures concerning such use, of a credit-based insurance score of a consumer by any person engaged in the business of insurance;

(4) with respect to the frequency of any disclosure under section 612(a), except that this paragraph shall not apply--

(A)   with respect to section 12-14.3-105(1)(d) of the Colorado Revised Statutes (as in effect on the date of enactment of the Fair and Accurate Credit Transactions Act of 2003);

(B)   with respect to section 10-1-393(29)(C) of the Georgia Code (as in effect on the date of enactment of the Fair and Accurate Credit Transactions Act of 2003);

    (C)   with respect to section 1316.2 of title 10 of the Maine Revised Statutes (as in effect on the date of enactment of the Fair and Accurate Credit Transactions Act of 2003);

    (D)   with respect to sections 14-1209(a)(1) and 14-1209(b)(1)(i) of the Commercial Law Article of the Code of Maryland (as in effect on the date of enactment of the Fair and Accurate Credit Transactions Act of 2003);

    (E)   with respect to section 59(d) and section 59(e) of chapter 93 of the General Laws of Massachusetts (as in effect on the date of enactment of the Fair and Accurate Credit Transactions Act of 2003);

    (F)   with respect to section 56:11-37.10(a)(1) of the New Jersey Revised Statutes (as in effect on the date of enactment of the Fair and Accurate Credit Transactions Act of 2003); or

    (G)   with respect to section 2480c(a)(1) of title 9 of the Vermont Statutes Annotated (as in effect on the date of enactment of the Fair and Accurate Credit Transactions Act of 2003); or

(5) with respect to the conduct required by the specific provisions of--

    (A)   section 605(g);

    (B)   section 605A;

    (C)   section 605B;

    (D)   section 609(a)(1)(A);

    (E)   section 612(a);

    (F)   subsections (e), (f), and (g) of section 615;

    (G)   section 621(f);

    (H)   section 623(a)(6); or

    (I)   section 628.

(c) *Definition of firm offer of credit or insurance.* Notwithstanding any definition of the term "firm offer of credit or insurance" (or any equivalent term) under the laws of any State, the definition of that term contained in section 603(*l*) [§ 1681a] shall be construed to apply in the enforcement and interpretation of the laws of any State governing consumer reports.

(d) *Limitations.* Subsections (b) and (c) do not affect any settlement, agreement, or consent judgment between any State Attorney General and any consumer reporting agency in effect on the date of enactment of the Consumer Credit Reporting Reform Act of 1996.

§ 626. Disclosures to FBI for counterintelligence purposes [15 U.S.C. § 1681u]

(a) *Identity of financial institutions.* Notwithstanding section 604 [§ 1681b] or any other provision of this title, a consumer reporting agency shall furnish to the Federal Bureau of Investigation the names and addresses of all financial institutions (as that term is defined in section 1101 of the Right to Financial Privacy Act of 1978 [12 U.S.C. § 3401]) at which a consumer maintains or has maintained an account, to the extent that information is in the files of the agency, when presented with a written request for that information, signed by the Director of the Federal Bureau of Investigation, or the Director's designee in a position not lower than Deputy Assistant Director at Bureau headquarters or a Special Agent in Charge of a Bureau field office designated by the Director, which certifies compliance with this section. The Director or the Director's designee may make such a certification only if the Director or the Director's designee has determined in writing, that such information is sought for the conduct of an authorized investigation to protect against international terrorism or clandestine intelligence activities, provided that such an investigation of a United States person is not conducted solely upon the basis of activities protected by the first amendment to the Constitution of the United States.

(b) *Identifying information.* Notwithstanding the provisions of section 604 [§ 1681b] or any other provision of this title, a consumer reporting agency shall furnish identifying information respecting a consumer, limited to name, address, former addresses, places of employment, or former places of employment, to the Federal Bureau of Investigation when presented with a written request, signed by the Director or the Director's designee, which certifies compliance with this subsection. The Director or the Director's designee in a position not lower than Deputy Assistant Director at Bureau headquarters or a Special Agent in Charge of a Bureau field office designated by the Director may make such a certification only if the Director or the Director's designee has determined in writing that such information is sought for the conduct of an authorized investigation to protect against international terrorism or clandestine intelligence activities, provided that such an investigation of a United States person is not conducted solely upon the basis of activities protected by the first amendment to the Constitution of the United States.

(c) *Court order for disclosure of consumer reports.* Notwithstanding section 604 [§ 1681b] or any other provision of this title, if requested in writing by the Director of the Federal Bureau of Investigation, or a designee of the Director in a position not lower than Deputy Assistant Director at Bureau headquarters or a Special Agent in Charge of a Bureau field office designated by the Director, a court may issue an order ex parte directing a consumer reporting agency to furnish a consumer report to the Federal Bureau of Investigation, upon a showing in camera that the consumer report is sought for the conduct of an authorized investigation to protect against international terrorism or clandestine intelligence activities, provided that such an investigation of a United States person is not conducted solely upon the basis of activities protected by the first amendment to the Constitution of the United States. The terms of an order issued under this subsection shall not disclose that the order is issued for purposes of a counterintelligence investigation.

(d) *Confidentiality.* No consumer reporting agency or officer, employee, or agent of a consumer reporting agency shall disclose to any person, other than those officers, employees, or agents of a consumer reporting agency necessary to fulfill the requirement

to disclose information to the Federal Bureau of Investigation under this section, that the Federal Bureau of Investigation has sought or obtained the identity of financial institutions or a consumer report respecting any consumer under subsection (a), (b), or (c), and no consumer reporting agency or officer, employee, or agent of a consumer reporting agency shall include in any consumer report any information that would indicate that the Federal Bureau of Investigation has sought or obtained such information or a consumer report.

(e) *Payment of fees.* The Federal Bureau of Investigation shall, subject to the availability of appropriations, pay to the consumer reporting agency assembling or providing report or information in accordance with procedures established under this section a fee for reimbursement for such costs as are reasonably necessary and which have been directly incurred in searching, reproducing, or transporting books, papers, records, or other data required or requested to be produced under this section.

(f) *Limit on dissemination.* The Federal Bureau of Investigation may not disseminate information obtained pursuant to this section outside of the Federal Bureau of Investigation, except to other Federal agencies as may be necessary for the approval or conduct of a foreign counterintelligence investigation, or, where the information concerns a person subject to the Uniform Code of Military Justice, to appropriate investigative authorities within the military department concerned as may be necessary for the conduct of a joint foreign counterintelligence investigation.

(g) *Rules of construction.* Nothing in this section shall be construed to prohibit information from being furnished by the Federal Bureau of Investigation pursuant to a subpoena or court order, in connection with a judicial or administrative proceeding to enforce the provisions of this Act. Nothing in this section shall be construed to authorize or permit the withholding of information from the Congress.

(h) *Reports to Congress.* On a semiannual basis, the Attorney General shall fully inform the Permanent Select Committee on Intelligence and the Committee on Banking, Finance and Urban Affairs of the House of Representatives, and the Select Committee on Intelligence and the Committee on Banking, Housing, and Urban Affairs of the Senate concerning all requests made pursuant to subsections (a), (b), and (c).

(i) *Damages.* Any agency or department of the United States obtaining or disclosing any consumer reports, records, or information contained therein in violation of this section is liable to the consumer to whom such consumer reports, records, or information relate in an amount equal to the sum of

    (1) $100, without regard to the volume of consumer reports, records, or information involved;

    (2) any actual damages sustained by the consumer as a result of the disclosure;

    (3) if the violation is found to have been willful or intentional, such punitive damages as a court may allow; and

    (4) in the case of any successful action to enforce liability under this subsection, the costs of the action, together with reasonable attorney fees, as determined by the court.

(j) *Disciplinary actions for violations.* If a court determines that any agency or department of the United States has violated any provision of this section and the court finds that the circumstances surrounding the violation raise questions of whether or not an officer or employee of the agency or department acted willfully or intentionally with respect to the violation, the agency or department shall promptly initiate a proceeding to determine whether or not disciplinary action is warranted against the officer or employee who was responsible for the violation.

(k) *Good-faith exception.* Notwithstanding any other provision of this title, any consumer reporting agency or agent or employee thereof making disclosure of consumer reports or identifying information pursuant to this subsection in good-faith reliance upon a certification of the Federal Bureau of Investigation pursuant to provisions of this section shall not be liable to any person for such disclosure under this title, the constitution of any State, or any law or regulation of any State or any political subdivision of any State.

(l) *Limitation of remedies.* Notwithstanding any other provision of this title, the remedies and sanctions set forth in this section shall be the only judicial remedies and sanctions for violation of this section.

(m) *Injunctive relief.* In addition to any other remedy contained in this section, injunctive relief shall be available to require compliance with the procedures of this section. In the event of any successful action under this subsection, costs together with reasonable attorney fees, as determined by the court, may be recovered.

§ 627. Disclosures to governmental agencies for counterterrorism purposes [15 U.S.C. §1681v]

(a) *Disclosure.* Notwithstanding section 604 or any other provision of this title, a consumer reporting agency shall furnish a consumer report of a consumer and all other information in a consumer's file to a government agency authorized to conduct investigations of, or intelligence or counterintelligence activities or analysis related to, international terrorism when presented with a written certification by such government agency that such information is necessary for the agency's conduct or such investigation, activity or analysis.

(b) *Form of certification.* The certification described in subsection (a) shall be signed by a supervisory official designated by the head of a Federal agency or an officer of a Federal agency whose appointment to office is required to be made by the President, by and with the advice and consent of the Senate.

(c) *Confidentiality.* No consumer reporting agency, or officer, employee, or agent of such consumer reporting agency, shall disclose to any person, or specify in any consumer report, that a government agency has sought or obtained access to information under subsection (a).

(d) *Rule of construction.* Nothing in section 626 shall be construed to limit the authority of the Director of the Federal Bureau of Investigation under this section.

(e) *Safe harbor.* Notwithstanding any other provision of this title, any consumer reporting agency or agent or employee thereof making disclosure of consumer reports or other information pursuant to this section in good-faith reliance upon a certification of a governmental agency pursuant to the provisions of this section shall not be liable to any person for such disclosure under this subchapter, the constitution of any State, or any law or regulation of any State or any political subdivision of any State.

§ **628. Disposal of records** [15 U.S.C. §1681w]

(a) Regulations

See also 16 CFR Part 682
69 Fed. Reg. 68690 (11/24/04)

    (1) *In general.* Not later than 1 year after the date of enactment of this section, the Federal banking agencies, the National Credit Union Administration, and the Commission with respect to the entities that are subject to their respective enforcement authority under section 621, and the Securities and Exchange Commission, and in coordination as described in paragraph (2), shall issue final regulations requiring any person that maintains or otherwise possesses consumer information, or any compilation of consumer information, derived from consumer reports for a business purpose to properly dispose of any such information or compilation.

    (2) *Coordination.* Each agency required to prescribe regulations under paragraph (1) shall–

        (A)   consult and coordinate with each other such agency so that, to the extent possible, the regulations prescribed by each such agency are consistent and comparable with the regulations by each such other agency; and

        (B)   ensure that such regulations are consistent with the requirements and regulations issued pursuant to Public Law 106-102 and other provisions of Federal law.

    (3) *Exemption authority.* In issuing regulations under this section, the Federal banking agencies, the National Credit Union Administration, the Commission, and the Securities and Exchange Commission may exempt any person or class of persons from application of those regulations, as such agency deems appropriate to carry out the purpose of this section.

(b) *Rule of construction.* Nothing in this section shall be construed--

    (1) to require a person to maintain or destroy any record pertaining to a consumer that is not imposed under other law; or

    (2) to alter or affect any requirement imposed under any other provision of law to maintain or destroy such a record.

§ 629. Corporate and technological circumvention prohibited [15 U.S.C. §1681x]

The Commission shall prescribe regulations, to become effective not later than 90 days after the date of enactment of this section, to prevent a consumer reporting agency from circumventing or evading treatment as a consumer reporting agency described in section 603(p) for purposes of this title, including--

(1) by means of a corporate reorganization or restructuring, including a merger, acquisition, dissolution, divestiture, or asset sale of a consumer reporting agency; or

(2) by maintaining or merging public record and credit account information in a manner that is substantially equivalent to that described in paragraphs (1) and (2) of section 603(p), in the manner described in section 603(p).

See also 16 CFR Part 611
69 Fed. Reg. 8531 (02/24/04)
69 Fed. Reg. 29061 (05/20/04)

Legislative History

House Reports: No. 91-975 (Comm. on Banking and Currency) and
No. 91-1587 (Comm. of Conference)

Senate Reports: No. 91-1139 accompanying S. 3678 (Comm. on Banking and Currency)

Enactment: Public Law No. 91-508 (October 26, 1970):

Amendments: Public Law Nos. 95-473 (October 17, 1978)
95-598 (November 6, 1978)
98-443 (October 4, 1984)
101-73 (August 9, 1989)
102-242 (December 19, 1991)
102-537 (October 27, 1992)
102-550 (October 28, 1992)
103-325 (September 23, 1994)
104-88 (December 29, 1995)
104-93 (January 6, 1996)
104-193 (August 22, 1996)
104-208 (September 30, 1996)
105-107 (November 20, 1997)
105-347 (November 2, 1998)
106-102 (November 12, 1999)
107-56 (October 26, 2001)
108-159 (December 4, 2003)
109-351 (October 13, 2006)

The FACT Act:
Fair and Accurate Credit Transactions Act

PUBLIC LAW 108–159—DEC. 4, 2003

FAIR AND ACCURATE CREDIT TRANSACTIONS
ACT OF 2003

117 STAT. 1952 PUBLIC LAW 108–159—DEC. 4, 2003

Public Law 108–159
108th Congress

An Act

Dec. 4, 2003
[H.R. 2622]

To amend the Fair Credit Reporting Act, to prevent identity theft, improve resolution of consumer disputes, improve the accuracy of consumer records, make improvements in the use of, and consumer access to, credit information, and for other purposes.

Be it enacted by the Senate and House of Representatives of the United States of America in Congress assembled,

Fair and
Accurate Credit
Transactions Act
of 2003.
15 USC 1601
note.

SECTION 1. SHORT TITLE; TABLE OF CONTENTS.

(a) SHORT TITLE.—This Act may be cited as the "Fair and Accurate Credit Transactions Act of 2003".

(b) TABLE OF CONTENTS.—The table of contents for this Act is as follows:

SEC. 2. DEFINITIONS.

15 USC 1681 note.

As used in this Act—

(1) the term "Board" means the Board of Governors of the Federal Reserve System;

(2) the term "Commission", other than as used in title V, means the Federal Trade Commission;

(3) the terms "consumer", "consumer report", "consumer reporting agency", "creditor", "Federal banking agencies", and "financial institution" have the same meanings as in section 603 of the Fair Credit Reporting Act, as amended by this Act; and

(4) the term "affiliates" means persons that are related by common ownership or affiliated by corporate control.

SEC. 3. EFFECTIVE DATES.

15 USC 1681 note.

Except as otherwise specifically provided in this Act and the amendments made by this Act—

Regulations.

(1) before the end of the 2-month period beginning on the date of enactment of this Act, the Board and the Commission shall jointly prescribe regulations in final form establishing effective dates for each provision of this Act; and

(2) the regulations prescribed under paragraph (1) shall establish effective dates that are as early as possible, while allowing a reasonable time for the implementation of the provisions of this Act, but in no case shall any such effective date be later than 10 months after the date of issuance of such regulations in final form.

117 STAT. 1954   PUBLIC LAW 108–159—DEC. 4, 2003

TITLE I—IDENTITY THEFT PREVENTION AND CREDIT HISTORY RESTORATION

Subtitle A—Identity Theft Prevention

SEC. 111. AMENDMENT TO DEFINITIONS.

Section 603 of the Fair Credit Reporting Act (15 U.S.C. 1681a) is amended by adding at the end the following:

"(q) DEFINITIONS RELATING TO FRAUD ALERTS.—

"(1) ACTIVE DUTY MILITARY CONSUMER.—The term 'active duty military consumer' means a consumer in military service who—

"(A) is on active duty (as defined in section 101(d)(1) of title 10, United States Code) or is a reservist performing duty under a call or order to active duty under a provision of law referred to in section 101(a)(13) of title 10, United States Code; and

"(B) is assigned to service away from the usual duty station of the consumer.

"(2) FRAUD ALERT; ACTIVE DUTY ALERT.—The terms 'fraud alert' and 'active duty alert' mean a statement in the file of a consumer that—

"(A) notifies all prospective users of a consumer report relating to the consumer that the consumer may be a victim of fraud, including identity theft, or is an active duty military consumer, as applicable; and

"(B) is presented in a manner that facilitates a clear and conspicuous view of the statement described in subparagraph (A) by any person requesting such consumer report.

"(3) IDENTITY THEFT.—The term 'identity theft' means a fraud committed using the identifying information of another person, subject to such further definition as the Commission may prescribe, by regulation.

"(4) IDENTITY THEFT REPORT.—The term 'identity theft report' has the meaning given that term by rule of the Commission, and means, at a minimum, a report—

"(A) that alleges an identity theft;

"(B) that is a copy of an official, valid report filed by a consumer with an appropriate Federal, State, or local law enforcement agency, including the United States Postal Inspection Service, or such other government agency deemed appropriate by the Commission; and

"(C) the filing of which subjects the person filing the report to criminal penalties relating to the filing of false information if, in fact, the information in the report is false.

"(5) NEW CREDIT PLAN.—The term 'new credit plan' means a new account under an open end credit plan (as defined in section 103(i) of the Truth in Lending Act) or a new credit transaction not under an open end credit plan.

"(r) CREDIT AND DEBIT RELATED TERMS—

"(1) CARD ISSUER.—The term 'card issuer' means—

"(A) a credit card issuer, in the case of a credit card; and

PUBLIC LAW 108–159—DEC. 4, 2003   117 STAT. 1955

"(B) a debit card issuer, in the case of a debit card.
"(2) CREDIT CARD.—The term 'credit card' has the same meaning as in section 103 of the Truth in Lending Act.
"(3) DEBIT CARD.—The term 'debit card' means any card issued by a financial institution to a consumer for use in initiating an electronic fund transfer from the account of the consumer at such financial institution, for the purpose of transferring money between accounts or obtaining money, property, labor, or services.
"(4) ACCOUNT AND ELECTRONIC FUND TRANSFER.—The terms 'account' and 'electronic fund transfer' have the same meanings as in section 903 of the Electronic Fund Transfer Act.
"(5) CREDIT AND CREDITOR.—The terms 'credit' and 'creditor' have the same meanings as in section 702 of the Equal Credit Opportunity Act.
"(s) FEDERAL BANKING AGENCY.—The term 'Federal banking agency' has the same meaning as in section 3 of the Federal Deposit Insurance Act.
"(t) FINANCIAL INSTITUTION.—The term 'financial institution' means a State or National bank, a State or Federal savings and loan association, a mutual savings bank, a State or Federal credit union, or any other person that, directly or indirectly, holds a transaction account (as defined in section 19(b) of the Federal Reserve Act) belonging to a consumer.
"(u) RESELLER.—The term 'reseller' means a consumer reporting agency that—
       "(1) assembles and merges information contained in the database of another consumer reporting agency or multiple consumer reporting agencies concerning any consumer for purposes of furnishing such information to any third party, to the extent of such activities; and
       "(2) does not maintain a database of the assembled or merged information from which new consumer reports are produced.
"(v) COMMISSION.—The term 'Commission' means the Federal Trade Commission.
"(w) NATIONWIDE SPECIALTY CONSUMER REPORTING AGENCY.— The term 'nationwide specialty consumer reporting agency' means a consumer reporting agency that compiles and maintains files on consumers on a nationwide basis relating to—
       "(1) medical records or payments;
       "(2) residential or tenant history;
       "(3) check writing history;
       "(4) employment history; or
       "(5) insurance claims.".

SEC. 112. FRAUD ALERTS AND ACTIVE DUTY ALERTS.

   (a) FRAUD ALERTS.—The Fair Credit Reporting Act (15 U.S.C. 1681 et seq.) is amended by inserting after section 605 the following:

"§ 605A. Identity theft prevention; fraud alerts and active   15 USC 1681c–1.
            duty alerts

   "(a) ONE-CALL FRAUD ALERTS.—
       "(1) INITIAL ALERTS.—Upon the direct request of a consumer, or an individual acting on behalf of or as a personal representative of a consumer, who asserts in good faith a suspicion that the consumer has been or is about to become a

117 STAT. 1956 PUBLIC LAW 108–159—DEC. 4, 2003

victim of fraud or related crime, including identity theft, a consumer reporting agency described in section 603(p) that maintains a file on the consumer and has received appropriate proof of the identity of the requester shall—

"(A) include a fraud alert in the file of that consumer, and also provide that alert along with any credit score generated in using that file, for a period of not less than 90 days, beginning on the date of such request, unless the consumer or such representative requests that such fraud alert be removed before the end of such period, and the agency has received appropriate proof of the identity of the requester for such purpose; and

"(B) refer the information regarding the fraud alert under this paragraph to each of the other consumer reporting agencies described in section 603(p), in accordance with procedures developed under section 621(f).

"(2) ACCESS TO FREE REPORTS.—In any case in which a consumer reporting agency includes a fraud alert in the file of a consumer pursuant to this subsection, the consumer reporting agency shall—

"(A) disclose to the consumer that the consumer may request a free copy of the file of the consumer pursuant to section 612(d); and

Deadline.

"(B) provide to the consumer all disclosures required to be made under section 609, without charge to the consumer, not later than 3 business days after any request described in subparagraph (A).

"(b) EXTENDED ALERTS.—

"(1) IN GENERAL.—Upon the direct request of a consumer, or an individual acting on behalf of or as a personal representative of a consumer, who submits an identity theft report to a consumer reporting agency described in section 603(p) that maintains a file on the consumer, if the agency has received appropriate proof of the identity of the requester, the agency shall—

"(A) include a fraud alert in the file of that consumer, and also provide that alert along with any credit score generated in using that file, during the 7-year period beginning on the date of such request, unless the consumer or such representative requests that such fraud alert be removed before the end of such period and the agency has received appropriate proof of the identity of the requester for such purpose;

"(B) during the 5-year period beginning on the date of such request, exclude the consumer from any list of consumers prepared by the consumer reporting agency and provided to any third party to offer credit or insurance to the consumer as part of a transaction that was not initiated by the consumer, unless the consumer or such representative requests that such exclusion be rescinded before the end of such period; and

"(C) refer the information regarding the extended fraud alert under this paragraph to each of the other consumer reporting agencies described in section 603(p), in accordance with procedures developed under section 621(f).

"(2) ACCESS TO FREE REPORTS.—In any case in which a consumer reporting agency includes a fraud alert in the file

PUBLIC LAW 108–159—DEC. 4, 2003   117 STAT. 1957

of a consumer pursuant to this subsection, the consumer reporting agency shall—

"(A) disclose to the consumer that the consumer may request 2 free copies of the file of the consumer pursuant to section 612(d) during the 12-month period beginning on the date on which the fraud alert was included in the file; and

"(B) provide to the consumer all disclosures required to be made under section 609, without charge to the consumer, not later than 3 business days after any request described in subparagraph (A). *Deadline.*

"(c) ACTIVE DUTY ALERTS.—Upon the direct request of an active duty military consumer, or an individual acting on behalf of or as a personal representative of an active duty military consumer, a consumer reporting agency described in section 603(p) that maintains a file on the active duty military consumer and has received appropriate proof of the identity of the requester shall—

"(1) include an active duty alert in the file of that active duty military consumer, and also provide that alert along with any credit score generated in using that file, during a period of not less than 12 months, or such longer period as the Commission shall determine, by regulation, beginning on the date of the request, unless the active duty military consumer or such representative requests that such fraud alert be removed before the end of such period, and the agency has received appropriate proof of the identity of the requester for such purpose;

"(2) during the 2-year period beginning on the date of such request, exclude the active duty military consumer from any list of consumers prepared by the consumer reporting agency and provided to any third party to offer credit or insurance to the consumer as part of a transaction that was not initiated by the consumer, unless the consumer requests that such exclusion be rescinded before the end of such period; and

"(3) refer the information regarding the active duty alert to each of the other consumer reporting agencies described in section 603(p), in accordance with procedures developed under section 621(f).

"(d) PROCEDURES.—Each consumer reporting agency described in section 603(p) shall establish policies and procedures to comply with this section, including procedures that inform consumers of the availability of initial, extended, and active duty alerts and procedures that allow consumers and active duty military consumers to request initial, extended, or active duty alerts (as applicable) in a simple and easy manner, including by telephone.

"(e) REFERRALS OF ALERTS.—Each consumer reporting agency described in section 603(p) that receives a referral of a fraud alert or active duty alert from another consumer reporting agency pursuant to this section shall, as though the agency received the request from the consumer directly, follow the procedures required under—

"(1) paragraphs (1)(A) and (2) of subsection (a), in the case of a referral under subsection (a)(1)(B);

"(2) paragraphs (1)(A), (1)(B), and (2) of subsection (b), in the case of a referral under subsection (b)(1)(C); and

"(3) paragraphs (1) and (2) of subsection (c), in the case of a referral under subsection (c)(3).

117 STAT. 1958   PUBLIC LAW 108–159—DEC. 4, 2003

"(f) DUTY OF RESELLER TO RECONVEY ALERT.—A reseller shall include in its report any fraud alert or active duty alert placed in the file of a consumer pursuant to this section by another consumer reporting agency.

"(g) DUTY OF OTHER CONSUMER REPORTING AGENCIES TO PROVIDE CONTACT INFORMATION.—If a consumer contacts any consumer reporting agency that is not described in section 603(p) to communicate a suspicion that the consumer has been or is about to become a victim of fraud or related crime, including identity theft, the agency shall provide information to the consumer on how to contact the Commission and the consumer reporting agencies described in section 603(p) to obtain more detailed information and request alerts under this section.

"(h) LIMITATIONS ON USE OF INFORMATION FOR CREDIT EXTENSIONS.—

"(1) REQUIREMENTS FOR INITIAL AND ACTIVE DUTY ALERTS.—

"(A) NOTIFICATION.—Each initial fraud alert and active duty alert under this section shall include information that notifies all prospective users of a consumer report on the consumer to which the alert relates that the consumer does not authorize the establishment of any new credit plan or extension of credit, other than under an open-end credit plan (as defined in section 103(i)), in the name of the consumer, or issuance of an additional card on an existing credit account requested by a consumer, or any increase in credit limit on an existing credit account requested by a consumer, except in accordance with subparagraph (B).

"(B) LIMITATION ON USERS.—

"(i) IN GENERAL.—No prospective user of a consumer report that includes an initial fraud alert or an active duty alert in accordance with this section may establish a new credit plan or extension of credit, other than under an open-end credit plan (as defined in section 103(i)), in the name of the consumer, or issue an additional card on an existing credit account requested by a consumer, or grant any increase in credit limit on an existing credit account requested by a consumer, unless the user utilizes reasonable policies and procedures to form a reasonable belief that the user knows the identity of the person making the request.

"(ii) VERIFICATION.—If a consumer requesting the alert has specified a telephone number to be used for identity verification purposes, before authorizing any new credit plan or extension described in clause (i) in the name of such consumer, a user of such consumer report shall contact the consumer using that telephone number or take reasonable steps to verify the consumer's identity and confirm that the application for a new credit plan is not the result of identity theft.

"(2) REQUIREMENTS FOR EXTENDED ALERTS.—

"(A) NOTIFICATION.—Each extended alert under this section shall include information that provides all prospective users of a consumer report relating to a consumer with—

PUBLIC LAW 108–159—DEC. 4, 2003   117 STAT. 1959

"(i) notification that the consumer does not authorize the establishment of any new credit plan or extension of credit described in clause (i), other than under an open-end credit plan (as defined in section 103(i)), in the name of the consumer, or issuance of an additional card on an existing credit account requested by a consumer, or any increase in credit limit on an existing credit account requested by a consumer, except in accordance with subparagraph (B); and

"(ii) a telephone number or other reasonable contact method designated by the consumer.

"(B) LIMITATION ON USERS.—No prospective user of a consumer report or of a credit score generated using the information in the file of a consumer that includes an extended fraud alert in accordance with this section may establish a new credit plan or extension of credit, other than under an open-end credit plan (as defined in section 103(i)), in the name of the consumer, or issue an additional card on an existing credit account requested by a consumer, or any increase in credit limit on an existing credit account requested by a consumer, unless the user contacts the consumer in person or using the contact method described in subparagraph (A)(ii) to confirm that the application for a new credit plan or increase in credit limit, or request for an additional card is not the result of identity theft.".

(b) RULEMAKING.—The Commission shall prescribe regulations to define what constitutes appropriate proof of identity for purposes of sections 605A, 605B, and 609(a)(1) of the Fair Credit Reporting Act, as amended by this Act.

15 USC 1681c–1 note.

SEC. 113. TRUNCATION OF CREDIT CARD AND DEBIT CARD ACCOUNT NUMBERS.

Section 605 of the Fair Credit Reporting Act (15 U.S.C. 1681c) is amended by adding at the end the following:

"(g) TRUNCATION OF CREDIT CARD AND DEBIT CARD NUMBERS.—

"(1) IN GENERAL.—Except as otherwise provided in this subsection, no person that accepts credit cards or debit cards for the transaction of business shall print more than the last 5 digits of the card number or the expiration date upon any receipt provided to the cardholder at the point of the sale or transaction.

"(2) LIMITATION.—This subsection shall apply only to receipts that are electronically printed, and shall not apply to transactions in which the sole means of recording a credit card or debit card account number is by handwriting or by an imprint or copy of the card.

Applicability.

"(3) EFFECTIVE DATE.—This subsection shall become effective—

"(A) 3 years after the date of enactment of this subsection, with respect to any cash register or other machine or device that electronically prints receipts for credit card or debit card transactions that is in use before January 1, 2005; and

"(B) 1 year after the date of enactment of this subsection, with respect to any cash register or other machine

117 STAT. 1960   PUBLIC LAW 108–159—DEC. 4, 2003

or device that electronically prints receipts for credit card or debit card transactions that is first put into use on or after January 1, 2005.".

SEC. 114. ESTABLISHMENT OF PROCEDURES FOR THE IDENTIFICA-TION OF POSSIBLE INSTANCES OF IDENTITY THEFT.

Section 615 of the Fair Credit Reporting Act (15 U.S.C. 1681m) is amended—

(1) by striking "(e)" at the end; and

(2) by adding at the end the following:

"(e) RED FLAG GUIDELINES AND REGULATIONS REQUIRED.—

"(1) GUIDELINES.—The Federal banking agencies, the National Credit Union Administration, and the Commission shall jointly, with respect to the entities that are subject to their respective enforcement authority under section 621—

"(A) establish and maintain guidelines for use by each financial institution and each creditor regarding identity theft with respect to account holders at, or customers of, such entities, and update such guidelines as often as necessary;

"(B) prescribe regulations requiring each financial institution and each creditor to establish reasonable policies and procedures for implementing the guidelines established pursuant to subparagraph (A), to identify possible risks to account holders or customers or to the safety and soundness of the institution or customers; and

"(C) prescribe regulations applicable to card issuers to ensure that, if a card issuer receives notification of a change of address for an existing account, and within a short period of time (during at least the first 30 days after such notification is received) receives a request for an additional or replacement card for the same account, the card issuer may not issue the additional or replacement card, unless the card issuer, in accordance with reasonable policies and procedures—

"(i) notifies the cardholder of the request at the former address of the cardholder and provides to the cardholder a means of promptly reporting incorrect address changes;

"(ii) notifies the cardholder of the request by such other means of communication as the cardholder and the card issuer previously agreed to; or

"(iii) uses other means of assessing the validity of the change of address, in accordance with reasonable policies and procedures established by the card issuer in accordance with the regulations prescribed under subparagraph (B).

"(2) CRITERIA.—

"(A) IN GENERAL.—In developing the guidelines required by paragraph (1)(A), the agencies described in paragraph (1) shall identify patterns, practices, and specific forms of activity that indicate the possible existence of identity theft.

"(B) INACTIVE ACCOUNTS.—In developing the guidelines required by paragraph (1)(A), the agencies described in paragraph (1) shall consider including reasonable guidelines providing that when a transaction occurs with respect

PUBLIC LAW 108–159—DEC. 4, 2003   117 STAT. 1961

to a credit or deposit account that has been inactive for more than 2 years, the creditor or financial institution shall follow reasonable policies and procedures that provide for notice to be given to a consumer in a manner reasonably designed to reduce the likelihood of identity theft with respect to such account.

"(3) CONSISTENCY WITH VERIFICATION REQUIREMENTS.— Guidelines established pursuant to paragraph (1) shall not be inconsistent with the policies and procedures required under section 5318(l) of title 31, United States Code.".

SEC. 115. AUTHORITY TO TRUNCATE SOCIAL SECURITY NUMBERS.

Section 609(a)(1) of the Fair Credit Reporting Act (15 U.S.C. 1681g(a)(1)) is amended by striking "except that nothing" and inserting the following: "except that—

"(A) if the consumer to whom the file relates requests that the first 5 digits of the social security number (or similar identification number) of the consumer not be included in the disclosure and the consumer reporting agency has received appropriate proof of the identity of the requester, the consumer reporting agency shall so truncate such number in such disclosure; and

"(B) nothing".

Subtitle B—Protection and Restoration of Identity Theft Victim Credit History

SEC. 151. SUMMARY OF RIGHTS OF IDENTITY THEFT VICTIMS.

(a) IN GENERAL.—

(1) SUMMARY.—Section 609 of the Fair Credit Reporting Act (15 U.S.C. 1681g) is amended by adding at the end the following:

"(d) SUMMARY OF RIGHTS OF IDENTITY THEFT VICTIMS.—

"(1) IN GENERAL.—The Commission, in consultation with the Federal banking agencies and the National Credit Union Administration, shall prepare a model summary of the rights of consumers under this title with respect to the procedures for remedying the effects of fraud or identity theft involving credit, an electronic fund transfer, or an account or transaction at or with a financial institution or other creditor.

"(2) SUMMARY OF RIGHTS AND CONTACT INFORMATION.— Beginning 60 days after the date on which the model summary of rights is prescribed in final form by the Commission pursuant to paragraph (1), if any consumer contacts a consumer reporting agency and expresses a belief that the consumer is a victim of fraud or identity theft involving credit, an electronic fund transfer, or an account or transaction at or with a financial institution or other creditor, the consumer reporting agency shall, in addition to any other action that the agency may take, provide the consumer with a summary of rights that contains all of the information required by the Commission under paragraph (1), and information on how to contact the Commission to obtain more detailed information. *Effective date.*

"(e) INFORMATION AVAILABLE TO VICTIMS.—

"(1) IN GENERAL.—For the purpose of documenting fraudulent transactions resulting from identity theft, not later than *Deadline.*

30 days after the date of receipt of a request from a victim in accordance with paragraph (3), and subject to verification of the identity of the victim and the claim of identity theft in accordance with paragraph (2), a business entity that has provided credit to, provided for consideration products, goods, or services to, accepted payment from, or otherwise entered into a commercial transaction for consideration with, a person who has allegedly made unauthorized use of the means of identification of the victim, shall provide a copy of application and business transaction records in the control of the business entity, whether maintained by the business entity or by another person on behalf of the business entity, evidencing any transaction alleged to be a result of identity theft to—

"(A) the victim;

"(B) any Federal, State, or local government law enforcement agency or officer specified by the victim in such a request; or

"(C) any law enforcement agency investigating the identity theft and authorized by the victim to take receipt of records provided under this subsection.

"(2) VERIFICATION OF IDENTITY AND CLAIM.—Before a business entity provides any information under paragraph (1), unless the business entity, at its discretion, otherwise has a high degree of confidence that it knows the identity of the victim making a request under paragraph (1), the victim shall provide to the business entity—

"(A) as proof of positive identification of the victim, at the election of the business entity—

"(i) the presentation of a government-issued identification card;

"(ii) personally identifying information of the same type as was provided to the business entity by the unauthorized person; or

"(iii) personally identifying information that the business entity typically requests from new applicants or for new transactions, at the time of the victim's request for information, including any documentation described in clauses (i) and (ii); and

"(B) as proof of a claim of identity theft, at the election of the business entity—

"(i) a copy of a police report evidencing the claim of the victim of identity theft; and

"(ii) a properly completed—

"(I) copy of a standardized affidavit of identity theft developed and made available by the Commission; or

"(II) an affidavit of fact that is acceptable to the business entity for that purpose.

"(3) PROCEDURES.—The request of a victim under paragraph (1) shall—

"(A) be in writing;

"(B) be mailed to an address specified by the business entity, if any; and

"(C) if asked by the business entity, include relevant information about any transaction alleged to be a result of identity theft to facilitate compliance with this section including—

PUBLIC LAW 108–159—DEC. 4, 2003   117 STAT. 1963

"(i) if known by the victim (or if readily obtainable by the victim), the date of the application or transaction; and

"(ii) if known by the victim (or if readily obtainable by the victim), any other identifying information such as an account or transaction number.

"(4) NO CHARGE TO VICTIM.—Information required to be provided under paragraph (1) shall be so provided without charge.

"(5) AUTHORITY TO DECLINE TO PROVIDE INFORMATION.— A business entity may decline to provide information under paragraph (1) if, in the exercise of good faith, the business entity determines that—

"(A) this subsection does not require disclosure of the information;

"(B) after reviewing the information provided pursuant to paragraph (2), the business entity does not have a high degree of confidence in knowing the true identity of the individual requesting the information;

"(C) the request for the information is based on a misrepresentation of fact by the individual requesting the information relevant to the request for information; or

"(D) the information requested is Internet navigational data or similar information about a person's visit to a website or online service.

"(6) LIMITATION ON LIABILITY.—Except as provided in section 621, sections 616 and 617 do not apply to any violation of this subsection.

"(7) LIMITATION ON CIVIL LIABILITY.—No business entity may be held civilly liable under any provision of Federal, State, or other law for disclosure, made in good faith pursuant to this subsection.

"(8) NO NEW RECORDKEEPING OBLIGATION.—Nothing in this subsection creates an obligation on the part of a business entity to obtain, retain, or maintain information or records that are not otherwise required to be obtained, retained, or maintained in the ordinary course of its business or under other applicable law.

"(9) RULE OF CONSTRUCTION.—

"(A) IN GENERAL.—No provision of subtitle A of title V of Public Law 106–102, prohibiting the disclosure of financial information by a business entity to third parties shall be used to deny disclosure of information to the victim under this subsection.

"(B) LIMITATION.—Except as provided in subparagraph (A), nothing in this subsection permits a business entity to disclose information, including information to law enforcement under subparagraphs (B) and (C) of paragraph (1), that the business entity is otherwise prohibited from disclosing under any other applicable provision of Federal or State law.

"(10) AFFIRMATIVE DEFENSE.—In any civil action brought to enforce this subsection, it is an affirmative defense (which the defendant must establish by a preponderance of the evidence) for a business entity to file an affidavit or answer stating that—

117 STAT. 1964   PUBLIC LAW 108–159—DEC. 4, 2003

"(A) the business entity has made a reasonably diligent search of its available business records; and

"(B) the records requested under this subsection do not exist or are not reasonably available.

"(11) DEFINITION OF VICTIM.—For purposes of this subsection, the term 'victim' means a consumer whose means of identification or financial information has been used or transferred (or has been alleged to have been used or transferred) without the authority of that consumer, with the intent to commit, or to aid or abet, an identity theft or a similar crime.

"(12) EFFECTIVE DATE.—This subsection shall become effective 180 days after the date of enactment of this subsection.

Deadline.
Reports.
"(13) EFFECTIVENESS STUDY.—Not later than 18 months after the date of enactment of this subsection, the Comptroller General of the United States shall submit a report to Congress assessing the effectiveness of this provision.".

(2) RELATION TO STATE LAWS.—Section 625(b)(1) of the Fair Credit Reporting Act (15 U.S.C. 1681t(b)(1), as so redesignated) is amended by adding at the end the following new subparagraph:

"(G) section 609(e), relating to information available to victims under section 609(e);".

Deadline.
15 USC 1681c–1 note.
(b) PUBLIC CAMPAIGN TO PREVENT IDENTITY THEFT.—Not later than 2 years after the date of enactment of this Act, the Commission shall establish and implement a media and distribution campaign to teach the public how to prevent identity theft. Such campaign shall include existing Commission education materials, as well as radio, television, and print public service announcements, video cassettes, interactive digital video discs (DVD's) or compact audio discs (CD's), and Internet resources.

SEC. 152. BLOCKING OF INFORMATION RESULTING FROM IDENTITY THEFT.

(a) IN GENERAL.—The Fair Credit Reporting Act (15 U.S.C. 1681 et seq.) is amended by inserting after section 605A, as added by this Act, the following:

15 USC 1681c–2.
Deadline.
"§ 605B. Block of information resulting from identity theft

"(a) BLOCK.—Except as otherwise provided in this section, a consumer reporting agency shall block the reporting of any information in the file of a consumer that the consumer identifies as information that resulted from an alleged identity theft, not later than 4 business days after the date of receipt by such agency of—

"(1) appropriate proof of the identity of the consumer;

"(2) a copy of an identity theft report;

"(3) the identification of such information by the consumer; and

"(4) a statement by the consumer that the information is not information relating to any transaction by the consumer.

"(b) NOTIFICATION.—A consumer reporting agency shall promptly notify the furnisher of information identified by the consumer under subsection (a)—

"(1) that the information may be a result of identity theft;

"(2) that an identity theft report has been filed;

"(3) that a block has been requested under this section; and

PUBLIC LAW 108–159—DEC. 4, 2003   117 STAT. 1965

"(4) of the effective dates of the block.

"(c) AUTHORITY TO DECLINE OR RESCIND.—

"(1) IN GENERAL.—A consumer reporting agency may decline to block, or may rescind any block, of information relating to a consumer under this section, if the consumer reporting agency reasonably determines that—

"(A) the information was blocked in error or a block was requested by the consumer in error;

"(B) the information was blocked, or a block was requested by the consumer, on the basis of a material misrepresentation of fact by the consumer relevant to the request to block; or

"(C) the consumer obtained possession of goods, services, or money as a result of the blocked transaction or transactions.

"(2) NOTIFICATION TO CONSUMER.—If a block of information is declined or rescinded under this subsection, the affected consumer shall be notified promptly, in the same manner as consumers are notified of the reinsertion of information under section 611(a)(5)(B).

"(3) SIGNIFICANCE OF BLOCK.—For purposes of this subsection, if a consumer reporting agency rescinds a block, the presence of information in the file of a consumer prior to the blocking of such information is not evidence of whether the consumer knew or should have known that the consumer obtained possession of any goods, services, or money as a result of the block.

"(d) EXCEPTION FOR RESELLERS.—

"(1) NO RESELLER FILE.—This section shall not apply to a consumer reporting agency, if the consumer reporting agency—

"(A) is a reseller;

"(B) is not, at the time of the request of the consumer under subsection (a), otherwise furnishing or reselling a consumer report concerning the information identified by the consumer; and

"(C) informs the consumer, by any means, that the consumer may report the identity theft to the Commission to obtain consumer information regarding identity theft.

"(2) RESELLER WITH FILE.—The sole obligation of the consumer reporting agency under this section, with regard to any request of a consumer under this section, shall be to block the consumer report maintained by the consumer reporting agency from any subsequent use, if—

"(A) the consumer, in accordance with the provisions of subsection (a), identifies, to a consumer reporting agency, information in the file of the consumer that resulted from identity theft; and

"(B) the consumer reporting agency is a reseller of the identified information.

"(3) NOTICE.—In carrying out its obligation under paragraph (2), the reseller shall promptly provide a notice to the consumer of the decision to block the file. Such notice shall contain the name, address, and telephone number of each consumer reporting agency from which the consumer information was obtained for resale.

"(e) EXCEPTION FOR VERIFICATION COMPANIES.—The provisions of this section do not apply to a check services company, acting as such, which issues authorizations for the purpose of approving or processing negotiable instruments, electronic fund transfers, or similar methods of payments, except that, beginning 4 business days after receipt of information described in paragraphs (1) through (3) of subsection (a), a check services company shall not report to a national consumer reporting agency described in section 603(p), any information identified in the subject identity theft report as resulting from identity theft.

"(f) ACCESS TO BLOCKED INFORMATION BY LAW ENFORCEMENT AGENCIES.—No provision of this section shall be construed as requiring a consumer reporting agency to prevent a Federal, State, or local law enforcement agency from accessing blocked information in a consumer file to which the agency could otherwise obtain access under this title.".

(b) CLERICAL AMENDMENT.—The table of sections for the Fair Credit Reporting Act (15 U.S.C. 1681 et seq.) is amended by inserting after the item relating to section 605 the following new items:

"605A. Identity theft prevention; fraud alerts and active duty alerts.
"605B. Block of information resulting from identity theft.".

Procedures.

SEC. 153. COORDINATION OF IDENTITY THEFT COMPLAINT INVESTIGATIONS.

Section 621 of the Fair Credit Reporting Act (15 U.S.C. 1681s) is amended by adding at the end the following:

"(f) COORDINATION OF CONSUMER COMPLAINT INVESTIGATIONS.—

"(1) IN GENERAL.—Each consumer reporting agency described in section 603(p) shall develop and maintain procedures for the referral to each other such agency of any consumer complaint received by the agency alleging identity theft, or requesting a fraud alert under section 605A or a block under section 605B.

"(2) MODEL FORM AND PROCEDURE FOR REPORTING IDENTITY THEFT.—The Commission, in consultation with the Federal banking agencies and the National Credit Union Administration, shall develop a model form and model procedures to be used by consumers who are victims of identity theft for contacting and informing creditors and consumer reporting agencies of the fraud.

"(3) ANNUAL SUMMARY REPORTS.—Each consumer reporting agency described in section 603(p) shall submit an annual summary report to the Commission on consumer complaints received by the agency on identity theft or fraud alerts.".

SEC. 154. PREVENTION OF REPOLLUTION OF CONSUMER REPORTS.

(a) PREVENTION OF REINSERTION OF ERRONEOUS INFORMATION.—Section 623(a) of the Fair Credit Reporting Act (15 U.S.C. 1681s–2(a)) is amended by adding at the end the following:

"(6) DUTIES OF FURNISHERS UPON NOTICE OF IDENTITY THEFT-RELATED INFORMATION.—

"(A) REASONABLE PROCEDURES.—A person that furnishes information to any consumer reporting agency shall have in place reasonable procedures to respond to any notification that it receives from a consumer reporting agency under section 605B relating to information resulting

PUBLIC LAW 108–159—DEC. 4, 2003   117 STAT. 1967

from identity theft, to prevent that person from refurnishing such blocked information.

"(B) INFORMATION ALLEGED TO RESULT FROM IDENTITY THEFT.—If a consumer submits an identity theft report to a person who furnishes information to a consumer reporting agency at the address specified by that person for receiving such reports stating that information maintained by such person that purports to relate to the consumer resulted from identity theft, the person may not furnish such information that purports to relate to the consumer to any consumer reporting agency, unless the person subsequently knows or is informed by the consumer that the information is correct.".

(b) PROHIBITION ON SALE OR TRANSFER OF DEBT CAUSED BY IDENTITY THEFT.—Section 615 of the Fair Credit Reporting Act (15 U.S.C. 1681m), as amended by this Act, is amended by adding at the end the following:

"(f) PROHIBITION ON SALE OR TRANSFER OF DEBT CAUSED BY IDENTITY THEFT.—

"(1) IN GENERAL.—No person shall sell, transfer for consideration, or place for collection a debt that such person has been notified under section 605B has resulted from identity theft.

"(2) APPLICABILITY.—The prohibitions of this subsection shall apply to all persons collecting a debt described in paragraph (1) after the date of a notification under paragraph (1).

"(3) RULE OF CONSTRUCTION.—Nothing in this subsection shall be construed to prohibit—

"(A) the repurchase of a debt in any case in which the assignee of the debt requires such repurchase because the debt has resulted from identity theft;

"(B) the securitization of a debt or the pledging of a portfolio of debt as collateral in connection with a borrowing; or

"(C) the transfer of debt as a result of a merger, acquisition, purchase and assumption transaction, or transfer of substantially all of the assets of an entity.".

SEC. 155. NOTICE BY DEBT COLLECTORS WITH RESPECT TO FRAUDULENT INFORMATION.

Section 615 of the Fair Credit Reporting Act (15 U.S.C. 1681m), as amended by this Act, is amended by adding at the end the following:

"(g) DEBT COLLECTOR COMMUNICATIONS CONCERNING IDENTITY THEFT.—If a person acting as a debt collector (as that term is defined in title VIII) on behalf of a third party that is a creditor or other user of a consumer report is notified that any information relating to a debt that the person is attempting to collect may be fraudulent or may be the result of identity theft, that person shall—

"(1) notify the third party that the information may be fraudulent or may be the result of identity theft; and

"(2) upon request of the consumer to whom the debt purportedly relates, provide to the consumer all information to which the consumer would otherwise be entitled if the consumer were not a victim of identity theft, but wished to dispute the debt under provisions of law applicable to that person.".

SEC. 156. STATUTE OF LIMITATIONS.

Section 618 of the Fair Credit Reporting Act (15 U.S.C. 1681p) is amended to read as follows:

"§ 618. Jurisdiction of courts; limitation of actions

"An action to enforce any liability created under this title may be brought in any appropriate United States district court, without regard to the amount in controversy, or in any other court of competent jurisdiction, not later than the earlier of—

"(1) 2 years after the date of discovery by the plaintiff of the violation that is the basis for such liability; or

"(2) 5 years after the date on which the violation that is the basis for such liability occurs.".

SEC. 157. STUDY ON THE USE OF TECHNOLOGY TO COMBAT IDENTITY THEFT.

(a) STUDY REQUIRED.—The Secretary of the Treasury shall conduct a study of the use of biometrics and other similar technologies to reduce the incidence and costs to society of identity theft by providing convincing evidence of who actually performed a given financial transaction.

(b) CONSULTATION.—The Secretary of the Treasury shall consult with Federal banking agencies, the Commission, and representatives of financial institutions, consumer reporting agencies, Federal, State, and local government agencies that issue official forms or means of identification, State prosecutors, law enforcement agencies, the biometric industry, and the general public in formulating and conducting the study required by subsection (a).

(c) AUTHORIZATION OF APPROPRIATIONS.—There are authorized to be appropriated to the Secretary of the Treasury for fiscal year 2004, such sums as may be necessary to carry out the provisions of this section.

Deadline.

(d) REPORT REQUIRED.—Before the end of the 180-day period beginning on the date of enactment of this Act, the Secretary shall submit a report to Congress containing the findings and conclusions of the study required under subsection (a), together with such recommendations for legislative or administrative actions as may be appropriate.

TITLE II—IMPROVEMENTS IN USE OF AND CONSUMER ACCESS TO CREDIT INFORMATION

SEC. 211. FREE CONSUMER REPORTS.

(a) IN GENERAL.—Section 612 of the Fair Credit Reporting Act (15 U.S.C. 1681j) is amended—

(1) by redesignating subsection (a) as subsection (f), and transferring it to the end of the section;

(2) by inserting before subsection (b) the following:

"(a) FREE ANNUAL DISCLOSURE.—

"(1) NATIONWIDE CONSUMER REPORTING AGENCIES.—

PUBLIC LAW 108–159—DEC. 4, 2003   117 STAT. 1969

"(A) IN GENERAL.—All consumer reporting agencies described in subsections (p) and (w) of section 603 shall make all disclosures pursuant to section 609 once during any 12-month period upon request of the consumer and without charge to the consumer.

"(B) CENTRALIZED SOURCE.—Subparagraph (A) shall apply with respect to a consumer reporting agency described in section 603(p) only if the request from the consumer is made using the centralized source established for such purpose in accordance with section 211(c) of the Fair and Accurate Credit Transactions Act of 2003.

Applicability.

"(C) NATIONWIDE SPECIALTY CONSUMER REPORTING AGENCY.—

"(i) IN GENERAL.—The Commission shall prescribe regulations applicable to each consumer reporting agency described in section 603(w) to require the establishment of a streamlined process for consumers to request consumer reports under subparagraph (A), which shall include, at a minimum, the establishment by each such agency of a toll-free telephone number for such requests.

Regulations.

"(ii) CONSIDERATIONS.—In prescribing regulations under clause (i), the Commission shall consider—

"(I) the significant demands that may be placed on consumer reporting agencies in providing such consumer reports;

"(II) appropriate means to ensure that consumer reporting agencies can satisfactorily meet those demands, including the efficacy of a system of staggering the availability to consumers of such consumer reports; and

"(III) the ease by which consumers should be able to contact consumer reporting agencies with respect to access to such consumer reports.

"(iii) DATE OF ISSUANCE.—The Commission shall issue the regulations required by this subparagraph in final form not later than 6 months after the date of enactment of the Fair and Accurate Credit Transactions Act of 2003.

Deadline.

"(iv) CONSIDERATION OF ABILITY TO COMPLY.—The regulations of the Commission under this subparagraph shall establish an effective date by which each nationwide specialty consumer reporting agency (as defined in section 603(w)) shall be required to comply with subsection (a), which effective date—

Effective date.

"(I) shall be established after consideration of the ability of each nationwide specialty consumer reporting agency to comply with subsection (a); and

"(II) shall be not later than 6 months after the date on which such regulations are issued in final form (or such additional period not to exceed 3 months, as the Commission determines appropriate).

Deadline.

"(2) TIMING.—A consumer reporting agency shall provide a consumer report under paragraph (1) not later than 15 days

Deadline.

117 STAT. 1970   PUBLIC LAW 108–159—DEC. 4, 2003

after the date on which the request is received under paragraph (1).

Deadline.

"(3) REINVESTIGATIONS.—Notwithstanding the time periods specified in section 611(a)(1), a reinvestigation under that section by a consumer reporting agency upon a request of a consumer that is made after receiving a consumer report under this subsection shall be completed not later than 45 days after the date on which the request is received.

"(4) EXCEPTION FOR FIRST 12 MONTHS OF OPERATION.—This subsection shall not apply to a consumer reporting agency that has not been furnishing consumer reports to third parties on a continuing basis during the 12-month period preceding a request under paragraph (1), with respect to consumers residing nationwide.";

(3) by redesignating subsection (d) as subsection (e);

(4) by inserting before subsection (e), as redesignated, the following:

"(d) FREE DISCLOSURES IN CONNECTION WITH FRAUD ALERTS.—Upon the request of a consumer, a consumer reporting agency described in section 603(p) shall make all disclosures pursuant to section 609 without charge to the consumer, as provided in subsections (a)(2) and (b)(2) of section 605A, as applicable.";

(5) in subsection (e), as redesignated, by striking "subsection (a)" and inserting "subsection (f)"; and

(6) in subsection (f), as redesignated, by striking "Except as provided in subsections (b), (c), and (d), a" and inserting "In the case of a request from a consumer other than a request that is covered by any of subsections (a) through (d), a".

(b) CIRCUMVENTION PROHIBITED.—The Fair Credit Reporting Act (15 U.S.C. 1681 et seq.) is amended by adding after section 628, as added by section 216 of this Act, the following new section:

15 USC 1681x.

"§ 629. Corporate and technological circumvention prohibited

Regulations.
Effective date.

"The Commission shall prescribe regulations, to become effective not later than 90 days after the date of enactment of this section, to prevent a consumer reporting agency from circumventing or evading treatment as a consumer reporting agency described in section 603(p) for purposes of this title, including—

"(1) by means of a corporate reorganization or restructuring, including a merger, acquisition, dissolution, divestiture, or asset sale of a consumer reporting agency; or

"(2) by maintaining or merging public record and credit account information in a manner that is substantially equivalent to that described in paragraphs (1) and (2) of section 603(p), in the manner described in section 603(p).".

(c) SUMMARY OF RIGHTS TO OBTAIN AND DISPUTE INFORMATION IN CONSUMER REPORTS AND TO OBTAIN CREDIT SCORES.—Section 609(c) of the Fair Credit Reporting Act (15 U.S.C. 1681g) is amended to read as follows:

"(c) SUMMARY OF RIGHTS TO OBTAIN AND DISPUTE INFORMATION IN CONSUMER REPORTS AND TO OBTAIN CREDIT SCORES.—

"(1) COMMISSION SUMMARY OF RIGHTS REQUIRED.—

"(A) IN GENERAL.—The Commission shall prepare a model summary of the rights of consumers under this title.

PUBLIC LAW 108–159—DEC. 4, 2003   117 STAT. 1971

"(B) CONTENT OF SUMMARY.—The summary of rights prepared under subparagraph (A) shall include a description of—

"(i) the right of a consumer to obtain a copy of a consumer report under subsection (a) from each consumer reporting agency;

"(ii) the frequency and circumstances under which a consumer is entitled to receive a consumer report without charge under section 612;

"(iii) the right of a consumer to dispute information in the file of the consumer under section 611;

"(iv) the right of a consumer to obtain a credit score from a consumer reporting agency, and a description of how to obtain a credit score;

"(v) the method by which a consumer can contact, and obtain a consumer report from, a consumer reporting agency without charge, as provided in the regulations of the Commission prescribed under section 211(c) of the Fair and Accurate Credit Transactions Act of 2003; and

"(vi) the method by which a consumer can contact, and obtain a consumer report from, a consumer reporting agency described in section 603(w), as provided in the regulations of the Commission prescribed under section 612(a)(1)(C).

"(C) AVAILABILITY OF SUMMARY OF RIGHTS.—The Commission shall—

Public information.

"(i) actively publicize the availability of the summary of rights prepared under this paragraph;

"(ii) conspicuously post on its Internet website the availability of such summary of rights; and

"(iii) promptly make such summary of rights available to consumers, on request.

"(2) SUMMARY OF RIGHTS REQUIRED TO BE INCLUDED WITH AGENCY DISCLOSURES.—A consumer reporting agency shall provide to a consumer, with each written disclosure by the agency to the consumer under this section—

"(A) the summary of rights prepared by the Commission under paragraph (1);

"(B) in the case of a consumer reporting agency described in section 603(p), a toll-free telephone number established by the agency, at which personnel are accessible to consumers during normal business hours;

"(C) a list of all Federal agencies responsible for enforcing any provision of this title, and the address and any appropriate phone number of each such agency, in a form that will assist the consumer in selecting the appropriate agency;

"(D) a statement that the consumer may have additional rights under State law, and that the consumer may wish to contact a State or local consumer protection agency or a State attorney general (or the equivalent thereof) to learn of those rights; and

"(E) a statement that a consumer reporting agency is not required to remove accurate derogatory information from the file of a consumer, unless the information is outdated under section 605 or cannot be verified.".

15 USC 1681j
note.

(d) RULEMAKING REQUIRED.—

(1) IN GENERAL.—The Commission shall prescribe regulations applicable to consumer reporting agencies described in section 603(p) of the Fair Credit Reporting Act, to require the establishment of—

(A) a centralized source through which consumers may obtain a consumer report from each such consumer reporting agency, using a single request, and without charge to the consumer, as provided in section 612(a) of the Fair Credit Reporting Act (as amended by this section); and

(B) a standardized form for a consumer to make such a request for a consumer report by mail or through an Internet website.

(2) CONSIDERATIONS.—In prescribing regulations under paragraph (1), the Commission shall consider—

(A) the significant demands that may be placed on consumer reporting agencies in providing such consumer reports;

(B) appropriate means to ensure that consumer reporting agencies can satisfactorily meet those demands, including the efficacy of a system of staggering the availability to consumers of such consumer reports; and

(C) the ease by which consumers should be able to contact consumer reporting agencies with respect to access to such consumer reports.

(3) CENTRALIZED SOURCE.—The centralized source for a request for a consumer report from a consumer required by this subsection shall provide for—

(A) a toll-free telephone number for such purpose;

(B) use of an Internet website for such purpose; and

(C) a process for requests by mail for such purpose.

(4) TRANSITION.—The regulations of the Commission under paragraph (1) shall provide for an orderly transition by consumer reporting agencies described in section 603(p) of the Fair Credit Reporting Act to the centralized source for consumer report distribution required by section 612(a)(1)(B), as amended by this section, in a manner that—

(A) does not temporarily overwhelm such consumer reporting agencies with requests for disclosures of consumer reports beyond their capacity to deliver; and

(B) does not deny creditors, other users, and consumers access to consumer reports on a time-sensitive basis for specific purposes, such as home purchases or suspicions of identity theft, during the transition period.

(5) TIMING.—Regulations required by this subsection shall—

Deadline.

(A) be issued in final form not later than 6 months after the date of enactment of this Act; and

Effective date.

(B) become effective not later than 6 months after the date on which they are issued in final form.

(6) SCOPE OF REGULATIONS.—

(A) IN GENERAL.—The Commission shall, by rule, determine whether to require a consumer reporting agency that compiles and maintains files on consumers on substantially a nationwide basis, other than one described in section

603(p) of the Fair Credit Reporting Act, to make free consumer reports available upon consumer request, and if so, whether such consumer reporting agencies should make such free reports available through the centralized source described in paragraph (1)(A).

(B) CONSIDERATIONS.—Before making any determination under subparagraph (A), the Commission shall consider—

(i) the number of requests for consumer reports to, and the number of consumer reports generated by, the consumer reporting agency, in comparison with consumer reporting agencies described in subsections (p) and (w) of section 603 of the Fair Credit Reporting Act;

(ii) the overall scope of the operations of the consumer reporting agency;

(iii) the needs of consumers for access to consumer reports provided by consumer reporting agencies free of charge;

(iv) the costs of providing access to consumer reports by consumer reporting agencies free of charge; and

(v) the effects on the ongoing competitive viability of such consumer reporting agencies if such free access is required.

SEC. 212. DISCLOSURE OF CREDIT SCORES.

(a) STATEMENT ON AVAILABILITY OF CREDIT SCORES.—Section 609(a) of the Fair Credit Reporting Act (15 U.S.C. 1681g(a)) is amended by adding at the end the following new paragraph:

"(6) If the consumer requests the credit file and not the credit score, a statement that the consumer may request and obtain a credit score.".

(b) DISCLOSURE OF CREDIT SCORES.—Section 609 of the Fair Credit Reporting Act (15 U.S.C. 1681g), as amended by this Act, is amended by adding at the end the following:

"(f) DISCLOSURE OF CREDIT SCORES.—

"(1) IN GENERAL.—Upon the request of a consumer for a credit score, a consumer reporting agency shall supply to the consumer a statement indicating that the information and credit scoring model may be different than the credit score that may be used by the lender, and a notice which shall include—

"(A) the current credit score of the consumer or the most recent credit score of the consumer that was previously calculated by the credit reporting agency for a purpose related to the extension of credit;

"(B) the range of possible credit scores under the model used;

"(C) all of the key factors that adversely affected the credit score of the consumer in the model used, the total number of which shall not exceed 4, subject to paragraph (9);

"(D) the date on which the credit score was created; and

"(E) the name of the person or entity that provided the credit score or credit file upon which the credit score was created.

"(2) DEFINITIONS.—For purposes of this subsection, the following definitions shall apply:

"(A) CREDIT SCORE.—The term 'credit score'—

"(i) means a numerical value or a categorization derived from a statistical tool or modeling system used by a person who makes or arranges a loan to predict the likelihood of certain credit behaviors, including default (and the numerical value or the categorization derived from such analysis may also be referred to as a 'risk predictor' or 'risk score'); and

"(ii) does not include—

"(I) any mortgage score or rating of an automated underwriting system that considers one or more factors in addition to credit information, including the loan to value ratio, the amount of down payment, or the financial assets of a consumer; or

"(II) any other elements of the underwriting process or underwriting decision.

"(B) KEY FACTORS.—The term 'key factors' means all relevant elements or reasons adversely affecting the credit score for the particular individual, listed in the order of their importance based on their effect on the credit score.

"(3) TIMEFRAME AND MANNER OF DISCLOSURE.—The information required by this subsection shall be provided in the same timeframe and manner as the information described in subsection (a).

"(4) APPLICABILITY TO CERTAIN USES.—This subsection shall not be construed so as to compel a consumer reporting agency to develop or disclose a score if the agency does not—

"(A) distribute scores that are used in connection with residential real property loans; or

"(B) develop scores that assist credit providers in understanding the general credit behavior of a consumer and predicting the future credit behavior of the consumer.

"(5) APPLICABILITY TO CREDIT SCORES DEVELOPED BY ANOTHER PERSON.—

"(A) IN GENERAL.—This subsection shall not be construed to require a consumer reporting agency that distributes credit scores developed by another person or entity to provide a further explanation of them, or to process a dispute arising pursuant to section 611, except that the consumer reporting agency shall provide the consumer with the name and address and website for contacting the person or entity who developed the score or developed the methodology of the score.

"(B) EXCEPTION.—This paragraph shall not apply to a consumer reporting agency that develops or modifies scores that are developed by another person or entity.

"(6) MAINTENANCE OF CREDIT SCORES NOT REQUIRED.—This subsection shall not be construed to require a consumer reporting agency to maintain credit scores in its files.

"(7) COMPLIANCE IN CERTAIN CASES.—In complying with this subsection, a consumer reporting agency shall—

PUBLIC LAW 108–159—DEC. 4, 2003   117 STAT. 1975

"(A) supply the consumer with a credit score that is derived from a credit scoring model that is widely distributed to users by that consumer reporting agency in connection with residential real property loans or with a credit score that assists the consumer in understanding the credit scoring assessment of the credit behavior of the consumer and predictions about the future credit behavior of the consumer; and

"(B) a statement indicating that the information and credit scoring model may be different than that used by the lender.

"(8) FAIR AND REASONABLE FEE.—A consumer reporting agency may charge a fair and reasonable fee, as determined by the Commission, for providing the information required under this subsection.

"(9) USE OF ENQUIRIES AS A KEY FACTOR.—If a key factor that adversely affects the credit score of a consumer consists of the number of enquiries made with respect to a consumer report, that factor shall be included in the disclosure pursuant to paragraph (1)(C) without regard to the numerical limitation in such paragraph.".

(c) DISCLOSURE OF CREDIT SCORES BY CERTAIN MORTGAGE LENDERS.—Section 609 of the Fair Credit Reporting Act (15 U.S.C. 1681g), as amended by this Act, is amended by adding at the end the following:

"(g) DISCLOSURE OF CREDIT SCORES BY CERTAIN MORTGAGE LENDERS.—

"(1) IN GENERAL.—Any person who makes or arranges loans and who uses a consumer credit score, as defined in subsection (f), in connection with an application initiated or sought by a consumer for a closed end loan or the establishment of an open end loan for a consumer purpose that is secured by 1 to 4 units of residential real property (hereafter in this subsection referred as the 'lender') shall provide the following to the consumer as soon as reasonably practicable:

"(A) INFORMATION REQUIRED UNDER SUBSECTION (f).—

"(i) IN GENERAL.—A copy of the information identified in subsection (f) that was obtained from a consumer reporting agency or was developed and used by the user of the information.

"(ii) NOTICE UNDER SUBPARAGRAPH (D).—In addition to the information provided to it by a third party that provided the credit score or scores, a lender is only required to provide the notice contained in subparagraph (D).

"(B) DISCLOSURES IN CASE OF AUTOMATED UNDERWRITING SYSTEM.—

"(i) IN GENERAL.—If a person that is subject to this subsection uses an automated underwriting system to underwrite a loan, that person may satisfy the obligation to provide a credit score by disclosing a credit score and associated key factors supplied by a consumer reporting agency.

"(ii) NUMERICAL CREDIT SCORE.—However, if a numerical credit score is generated by an automated underwriting system used by an enterprise, and that score is disclosed to the person, the score shall be

117 STAT. 1976

PUBLIC LAW 108–159—DEC. 4, 2003

disclosed to the consumer consistent with subparagraph (C).

"(iii) ENTERPRISE DEFINED.—For purposes of this subparagraph, the term 'enterprise' has the same meaning as in paragraph (6) of section 1303 of the Federal Housing Enterprises Financial Safety and Soundness Act of 1992.

"(C) DISCLOSURES OF CREDIT SCORES NOT OBTAINED FROM A CONSUMER REPORTING AGENCY.—A person that is subject to the provisions of this subsection and that uses a credit score, other than a credit score provided by a consumer reporting agency, may satisfy the obligation to provide a credit score by disclosing a credit score and associated key factors supplied by a consumer reporting agency.

"(D) NOTICE TO HOME LOAN APPLICANTS.—A copy of the following notice, which shall include the name, address, and telephone number of each consumer reporting agency providing a credit score that was used:

'NOTICE TO THE HOME LOAN APPLICANT

'In connection with your application for a home loan, the lender must disclose to you the score that a consumer reporting agency distributed to users and the lender used in connection with your home loan, and the key factors affecting your credit scores.

'The credit score is a computer generated summary calculated at the time of the request and based on information that a consumer reporting agency or lender has on file. The scores are based on data about your credit history and payment patterns. Credit scores are important because they are used to assist the lender in determining whether you will obtain a loan. They may also be used to determine what interest rate you may be offered on the mortgage. Credit scores can change over time, depending on your conduct, how your credit history and payment patterns change, and how credit scoring technologies change.

'Because the score is based on information in your credit history, it is very important that you review the credit-related information that is being furnished to make sure it is accurate. Credit records may vary from one company to another.

'If you have questions about your credit score or the credit information that is furnished to you, contact the consumer reporting agency at the address and telephone number provided with this notice, or contact the lender, if the lender developed or generated the credit score. The consumer reporting agency plays no part in the decision to take any action on the loan application and is unable to provide you with specific reasons for the decision on a loan application.

'If you have questions concerning the terms of the loan, contact the lender.'.

"(E) ACTIONS NOT REQUIRED UNDER THIS SUBSECTION.— This subsection shall not require any person to—

"(i) explain the information provided pursuant to subsection (f);

"(ii) disclose any information other than a credit score or key factors, as defined in subsection (f);

PUBLIC LAW 108–159—DEC. 4, 2003   117 STAT. 1977

"(iii) disclose any credit score or related information obtained by the user after a loan has closed;

"(iv) provide more than 1 disclosure per loan transaction; or

"(v) provide the disclosure required by this subsection when another person has made the disclosure to the consumer for that loan transaction.

"(F) NO OBLIGATION FOR CONTENT.—

"(i) IN GENERAL.—The obligation of any person pursuant to this subsection shall be limited solely to providing a copy of the information that was received from the consumer reporting agency.

"(ii) LIMIT ON LIABILITY.—No person has liability under this subsection for the content of that information or for the omission of any information within the report provided by the consumer reporting agency.

"(G) PERSON DEFINED AS EXCLUDING ENTERPRISE.—As used in this subsection, the term 'person' does not include an enterprise (as defined in paragraph (6) of section 1303 of the Federal Housing Enterprises Financial Safety and Soundness Act of 1992).

"(2) PROHIBITION ON DISCLOSURE CLAUSES NULL AND VOID.—

"(A) IN GENERAL.—Any provision in a contract that prohibits the disclosure of a credit score by a person who makes or arranges loans or a consumer reporting agency is void.

"(B) NO LIABILITY FOR DISCLOSURE UNDER THIS SUBSECTION.—A lender shall not have liability under any contractual provision for disclosure of a credit score pursuant to this subsection.".

(d) INCLUSION OF KEY FACTOR IN CREDIT SCORE INFORMATION IN CONSUMER REPORT.—Section 605(d) of the Fair Credit Reporting Act (15 U.S.C. 1681c(d)) is amended—

(1) by striking "DISCLOSED.—Any consumer reporting agency" and inserting "DISCLOSED.—

"(1) TITLE 11 INFORMATION.—Any consumer reporting agency"; and

(2) by adding at the end the following new paragraph:

"(2) KEY FACTOR IN CREDIT SCORE INFORMATION.—Any consumer reporting agency that furnishes a consumer report that contains any credit score or any other risk score or predictor on any consumer shall include in the report a clear and conspicuous statement that a key factor (as defined in section 609(f)(2)(B)) that adversely affected such score or predictor was the number of enquiries, if such a predictor was in fact a key factor that adversely affected such score. This paragraph shall not apply to a check services company, acting as such, which issues authorizations for the purpose of approving or processing negotiable instruments, electronic fund transfers, or similar methods of payments, but only to the extent that such company is engaged in such activities.".

(e) TECHNICAL AND CONFORMING AMENDMENTS.—Section 625(b) of the Fair Credit Reporting Act (15 U.S.C. 1681t(b)), as so designated by section 214 of this Act, is amended—

(1) by striking "or" at the end of paragraph (2); and

(2) by striking paragraph (3) and inserting the following:

117 STAT. 1978　　PUBLIC LAW 108–159—DEC. 4, 2003

"(3) with respect to the disclosures required to be made under subsection (c), (d), (e), or (g) of section 609, or subsection (f) of section 609 relating to the disclosure of credit scores for credit granting purposes, except that this paragraph—

"(A) shall not apply with respect to sections 1785.10, 1785.16, and 1785.20.2 of the California Civil Code (as in effect on the date of enactment of the Fair and Accurate Credit Transactions Act of 2003) and section 1785.15 through section 1785.15.2 of such Code (as in effect on such date);

"(B) shall not apply with respect to sections 5–3–106(2) and 212–14.3–104.3 of the Colorado Revised Statutes (as in effect on the date of enactment of the Fair and Accurate Credit Transactions Act of 2003); and

"(C) shall not be construed as limiting, annulling, affecting, or superseding any provision of the laws of any State regulating the use in an insurance activity, or regulating disclosures concerning such use, of a credit-based insurance score of a consumer by any person engaged in the business of insurance;

"(4) with respect to the frequency of any disclosure under section 612(a), except that this paragraph shall not apply—

"(A) with respect to section 12–14.3–105(1)(d) of the Colorado Revised Statutes (as in effect on the date of enactment of the Fair and Accurate Credit Transactions Act of 2003);

"(B) with respect to section 10–1–393(29)(C) of the Georgia Code (as in effect on the date of enactment of the Fair and Accurate Credit Transactions Act of 2003);

"(C) with respect to section 1316.2 of title 10 of the Maine Revised Statutes (as in effect on the date of enactment of the Fair and Accurate Credit Transactions Act of 2003);

"(D) with respect to sections 14–1209(a)(1) and 14–1209(b)(1)(i) of the Commercial Law Article of the Code of Maryland (as in effect on the date of enactment of the Fair and Accurate Credit Transactions Act of 2003);

"(E) with respect to section 59(d) and section 59(e) of chapter 93 of the General Laws of Massachusetts (as in effect on the date of enactment of the Fair and Accurate Credit Transactions Act of 2003);

"(F) with respect to section 56:11–37.10(a)(1) of the New Jersey Revised Statutes (as in effect on the date of enactment of the Fair and Accurate Credit Transactions Act of 2003); or

"(G) with respect to section 2480c(a)(1) of title 9 of the Vermont Statutes Annotated (as in effect on the date of enactment of the Fair and Accurate Credit Transactions Act of 2003); or".

SEC. 213. ENHANCED DISCLOSURE OF THE MEANS AVAILABLE TO OPT OUT OF PRESCREENED LISTS.

(a) NOTICE AND RESPONSE FORMAT FOR USERS OF REPORTS.—Section 615(d)(2) of the Fair Credit Reporting Act (15 U.S.C. 1681m(d)(2)) is amended to read as follows:

"(2) DISCLOSURE OF ADDRESS AND TELEPHONE NUMBER; FORMAT.—A statement under paragraph (1) shall—

"(A) include the address and toll-free telephone number of the appropriate notification system established under section 604(e); and

"(B) be presented in such format and in such type size and manner as to be simple and easy to understand, as established by the Commission, by rule, in consultation with the Federal banking agencies and the National Credit Union Administration.".

(b) RULEMAKING SCHEDULE.—Regulations required by section 615(d)(2) of the Fair Credit Reporting Act, as amended by this section, shall be issued in final form not later than 1 year after the date of enactment of this Act.

Deadline.
15 USC 1681m
note.

(c) DURATION OF ELECTIONS.—Section 604(e) of the Fair Credit Reporting Act (15 U.S.C. 1681b(e)) is amended in each of paragraphs (3)(A) and (4)(B)(i)), by striking "2-year period" each place that term appears and inserting "5-year period".

(d) PUBLIC AWARENESS CAMPAIGN.—The Commission shall actively publicize and conspicuously post on its website any address and the toll-free telephone number established as part of a notification system for opting out of prescreening under section 604(e) of the Fair Credit Reporting Act (15 U.S.C. 1681b(e)), and otherwise take measures to increase public awareness regarding the availability of the right to opt out of prescreening.

Internet.
15 USC 1681b
note.

(e) ANALYSIS OF FURTHER RESTRICTIONS ON OFFERS OF CREDIT OR INSURANCE.—

15 USC 1601
note.

(1) IN GENERAL.—The Board shall conduct a study of—

(A) the ability of consumers to avoid receiving written offers of credit or insurance in connection with transactions not initiated by the consumer; and

(B) the potential impact that any further restrictions on providing consumers with such written offers of credit or insurance would have on consumers.

(2) REPORT.—The Board shall submit a report summarizing the results of the study required under paragraph (1) to the Congress not later than 12 months after the date of enactment of this Act, together with such recommendations for legislative or administrative action as the Board may determine to be appropriate.

Deadline.

(3) CONTENT OF REPORT.—The report described in paragraph (2) shall address the following issues:

(A) The current statutory or voluntary mechanisms that are available to a consumer to notify lenders and insurance providers that the consumer does not wish to receive written offers of credit or insurance.

(B) The extent to which consumers are currently utilizing existing statutory and voluntary mechanisms to avoid receiving offers of credit or insurance.

(C) The benefits provided to consumers as a result of receiving written offers of credit or insurance.

(D) Whether consumers incur significant costs or are otherwise adversely affected by the receipt of written offers of credit or insurance.

(E) Whether further restricting the ability of lenders and insurers to provide written offers of credit or insurance to consumers would affect—

(i) the cost consumers pay to obtain credit or insurance;

117 STAT. 1980   PUBLIC LAW 108–159—DEC. 4, 2003

        (ii) the availability of credit or insurance;
        (iii) consumers' knowledge about new or alternative products and services;
        (iv) the ability of lenders or insurers to compete with one another; and
        (v) the ability to offer credit or insurance products to consumers who have been traditionally underserved.

SEC. 214. AFFILIATE SHARING.

    (a) LIMITATION.—The Fair Credit Reporting Act (15 U.S.C. 1601 et seq.) is amended—
        (1) by redesignating sections 624 (15 U.S.C. 1681t), 625 (15 U.S.C. 1681u), and 626 (15 U.S.C. 6181v) as sections 625, 626, and 627, respectively; and
        (2) by inserting after section 623 the following:

15 USC 1681s–3.

"§ 624. Affiliate sharing

    "(a) SPECIAL RULE FOR SOLICITATION FOR PURPOSES OF MARKETING.—
        "(1) NOTICE.—Any person that receives from another person related to it by common ownership or affiliated by corporate control a communication of information that would be a consumer report, but for clauses (i), (ii), and (iii) of section 603(d)(2)(A), may not use the information to make a solicitation for marketing purposes to a consumer about its products or services, unless—
            "(A) it is clearly and conspicuously disclosed to the consumer that the information may be communicated among such persons for purposes of making such solicitations to the consumer; and
            "(B) the consumer is provided an opportunity and a simple method to prohibit the making of such solicitations to the consumer by such person.
        "(2) CONSUMER CHOICE.—
            "(A) IN GENERAL.—The notice required under paragraph (1) shall allow the consumer the opportunity to prohibit all solicitations referred to in such paragraph, and may allow the consumer to choose from different options when electing to prohibit the sending of such solicitations, including options regarding the types of entities and information covered, and which methods of delivering solicitations the consumer elects to prohibit.
            "(B) FORMAT.—Notwithstanding subparagraph (A), the notice required under paragraph (1) shall be clear, conspicuous, and concise, and any method provided under paragraph (1)(B) shall be simple. The regulations prescribed to implement this section shall provide specific guidance regarding how to comply with such standards.
        "(3) DURATION.—
            "(A) IN GENERAL.—The election of a consumer pursuant to paragraph (1)(B) to prohibit the making of solicitations shall be effective for at least 5 years, beginning on the date on which the person receives the election of the consumer, unless the consumer requests that such election be revoked.
            "(B) NOTICE UPON EXPIRATION OF EFFECTIVE PERIOD.—At such time as the election of a consumer pursuant to

PUBLIC LAW 108–159—DEC. 4, 2003   117 STAT. 1981

paragraph (1)(B) is no longer effective, a person may not use information that the person receives in the manner described in paragraph (1) to make any solicitation for marketing purposes to the consumer, unless the consumer receives a notice and an opportunity, using a simple method, to extend the opt-out for another period of at least 5 years, pursuant to the procedures described in paragraph (1).

"(4) SCOPE.—This section shall not apply to a person—

"(A) using information to make a solicitation for marketing purposes to a consumer with whom the person has a pre-existing business relationship;

"(B) using information to facilitate communications to an individual for whose benefit the person provides employee benefit or other services pursuant to a contract with an employer related to and arising out of the current employment relationship or status of the individual as a participant or beneficiary of an employee benefit plan;

"(C) using information to perform services on behalf of another person related by common ownership or affiliated by corporate control, except that this subparagraph shall not be construed as permitting a person to send solicitations on behalf of another person, if such other person would not be permitted to send the solicitation on its own behalf as a result of the election of the consumer to prohibit solicitations under paragraph (1)(B);

"(D) using information in response to a communication initiated by the consumer;

"(E) using information in response to solicitations authorized or requested by the consumer; or

"(F) if compliance with this section by that person would prevent compliance by that person with any provision of State insurance laws pertaining to unfair discrimination in any State in which the person is lawfully doing business.

"(5) NO RETROACTIVITY.—This subsection shall not prohibit the use of information to send a solicitation to a consumer if such information was received prior to the date on which persons are required to comply with regulations implementing this subsection.

"(b) NOTICE FOR OTHER PURPOSES PERMISSIBLE.—A notice or other disclosure under this section may be coordinated and consolidated with any other notice required to be issued under any other provision of law by a person that is subject to this section, and a notice or other disclosure that is equivalent to the notice required by subsection (a), and that is provided by a person described in subsection (a) to a consumer together with disclosures required by any other provision of law, shall satisfy the requirements of subsection (a).

"(c) USER REQUIREMENTS.—Requirements with respect to the use by a person of information received from another person related to it by common ownership or affiliated by corporate control, such as the requirements of this section, constitute requirements with respect to the exchange of information among persons affiliated by common ownership or common corporate control, within the meaning of section 625(b)(2).

117 STAT. 1982   PUBLIC LAW 108–159—DEC. 4, 2003

"(d) DEFINITIONS.—For purposes of this section, the following definitions shall apply:

"(1) PRE-EXISTING BUSINESS RELATIONSHIP.—The term 'pre-existing business relationship' means a relationship between a person, or a person's licensed agent, and a consumer, based on—

"(A) a financial contract between a person and a consumer which is in force;

"(B) the purchase, rental, or lease by the consumer of that person's goods or services, or a financial transaction (including holding an active account or a policy in force or having another continuing relationship) between the consumer and that person during the 18-month period immediately preceding the date on which the consumer is sent a solicitation covered by this section;

"(C) an inquiry or application by the consumer regarding a product or service offered by that person, during the 3-month period immediately preceding the date on which the consumer is sent a solicitation covered by this section; or

"(D) any other pre-existing customer relationship defined in the regulations implementing this section.

"(2) SOLICITATION.—The term 'solicitation' means the marketing of a product or service initiated by a person to a particular consumer that is based on an exchange of information described in subsection (a), and is intended to encourage the consumer to purchase such product or service, but does not include communications that are directed at the general public or determined not to be a solicitation by the regulations prescribed under this section.".

15 USC 1681s–3 note.

(b) RULEMAKING REQUIRED.—

(1) IN GENERAL.—The Federal banking agencies, the National Credit Union Administration, and the Commission, with respect to the entities that are subject to their respective enforcement authority under section 621 of the Fair Credit Reporting Act and the Securities and Exchange Commission, and in coordination as described in paragraph (2), shall prescribe regulations to implement section 624 of the Fair Credit Reporting Act, as added by this section.

(2) COORDINATION.—Each agency required to prescribe regulations under paragraph (1) shall consult and coordinate with each other such agency so that, to the extent practicable, the regulations prescribed by each such entity are consistent and comparable with the regulations prescribed by each other such agency.

(3) CONSIDERATIONS.—In promulgating regulations under this subsection, each agency referred to in paragraph (1) shall—

(A) ensure that affiliate sharing notification methods provide a simple means for consumers to make determinations and choices under section 624 of the Fair Credit Reporting Act, as added by this section;

(B) consider the affiliate sharing notification practices employed on the date of enactment of this Act by persons that will be subject to that section 624; and

(C) ensure that notices and disclosures may be coordinated and consolidated, as provided in subsection (b) of that section 624.

PUBLIC LAW 108–159—DEC. 4, 2003 117 STAT. 1983

(4) TIMING.—Regulations required by this subsection shall—

(A) be issued in final form not later than 9 months after the date of enactment of this Act; and

Deadline.

(B) become effective not later than 6 months after the date on which they are issued in final form.

Effective date.

(c) TECHNICAL AND CONFORMING AMENDMENTS.—

(1) DEFINITIONS.—Section 603(d)(2)(A) of the Fair Credit Reporting Act (15 U.S.C. 1681(d)(2)(A)) is amended by inserting "subject to section 624," after "(A)".

15 USC 1681a.

(2) RELATION TO STATE LAWS.—Section 625(b)(1) of the Fair Credit Reporting Act (15 U.S.C. 1681t(b)(1)), as so designated by subsection (a) of this section, is amended—

(A) by striking "or" after the semicolon at the end of subparagraph (E); and

(B) by adding at the end the following new subparagraph:

"(H) section 624, relating to the exchange and use of information to make a solicitation for marketing purposes; or".

(3) CROSS REFERENCE CORRECTION.—Section 627(d) of the Fair Credit Reporting Act (15 U.S.C. 1681v(d)), as so designated by subsection (a) of this section, is amended by striking "section 625" and inserting "section 626".

(4) TABLE OF SECTIONS.—The table of sections for title VI of the Consumer Credit Protection Act (15 U.S.C. 1601 et seq.) is amended by striking the items relating to sections 624 through 626 and inserting the following:

"624. Affiliate sharing.
"625. Relation to State laws.
"626. Disclosures to FBI for counterintelligence purposes.
"627. Disclosures to governmental agencies for counterintelligence purposes.".

(e) STUDIES OF INFORMATION SHARING PRACTICES.—

15 USC 1681s–3 note.

(1) IN GENERAL.—The Federal banking agencies, the National Credit Union Administration, and the Commission shall jointly conduct regular studies of the consumer information sharing practices by financial institutions and other persons that are creditors or users of consumer reports with their affiliates.

(2) MATTERS FOR STUDY.—In conducting the studies required by paragraph (1), the agencies described in paragraph (1) shall—

(A) identify—

(i) the purposes for which financial institutions and other creditors and users of consumer reports share consumer information;

(ii) the types of information shared by such entities with their affiliates;

(iii) the number of choices provided to consumers with respect to the control of such sharing, and the degree to and manner in which consumers exercise such choices, if at all; and

(iv) whether such entities share or may share personally identifiable transaction or experience information with affiliates for purposes—

(I) that are related to employment or hiring, including whether the person that is the subject

117 STAT. 1984   PUBLIC LAW 108–159—DEC. 4, 2003

of such information is given notice of such sharing, and the specific uses of such shared information; or

> (II) of general publication of such information; and

(B) specifically examine the information sharing practices that financial institutions and other creditors and users of consumer reports and their affiliates employ for the purpose of making underwriting decisions or credit evaluations of consumers.

(3) REPORTS.—

(A) INITIAL REPORT.—Not later than 3 years after the date of enactment of this Act, the Federal banking agencies, the National Credit Union Administration, and the Commission shall jointly submit a report to the Congress on the results of the initial study conducted in accordance with this subsection, together with any recommendations for legislative or regulatory action.

(B) FOLLOWUP REPORTS.—The Federal banking agencies, the National Credit Union Administration, and the Commission shall, not less frequently than once every 3 years following the date of submission of the initial report under subparagraph (A), jointly submit a report to the Congress that, together with any recommendations for legislative or regulatory action—

> (i) documents any changes in the areas of study referred to in paragraph (2)(A) occurring since the date of submission of the previous report;

> (ii) identifies any changes in the practices of financial institutions and other creditors and users of consumer reports in sharing consumer information with their affiliates for the purpose of making underwriting decisions or credit evaluations of consumers occurring since the date of submission of the previous report; and

> (iii) examines the effects that changes described in clause (ii) have had, if any, on the degree to which such affiliate sharing practices reduce the need for financial institutions, creditors, and other users of consumer reports to rely on consumer reports for such decisions.

15 USC 1681 note.

SEC. 215. STUDY OF EFFECTS OF CREDIT SCORES AND CREDIT-BASED INSURANCE SCORES ON AVAILABILITY AND AFFORDABILITY OF FINANCIAL PRODUCTS.

(a) STUDY REQUIRED.—The Commission and the Board, in consultation with the Office of Fair Housing and Equal Opportunity of the Department of Housing and Urban Development, shall conduct a study of—

(1) the effects of the use of credit scores and credit-based insurance scores on the availability and affordability of financial products and services, including credit cards, mortgages, auto loans, and property and casualty insurance;

(2) the statistical relationship, utilizing a multivariate analysis that controls for prohibited factors under the Equal Credit Opportunity Act and other known risk factors, between credit

PUBLIC LAW 108–159—DEC. 4, 2003   117 STAT. 1985

scores and credit-based insurance scores and the quantifiable risks and actual losses experienced by businesses;

(3) the extent to which, if any, the use of credit scoring models, credit scores, and credit-based insurance scores impact on the availability and affordability of credit and insurance to the extent information is currently available or is available through proxies, by geography, income, ethnicity, race, color, religion, national origin, age, sex, marital status, and creed, including the extent to which the consideration or lack of consideration of certain factors by credit scoring systems could result in negative or differential treatment of protected classes under the Equal Credit Opportunity Act, and the extent to which, if any, the use of underwriting systems relying on these models could achieve comparable results through the use of factors with less negative impact; and

(4) the extent to which credit scoring systems are used by businesses, the factors considered by such systems, and the effects of variables which are not considered by such systems.

(b) PUBLIC PARTICIPATION.—The Commission shall seek public input about the prescribed methodology and research design of the study described in subsection (a), including from relevant Federal regulators, State insurance regulators, community, civil rights, consumer, and housing groups.

(c) REPORT REQUIRED.—

(1) IN GENERAL.—Before the end of the 24-month period *Deadline.* beginning on the date of enactment of this Act, the Commission shall submit a detailed report on the study conducted pursuant to subsection (a) to the Committee on Financial Services of the House of Representatives and the Committee on Banking, Housing, and Urban Affairs of the Senate.

(2) CONTENTS OF REPORT.—The report submitted under paragraph (1) shall include the findings and conclusions of the Commission, recommendations to address specific areas of concerns addressed in the study, and recommendations for legislative or administrative action that the Commission may determine to be necessary to ensure that credit and credit-based insurance scores are used appropriately and fairly to avoid negative effects.

SEC. 216. DISPOSAL OF CONSUMER REPORT INFORMATION AND RECORDS.

(a) IN GENERAL.—The Fair Credit Reporting Act (15 U.S.C. 1681 et seq.), as amended by this Act, is amended by adding at the end the following:

"§ 628. Disposal of records

15 USC 1681w.

"(a) REGULATIONS.—

"(1) IN GENERAL.—Not later than 1 year after the date *Deadline.* of enactment of this section, the Federal banking agencies, the National Credit Union Administration, and the Commission with respect to the entities that are subject to their respective enforcement authority under section 621, and the Securities and Exchange Commission, and in coordination as described in paragraph (2), shall issue final regulations requiring any person that maintains or otherwise possesses consumer information, or any compilation of consumer information,

117 STAT. 1986 PUBLIC LAW 108–159—DEC. 4, 2003

derived from consumer reports for a business purpose to properly dispose of any such information or compilation.

"(2) COORDINATION.—Each agency required to prescribe regulations under paragraph (1) shall—

"(A) consult and coordinate with each other such agency so that, to the extent possible, the regulations prescribed by each such agency are consistent and comparable with the regulations by each such other agency; and

"(B) ensure that such regulations are consistent with the requirements and regulations issued pursuant to Public Law 106–102 and other provisions of Federal law.

"(3) EXEMPTION AUTHORITY.—In issuing regulations under this section, the Federal banking agencies, the National Credit Union Administration, the Commission, and the Securities and Exchange Commission may exempt any person or class of persons from application of those regulations, as such agency deems appropriate to carry out the purpose of this section.

"(b) RULE OF CONSTRUCTION.—Nothing in this section shall be construed—

"(1) to require a person to maintain or destroy any record pertaining to a consumer that is not imposed under other law; or

"(2) to alter or affect any requirement imposed under any other provision of law to maintain or destroy such a record.".

(b) CLERICAL AMENDMENT.—The table of sections for title VI of the Consumer Credit Protection Act (15 U.S.C. 1601 et seq.) is amended by inserting after the item relating to section 627, as added by section 214 of this Act, the following:

"628. Disposal of records.
"629. Corporate and technological circumvention prohibited.".

SEC. 217. REQUIREMENT TO DISCLOSE COMMUNICATIONS TO A CONSUMER REPORTING AGENCY.

(a) IN GENERAL.—Section 623(a) of the Fair Credit Reporting Act (15 U.S.C. 1681s–2(a)) as amended by this Act, is amended by inserting after paragraph (6), the following new paragraph:

"(7) NEGATIVE INFORMATION.—

"(A) NOTICE TO CONSUMER REQUIRED.—

"(i) IN GENERAL.—If any financial institution that extends credit and regularly and in the ordinary course of business furnishes information to a consumer reporting agency described in section 603(p) furnishes negative information to such an agency regarding credit extended to a customer, the financial institution shall provide a notice of such furnishing of negative information, in writing, to the customer.

"(ii) NOTICE EFFECTIVE FOR SUBSEQUENT SUBMISSIONS.—After providing such notice, the financial institution may submit additional negative information to a consumer reporting agency described in section 603(p) with respect to the same transaction, extension of credit, account, or customer without providing additional notice to the customer.

"(B) TIME OF NOTICE.—

Deadline.

"(i) IN GENERAL.—The notice required under subparagraph (A) shall be provided to the customer prior to, or no later than 30 days after, furnishing

the negative information to a consumer reporting agency described in section 603(p).

"(ii) COORDINATION WITH NEW ACCOUNT DISCLO-SURES.—If the notice is provided to the customer prior to furnishing the negative information to a consumer reporting agency, the notice may not be included in the initial disclosures provided under section 127(a) of the Truth in Lending Act.

"(C) COORDINATION WITH OTHER DISCLOSURES.—The notice required under subparagraph (A)—

"(i) may be included on or with any notice of default, any billing statement, or any other materials provided to the customer; and

"(ii) must be clear and conspicuous.

"(D) MODEL DISCLOSURE.—

"(i) DUTY OF BOARD TO PREPARE.—The Board shall prescribe a brief model disclosure a financial institution may use to comply with subparagraph (A), which shall not exceed 30 words.

"(ii) USE OF MODEL NOT REQUIRED.—No provision of this paragraph shall be construed as requiring a financial institution to use any such model form pre-scribed by the Board.

"(iii) COMPLIANCE USING MODEL.—A financial institution shall be deemed to be in compliance with subparagraph (A) if the financial institution uses any such model form prescribed by the Board, or the finan-cial institution uses any such model form and rearranges its format.

"(E) USE OF NOTICE WITHOUT SUBMITTING NEGATIVE INFORMATION.—No provision of this paragraph shall be con-strued as requiring a financial institution that has provided a customer with a notice described in subparagraph (A) to furnish negative information about the customer to a consumer reporting agency.

"(F) SAFE HARBOR.—A financial institution shall not be liable for failure to perform the duties required by this paragraph if, at the time of the failure, the financial institution maintained reasonable policies and procedures to comply with this paragraph or the financial institution reasonably believed that the institution is prohibited, by law, from contacting the consumer.

"(G) DEFINITIONS.—For purposes of this paragraph, the following definitions shall apply:

"(i) NEGATIVE INFORMATION.—The term 'negative information' means information concerning a cus-tomer's delinquencies, late payments, insolvency, or any form of default.

"(ii) CUSTOMER; FINANCIAL INSTITUTION.—The terms 'customer' and 'financial institution' have the same meanings as in section 509 Public Law 106–102.".

(b) MODEL DISCLOSURE FORM.—Before the end of the 6-month period beginning on the date of enactment of this Act, the Board shall adopt the model disclosure required under the amendment

Deadline.
Federal Register, publication.
15 USC 1681s–2 note.

made by subsection (a) after notice duly given in the Federal Register and an opportunity for public comment in accordance with section 553 of title 5, United States Code.

TITLE III—ENHANCING THE ACCURACY OF CONSUMER REPORT INFORMATION

SEC. 311. RISK-BASED PRICING NOTICE.

(a) DUTIES OF USERS.—Section 615 of the Fair Credit Reporting Act (15 U.S.C. 1681m), as amended by this Act, is amended by adding at the end the following:

"(h) DUTIES OF USERS IN CERTAIN CREDIT TRANSACTIONS.—

"(1) IN GENERAL.—Subject to rules prescribed as provided in paragraph (6), if any person uses a consumer report in connection with an application for, or a grant, extension, or other provision of, credit on material terms that are materially less favorable than the most favorable terms available to a substantial proportion of consumers from or through that person, based in whole or in part on a consumer report, the person shall provide an oral, written, or electronic notice to the consumer in the form and manner required by regulations prescribed in accordance with this subsection.

"(2) TIMING.—The notice required under paragraph (1) may be provided at the time of an application for, or a grant, extension, or other provision of, credit or the time of communication of an approval of an application for, or grant, extension, or other provision of, credit, except as provided in the regulations prescribed under paragraph (6).

"(3) EXCEPTIONS.—No notice shall be required from a person under this subsection if—

"(A) the consumer applied for specific material terms and was granted those terms, unless those terms were initially specified by the person after the transaction was initiated by the consumer and after the person obtained a consumer report; or

"(B) the person has provided or will provide a notice to the consumer under subsection (a) in connection with the transaction.

"(4) OTHER NOTICE NOT SUFFICIENT.—A person that is required to provide a notice under subsection (a) cannot meet that requirement by providing a notice under this subsection.

"(5) CONTENT AND DELIVERY OF NOTICE.—A notice under this subsection shall, at a minimum—

"(A) include a statement informing the consumer that the terms offered to the consumer are set based on information from a consumer report;

"(B) identify the consumer reporting agency furnishing the report;

"(C) include a statement informing the consumer that the consumer may obtain a copy of a consumer report from that consumer reporting agency without charge; and

"(D) include the contact information specified by that consumer reporting agency for obtaining such consumer reports (including a toll-free telephone number established by the agency in the case of a consumer reporting agency described in section 603(p)).

PUBLIC LAW 108–159—DEC. 4, 2003 117 STAT. 1989

"(6) RULEMAKING.—

"(A) RULES REQUIRED.—The Commission and the Board shall jointly prescribe rules.

"(B) CONTENT.—Rules required by subparagraph (A) shall address, but are not limited to—

"(i) the form, content, time, and manner of delivery of any notice under this subsection;

"(ii) clarification of the meaning of terms used in this subsection, including what credit terms are material, and when credit terms are materially less favorable;

"(iii) exceptions to the notice requirement under this subsection for classes of persons or transactions regarding which the agencies determine that notice would not significantly benefit consumers;

"(iv) a model notice that may be used to comply with this subsection; and

"(v) the timing of the notice required under paragraph (1), including the circumstances under which the notice must be provided after the terms offered to the consumer were set based on information from a consumer report.

"(7) COMPLIANCE.—A person shall not be liable for failure to perform the duties required by this section if, at the time of the failure, the person maintained reasonable policies and procedures to comply with this section.

"(8) ENFORCEMENT.—

"(A) NO CIVIL ACTIONS.—Sections 616 and 617 shall not apply to any failure by any person to comply with this section.

"(B) ADMINISTRATIVE ENFORCEMENT.—This section shall be enforced exclusively under section 621 by the Federal agencies and officials identified in that section.".

(b) RELATION TO STATE LAWS.—Section 625(b)(1) of the Fair Credit Reporting Act (15 U.S.C. 1681t(b)(1)), as so designated by section 214 of this Act, is amended by adding at the end the following:

"(I) section 615(h), relating to the duties of users of consumer reports to provide notice with respect to terms in certain credit transactions;".

SEC. 312. PROCEDURES TO ENHANCE THE ACCURACY AND INTEGRITY OF INFORMATION FURNISHED TO CONSUMER REPORTING AGENCIES.

(a) ACCURACY GUIDELINES AND REGULATIONS.—Section 623 of the Fair Credit Reporting Act (15 U.S.C. 1681s–2) is amended by adding at the end the following:

"(e) ACCURACY GUIDELINES AND REGULATIONS REQUIRED.—

"(1) GUIDELINES.—The Federal banking agencies, the National Credit Union Administration, and the Commission shall, with respect to the entities that are subject to their respective enforcement authority under section 621, and in coordination as described in paragraph (2)—

"(A) establish and maintain guidelines for use by each person that furnishes information to a consumer reporting agency regarding the accuracy and integrity of the information relating to consumers that such entities furnish to

117 STAT. 1990 PUBLIC LAW 108–159—DEC. 4, 2003

consumer reporting agencies, and update such guidelines as often as necessary; and

"(B) prescribe regulations requiring each person that furnishes information to a consumer reporting agency to establish reasonable policies and procedures for implementing the guidelines established pursuant to subparagraph (A).

"(2) COORDINATION.—Each agency required to prescribe regulations under paragraph (1) shall consult and coordinate with each other such agency so that, to the extent possible, the regulations prescribed by each such entity are consistent and comparable with the regulations prescribed by each other such agency.

"(3) CRITERIA.—In developing the guidelines required by paragraph (1)(A), the agencies described in paragraph (1) shall—

"(A) identify patterns, practices, and specific forms of activity that can compromise the accuracy and integrity of information furnished to consumer reporting agencies;

"(B) review the methods (including technological means) used to furnish information relating to consumers to consumer reporting agencies;

"(C) determine whether persons that furnish information to consumer reporting agencies maintain and enforce policies to assure the accuracy and integrity of information furnished to consumer reporting agencies; and

"(D) examine the policies and processes that persons that furnish information to consumer reporting agencies employ to conduct reinvestigations and correct inaccurate information relating to consumers that has been furnished to consumer reporting agencies.".

(b) DUTY OF FURNISHERS TO PROVIDE ACCURATE INFORMATION.—Section 623(a)(1) of the Fair Credit Reporting Act (15 U.S.C. 1681s–2(a)(1)) is amended—

(1) in subparagraph (A), by striking "knows or consciously avoids knowing that the information is inaccurate" and inserting "knows or has reasonable cause to believe that the information is inaccurate"; and

(2) by adding at the end the following:

"(D) DEFINITION.—For purposes of subparagraph (A), the term 'reasonable cause to believe that the information is inaccurate' means having specific knowledge, other than solely allegations by the consumer, that would cause a reasonable person to have substantial doubts about the accuracy of the information.".

(c) ABILITY OF CONSUMER TO DISPUTE INFORMATION DIRECTLY WITH FURNISHER.—Section 623(a) of the Fair Credit Reporting Act (15 U.S.C. 1681s–2(a)), as amended by this Act, is amended by adding at the end the following:

"(8) ABILITY OF CONSUMER TO DISPUTE INFORMATION DIRECTLY WITH FURNISHER.—

Regulations.

"(A) IN GENERAL.—The Federal banking agencies, the National Credit Union Administration, and the Commission shall jointly prescribe regulations that shall identify the circumstances under which a furnisher shall be required to reinvestigate a dispute concerning the accuracy of

PUBLIC LAW 108–159—DEC. 4, 2003   117 STAT. 1991

information contained in a consumer report on the consumer, based on a direct request of a consumer.

"(B) CONSIDERATIONS.—In prescribing regulations under subparagraph (A), the agencies shall weigh—

"(i) the benefits to consumers with the costs on furnishers and the credit reporting system;

"(ii) the impact on the overall accuracy and integrity of consumer reports of any such requirements;

"(iii) whether direct contact by the consumer with the furnisher would likely result in the most expeditious resolution of any such dispute; and

"(iv) the potential impact on the credit reporting process if credit repair organizations, as defined in section 403(3), including entities that would be a credit repair organization, but for section 403(3)(B)(i), are able to circumvent the prohibition in subparagraph (G).

"(C) APPLICABILITY.—Subparagraphs (D) through (G) shall apply in any circumstance identified under the regulations promulgated under subparagraph (A).

"(D) SUBMITTING A NOTICE OF DISPUTE.—A consumer who seeks to dispute the accuracy of information shall provide a dispute notice directly to such person at the address specified by the person for such notices that—

"(i) identifies the specific information that is being disputed;

"(ii) explains the basis for the dispute; and

"(iii) includes all supporting documentation required by the furnisher to substantiate the basis of the dispute.

"(E) DUTY OF PERSON AFTER RECEIVING NOTICE OF DISPUTE.—After receiving a notice of dispute from a consumer pursuant to subparagraph (D), the person that provided the information in dispute to a consumer reporting agency shall—

"(i) conduct an investigation with respect to the disputed information;

"(ii) review all relevant information provided by the consumer with the notice;

"(iii) complete such person's investigation of the dispute and report the results of the investigation to the consumer before the expiration of the period under section 611(a)(1) within which a consumer reporting agency would be required to complete its action if the consumer had elected to dispute the information under that section; and

"(iv) if the investigation finds that the information reported was inaccurate, promptly notify each consumer reporting agency to which the person furnished the inaccurate information of that determination and provide to the agency any correction to that information that is necessary to make the information provided by the person accurate.

"(F) FRIVOLOUS OR IRRELEVANT DISPUTE.—

"(i) IN GENERAL.—This paragraph shall not apply if the person receiving a notice of a dispute from a consumer reasonably determines that the dispute is frivolous or irrelevant, including—

"(I) by reason of the failure of a consumer to provide sufficient information to investigate the disputed information; or

"(II) the submission by a consumer of a dispute that is substantially the same as a dispute previously submitted by or for the consumer, either directly to the person or through a consumer reporting agency under subsection (b), with respect to which the person has already performed the person's duties under this paragraph or subsection (b), as applicable.

"(ii) NOTICE OF DETERMINATION.—Upon making any determination under clause (i) that a dispute is frivolous or irrelevant, the person shall notify the consumer of such determination not later than 5 business days after making such determination, by mail or, if authorized by the consumer for that purpose, by any other means available to the person.

Deadline.

"(iii) CONTENTS OF NOTICE.—A notice under clause (ii) shall include—

"(I) the reasons for the determination under clause (i); and

"(II) identification of any information required to investigate the disputed information, which may consist of a standardized form describing the general nature of such information.

"(G) EXCLUSION OF CREDIT REPAIR ORGANIZATIONS.— This paragraph shall not apply if the notice of the dispute is submitted by, is prepared on behalf of the consumer by, or is submitted on a form supplied to the consumer by, a credit repair organization, as defined in section 403(3), or an entity that would be a credit repair organization, but for section 403(3)(B)(i).".

(d) FURNISHER LIABILITY EXCEPTION.—Section 623(a)(5) of the Fair Credit Reporting Act (15 U.S.C. 1681s–2(a)(5)) is amended—

(1) by striking "A person" and inserting the following:

"(A) IN GENERAL.—A person";

(2) by inserting "date of delinquency on the account, which shall be the" before "month";

(3) by inserting "on the account" before "that immediately preceded"; and

(4) by adding at the end the following:

"(B) RULE OF CONSTRUCTION.—For purposes of this paragraph only, and provided that the consumer does not dispute the information, a person that furnishes information on a delinquent account that is placed for collection, charged for profit or loss, or subjected to any similar action, complies with this paragraph, if—

"(i) the person reports the same date of delinquency as that provided by the creditor to which the account was owed at the time at which the commencement of the delinquency occurred, if the creditor previously reported that date of delinquency to a consumer reporting agency;

PUBLIC LAW 108–159—DEC. 4, 2003   117 STAT. 1993

"(ii) the creditor did not previously report the date of delinquency to a consumer reporting agency, and the person establishes and follows reasonable procedures to obtain the date of delinquency from the creditor or another reliable source and reports that date to a consumer reporting agency as the date of delinquency; or

"(iii) the creditor did not previously report the date of delinquency to a consumer reporting agency and the date of delinquency cannot be reasonably obtained as provided in clause (ii), the person establishes and follows reasonable procedures to ensure the date reported as the date of delinquency precedes the date on which the account is placed for collection, charged to profit or loss, or subjected to any similar action, and reports such date to the credit reporting agency.".

(e) LIABILITY AND ENFORCEMENT.—

(1) CIVIL LIABILITY.—Section 623 of the Fair Credit Reporting Act (15 U.S.C. 1681s–2) is amended by striking subsections (c) and (d) and inserting the following:

"(c) LIMITATION ON LIABILITY.—Except as provided in section 621(c)(1)(B), sections 616 and 617 do not apply to any violation of—

"(1) subsection (a) of this section, including any regulations issued thereunder;

"(2) subsection (e) of this section, except that nothing in this paragraph shall limit, expand, or otherwise affect liability under section 616 or 617, as applicable, for violations of subsection (b) of this section; or

"(3) subsection (e) of section 615.

"(d) LIMITATION ON ENFORCEMENT.—The provisions of law described in paragraphs (1) through (3) of subsection (c) (other than with respect to the exception described in paragraph (2) of subsection (c)) shall be enforced exclusively as provided under section 621 by the Federal agencies and officials and the State officials identified in section 621.".

(2) STATE ACTIONS.—Section 621(c) of the Fair Credit Reporting Act (15 U.S.C. 1681s(c)) is amended—

(A) in paragraph (1)(B)(ii), by striking "of section 623(a)" and inserting "described in any of paragraphs (1) through (3) of section 623(c)"; and

(B) in paragraph (5)—

(i) in each of subparagraphs (A) and (B), by striking "of section 623(a)(1)" each place that term appears and inserting "described in any of paragraphs (1) through (3) of section 623(c)"; and

(ii) by amending the paragraph heading to read as follows:

"(5) LIMITATIONS ON STATE ACTIONS FOR CERTAIN VIOLATIONS.—".

(f) RULE OF CONSTRUCTION.—Nothing in this section, the amendments made by this section, or any other provision of this Act shall be construed to affect any liability under section 616 or 617 of the Fair Credit Reporting Act (15 U.S.C. 1681n, 1681o) that existed on the day before the date of enactment of this Act.

15 USC 1681n note.

PUBLIC LAW 108–159—DEC. 4, 2003

SEC. 313. FTC AND CONSUMER REPORTING AGENCY ACTION CONCERNING COMPLAINTS.

(a) In General.—Section 611 of the Fair Credit Reporting Act (15 U.S.C. 1681i) is amended by adding at the end the following:

"(e) Treatment of Complaints and Report to Congress.—

"(1) In general.—The Commission shall—

Records.

"(A) compile all complaints that it receives that a file of a consumer that is maintained by a consumer reporting agency described in section 603(p) contains incomplete or inaccurate information, with respect to which, the consumer appears to have disputed the completeness or accuracy with the consumer reporting agency or otherwise utilized the procedures provided by subsection (a); and

"(B) transmit each such complaint to each consumer reporting agency involved.

"(2) Exclusion.—Complaints received or obtained by the Commission pursuant to its investigative authority under the Federal Trade Commission Act shall not be subject to paragraph (1).

"(3) Agency responsibilities.—Each consumer reporting agency described in section 603(p) that receives a complaint transmitted by the Commission pursuant to paragraph (1) shall—

"(A) review each such complaint to determine whether all legal obligations imposed on the consumer reporting agency under this title (including any obligation imposed by an applicable court or administrative order) have been met with respect to the subject matter of the complaint;

"(B) provide reports on a regular basis to the Commission regarding the determinations of and actions taken by the consumer reporting agency, if any, in connection with its review of such complaints; and

Records.

"(C) maintain, for a reasonable time period, records regarding the disposition of each such complaint that is sufficient to demonstrate compliance with this subsection.

"(4) Rulemaking authority.—The Commission may prescribe regulations, as appropriate to implement this subsection.

"(5) Annual report.—The Commission shall submit to the Committee on Banking, Housing, and Urban Affairs of the Senate and the Committee on Financial Services of the House of Representatives an annual report regarding information gathered by the Commission under this subsection.".

15 USC 1681i note.

(b) Prompt Investigation of Disputed Consumer Information.—

(1) Study required.—The Board and the Commission shall jointly study the extent to which, and the manner in which, consumer reporting agencies and furnishers of consumer information to consumer reporting agencies are complying with the procedures, time lines, and requirements under the Fair Credit Reporting Act for the prompt investigation of the disputed accuracy of any consumer information, the completeness of the information provided to consumer reporting agencies, and the prompt correction or deletion, in accordance with such Act, of any inaccurate or incomplete information or information that cannot be verified.

Deadline.

(2) Report required.—Before the end of the 12-month period beginning on the date of enactment of this Act, the

PUBLIC LAW 108–159—DEC. 4, 2003   117 STAT. 1995

Board and the Commission shall jointly submit a progress report to the Congress on the results of the study required under paragraph (1).

(3) CONSIDERATIONS.—In preparing the report required under paragraph (2), the Board and the Commission shall consider information relating to complaints compiled by the Commission under section 611(e) of the Fair Credit Reporting Act, as added by this section.

(4) RECOMMENDATIONS.—The report required under paragraph (2) shall include such recommendations as the Board and the Commission jointly determine to be appropriate for legislative or administrative action, to ensure that—

(A) consumer disputes with consumer reporting agencies over the accuracy or completeness of information in a consumer's file are promptly and fully investigated and any incorrect, incomplete, or unverifiable information is corrected or deleted immediately thereafter;

(B) furnishers of information to consumer reporting agencies maintain full and prompt compliance with the duties and responsibilities established under section 623 of the Fair Credit Reporting Act; and

(C) consumer reporting agencies establish and maintain appropriate internal controls and management review procedures for maintaining full and continuous compliance with the procedures, time lines, and requirements under the Fair Credit Reporting Act for the prompt investigation of the disputed accuracy of any consumer information and the prompt correction or deletion, in accordance with such Act, of any inaccurate or incomplete information or information that cannot be verified.

SEC. 314. IMPROVED DISCLOSURE OF THE RESULTS OF REINVESTIGATION.

(a) IN GENERAL.—Section 611(a)(5)(A) of the Fair Credit Reporting Act (15 U.S.C. 1681i(a)(5)(A)) is amended by striking "shall" and all that follows through the end of the subparagraph, and inserting the following: "shall—

"(i) promptly delete that item of information from the file of the consumer, or modify that item of information, as appropriate, based on the results of the reinvestigation; and

"(ii) promptly notify the furnisher of that information that the information has been modified or deleted from the file of the consumer.".

Notification.

(b) FURNISHER REQUIREMENTS RELATING TO INACCURATE, INCOMPLETE, OR UNVERIFIABLE INFORMATION.—Section 623(b)(1) of the Fair Credit Reporting Act (15 U.S.C. 1681s–2(b)(1)) is amended—

(1) in subparagraph (C), by striking "and" at the end; and

(2) in subparagraph (D), by striking the period at the end and inserting the following: "; and

"(E) if an item of information disputed by a consumer is found to be inaccurate or incomplete or cannot be verified after any reinvestigation under paragraph (1), for purposes

117 STAT. 1996   PUBLIC LAW 108–159—DEC. 4, 2003

of reporting to a consumer reporting agency only, as appropriate, based on the results of the reinvestigation promptly—

"(i) modify that item of information;

"(ii) delete that item of information; or

"(iii) permanently block the reporting of that item of information.".

SEC. 315. RECONCILING ADDRESSES.

Section 605 of the Fair Credit Reporting Act (15 U.S.C. 1681c), as amended by this Act, is amended by adding at the end the following:

"(h) NOTICE OF DISCREPANCY IN ADDRESS.—

"(1) IN GENERAL.—If a person has requested a consumer report relating to a consumer from a consumer reporting agency described in section 603(p), the request includes an address for the consumer that substantially differs from the addresses in the file of the consumer, and the agency provides a consumer report in response to the request, the consumer reporting agency shall notify the requester of the existence of the discrepancy.

"(2) REGULATIONS.—

"(A) REGULATIONS REQUIRED.—The Federal banking agencies, the National Credit Union Administration, and the Commission shall jointly, with respect to the entities that are subject to their respective enforcement authority under section 621, prescribe regulations providing guidance regarding reasonable policies and procedures that a user of a consumer report should employ when such user has received a notice of discrepancy under paragraph (1).

"(B) POLICIES AND PROCEDURES TO BE INCLUDED.—The regulations prescribed under subparagraph (A) shall describe reasonable policies and procedures for use by a user of a consumer report—

"(i) to form a reasonable belief that the user knows the identity of the person to whom the consumer report pertains; and

"(ii) if the user establishes a continuing relationship with the consumer, and the user regularly and in the ordinary course of business furnishes information to the consumer reporting agency from which the notice of discrepancy pertaining to the consumer was obtained, to reconcile the address of the consumer with the consumer reporting agency by furnishing such address to such consumer reporting agency as part of information regularly furnished by the user for the period in which the relationship is established.".

SEC. 316. NOTICE OF DISPUTE THROUGH RESELLER.

(a) REQUIREMENT FOR REINVESTIGATION OF DISPUTED INFORMATION UPON NOTICE FROM A RESELLER.—Section 611(a) of the Fair Credit Reporting Act (15 U.S.C. 1681i(a)(1)(A)) is amended—

(1) in paragraph (1)(A)—

(A) by striking "If the completeness" and inserting "Subject to subsection (f), if the completeness";

(B) by inserting ", or indirectly through a reseller," after "notifies the agency directly"; and

PUBLIC LAW 108–159—DEC. 4, 2003   117 STAT. 1997

(C) by inserting "or reseller" before the period at the end;

(2) in paragraph (2)(A)—

(A) by inserting "or a reseller" after "dispute from any consumer"; and

(B) by inserting "or reseller" before the period at the end; and

(3) in paragraph (2)(B), by inserting "or the reseller" after "from the consumer".

(b) REINVESTIGATION REQUIREMENT APPLICABLE TO RE-SELLERS.—Section 611 of the Fair Credit Reporting Act (15 U.S.C. 1681i), as amended by this Act, is amended by adding at the end the following:

"(f) REINVESTIGATION REQUIREMENT APPLICABLE TO RE-SELLERS.—

"(1) EXEMPTION FROM GENERAL REINVESTIGATION REQUIRE-MENT.—Except as provided in paragraph (2), a reseller shall be exempt from the requirements of this section.

"(2) ACTION REQUIRED UPON RECEIVING NOTICE OF A DIS-PUTE.—If a reseller receives a notice from a consumer of a dispute concerning the completeness or accuracy of any item of information contained in a consumer report on such consumer produced by the reseller, the reseller shall, within 5 business days of receiving the notice, and free of charge—   Deadline.

"(A) determine whether the item of information is incomplete or inaccurate as a result of an act or omission of the reseller; and

"(B) if—

"(i) the reseller determines that the item of information is incomplete or inaccurate as a result of an act or omission of the reseller, not later than 20 days after receiving the notice, correct the informa-tion in the consumer report or delete it; or   Deadline.

"(ii) if the reseller determines that the item of information is not incomplete or inaccurate as a result of an act or omission of the reseller, convey the notice of the dispute, together with all relevant information provided by the consumer, to each consumer reporting agency that provided the reseller with the information that is the subject of the dispute, using an address or a notification mechanism specified by the consumer reporting agency for such notices.

"(3) RESPONSIBILITY OF CONSUMER REPORTING AGENCY TO NOTIFY CONSUMER THROUGH RESELLER.—Upon the completion of a reinvestigation under this section of a dispute concerning the completeness or accuracy of any information in the file of a consumer by a consumer reporting agency that received notice of the dispute from a reseller under paragraph (2)—

"(A) the notice by the consumer reporting agency under paragraph (6), (7), or (8) of subsection (a) shall be provided to the reseller in lieu of the consumer; and

"(B) the reseller shall immediately reconvey such notice to the consumer, including any notice of a deletion by telephone in the manner required under paragraph (8)(A).

"(4) RESELLER REINVESTIGATIONS.—No provision of this sub-section shall be construed as prohibiting a reseller from con-ducting a reinvestigation of a consumer dispute directly.".

117 STAT. 1998   PUBLIC LAW 108–159—DEC. 4, 2003

(c) TECHNICAL AND CONFORMING AMENDMENT.—Section 611(a)(2)(B) of the Fair Credit Reporting Act (15 U.S.C. 1681i(a)(2)(B)) is amended in the subparagraph heading, by striking "FROM CONSUMER".

SEC. 317. REASONABLE REINVESTIGATION REQUIRED.

Section 611(a)(1)(A) of the Fair Credit Reporting Act (15 U.S.C. 1681i(a)(1)(A)) is amended by striking "shall reinvestigate free of charge" and inserting "shall, free of charge, conduct a reasonable reinvestigation to determine whether the disputed information is inaccurate".

15 USC 1681 note.

SEC. 318. FTC STUDY OF ISSUES RELATING TO THE FAIR CREDIT REPORTING ACT.

(a) STUDY REQUIRED.—

(1) IN GENERAL.—The Commission shall conduct a study on ways to improve the operation of the Fair Credit Reporting Act.

(2) AREAS FOR STUDY.—In conducting the study under paragraph (1), the Commission shall review—

(A) the efficacy of increasing the number of points of identifying information that a credit reporting agency is required to match to ensure that a consumer is the correct individual to whom a consumer report relates before releasing a consumer report to a user, including—

(i) the extent to which requiring additional points of such identifying information to match would—

(I) enhance the accuracy of credit reports; and

(II) combat the provision of incorrect consumer reports to users;

(ii) the extent to which requiring an exact match of the first and last name, social security number, and address and ZIP Code of the consumer would enhance the likelihood of increasing credit report accuracy; and

(iii) the effects of allowing consumer reporting agencies to use partial matches of social security numbers and name recognition software on the accuracy of credit reports;

(B) requiring notification to consumers when negative information has been added to their credit reports, including—

(i) the potential impact of such notification on the ability of consumers to identify errors on their credit reports; and

(ii) the potential impact of such notification on the ability of consumers to remove fraudulent information from their credit reports;

(C) the effects of requiring that a consumer who has experienced an adverse action based on a credit report receives a copy of the same credit report that the creditor relied on in taking the adverse action, including—

(i) the extent to which providing such reports to consumers would increase the ability of consumers to identify errors in their credit reports; and

(ii) the extent to which providing such reports to consumers would increase the ability of consumers

PUBLIC LAW 108–159—DEC. 4, 2003   117 STAT. 1999

to remove fraudulent information from their credit reports;

(D) any common financial transactions that are not generally reported to the consumer reporting agencies, but would provide useful information in determining the credit worthiness of consumers; and

(E) any actions that might be taken within a voluntary reporting system to encourage the reporting of the types of transactions described in subparagraph (D).

(3) COSTS AND BENEFITS.—With respect to each area of study described in paragraph (2), the Commission shall consider the extent to which such requirements would benefit consumers, balanced against the cost of implementing such provisions.

(b) REPORT REQUIRED.—Not later than 1 year after the date of enactment of this Act, the chairman of the Commission shall submit a report to the Committee on Banking, Housing, and Urban Affairs of the Senate and the Committee on Financial Services of the House of Representatives containing a detailed summary of the findings and conclusions of the study under this section, together with such recommendations for legislative or administrative actions as may be appropriate.

Deadline.

SEC. 319. FTC STUDY OF THE ACCURACY OF CONSUMER REPORTS.

15 USC 1681 note.

(a) STUDY REQUIRED.—Until the final report is submitted under subsection (b)(2), the Commission shall conduct an ongoing study of the accuracy and completeness of information contained in consumer reports prepared or maintained by consumer reporting agencies and methods for improving the accuracy and completeness of such information.

(b) BIENNIAL REPORTS REQUIRED.—

(1) INTERIM REPORTS.—The Commission shall submit an interim report to the Congress on the study conducted under subsection (a) at the end of the 1-year period beginning on the date of enactment of this Act and biennially thereafter for 8 years.

(2) FINAL REPORT.—The Commission shall submit a final report to the Congress on the study conducted under subsection (a) at the end of the 2-year period beginning on the date on which the final interim report is submitted to the Congress under paragraph (1).

(3) CONTENTS.—Each report submitted under this subsection shall contain a detailed summary of the findings and conclusions of the Commission with respect to the study required under subsection (a) and such recommendations for legislative and administrative action as the Commission may determine to be appropriate.

TITLE IV—LIMITING THE USE AND SHARING OF MEDICAL INFORMATION IN THE FINANCIAL SYSTEM

SEC. 411. PROTECTION OF MEDICAL INFORMATION IN THE FINANCIAL SYSTEM.

(a) IN GENERAL.—Section 604(g) of the Fair Credit Reporting Act (15 U.S.C. 1681b(g)) is amended to read as follows:

117 STAT. 2000   PUBLIC LAW 108–159—DEC. 4, 2003

"(g) PROTECTION OF MEDICAL INFORMATION.—

"(1) LIMITATION ON CONSUMER REPORTING AGENCIES.—A consumer reporting agency shall not furnish for employment purposes, or in connection with a credit or insurance transaction, a consumer report that contains medical information about a consumer, unless—

"(A) if furnished in connection with an insurance transaction, the consumer affirmatively consents to the furnishing of the report;

"(B) if furnished for employment purposes or in connection with a credit transaction—

"(i) the information to be furnished is relevant to process or effect the employment or credit transaction; and

"(ii) the consumer provides specific written consent for the furnishing of the report that describes in clear and conspicuous language the use for which the information will be furnished; or

"(C) the information to be furnished pertains solely to transactions, accounts, or balances relating to debts arising from the receipt of medical services, products, or devises, where such information, other than account status or amounts, is restricted or reported using codes that do not identify, or do not provide information sufficient to infer, the specific provider or the nature of such services, products, or devices, as provided in section 605(a)(6).

"(2) LIMITATION ON CREDITORS.—Except as permitted pursuant to paragraph (3)(C) or regulations prescribed under paragraph (5)(A), a creditor shall not obtain or use medical information pertaining to a consumer in connection with any determination of the consumer's eligibility, or continued eligibility, for credit.

"(3) ACTIONS AUTHORIZED BY FEDERAL LAW, INSURANCE ACTIVITIES AND REGULATORY DETERMINATIONS.—Section 603(d)(3) shall not be construed so as to treat information or any communication of information as a consumer report if the information or communication is disclosed—

"(A) in connection with the business of insurance or annuities, including the activities described in section 18B of the model Privacy of Consumer Financial and Health Information Regulation issued by the National Association of Insurance Commissioners (as in effect on January 1, 2003);

"(B) for any purpose permitted without authorization under the Standards for Individually Identifiable Health Information promulgated by the Department of Health and Human Services pursuant to the Health Insurance Portability and Accountability Act of 1996, or referred to under section 1179 of such Act, or described in section 502(e) of Public Law 106–102; or

"(C) as otherwise determined to be necessary and appropriate, by regulation or order and subject to paragraph (6), by the Commission, any Federal banking agency or the National Credit Union Administration (with respect to any financial institution subject to the jurisdiction of such agency or Administration under paragraph (1), (2), or (3) of section 621(b), or the applicable State insurance

PUBLIC LAW 108–159—DEC. 4, 2003   117 STAT. 2001

authority (with respect to any person engaged in providing insurance or annuities).

"(4) LIMITATION ON REDISCLOSURE OF MEDICAL INFORMATION.—Any person that receives medical information pursuant to paragraph (1) or (3) shall not disclose such information to any other person, except as necessary to carry out the purpose for which the information was initially disclosed, or as otherwise permitted by statute, regulation, or order.

"(5) REGULATIONS AND EFFECTIVE DATE FOR PARAGRAPH (2).—

"(A) REGULATIONS REQUIRED.—Each Federal banking agency and the National Credit Union Administration shall, subject to paragraph (6) and after notice and opportunity for comment, prescribe regulations that permit transactions under paragraph (2) that are determined to be necessary and appropriate to protect legitimate operational, transactional, risk, consumer, and other needs (and which shall include permitting actions necessary for administrative verification purposes), consistent with the intent of paragraph (2) to restrict the use of medical information for inappropriate purposes.

"(B) FINAL REGULATIONS REQUIRED.—The Federal banking agencies and the National Credit Union Administration shall issue the regulations required under subparagraph (A) in final form before the end of the 6-month period beginning on the date of enactment of the Fair and Accurate Credit Transactions Act of 2003.

Deadline.

"(6) COORDINATION WITH OTHER LAWS.—No provision of this subsection shall be construed as altering, affecting, or superseding the applicability of any other provision of Federal law relating to medical confidentiality.".

(b) RESTRICTION ON SHARING OF MEDICAL INFORMATION.—Section 603(d) of the Fair Credit Reporting Act (15 U.S.C. 1681a(d)) is amended—

(1) in paragraph (2), by striking "The term" and inserting "Except as provided in paragraph (3), the term"; and

(2) by adding at the end the following new paragraph:

"(3) RESTRICTION ON SHARING OF MEDICAL INFORMATION.—Except for information or any communication of information disclosed as provided in section 604(g)(3), the exclusions in paragraph (2) shall not apply with respect to information disclosed to any person related by common ownership or affiliated by corporate control, if the information is—

"(A) medical information;

"(B) an individualized list or description based on the payment transactions of the consumer for medical products or services; or

"(C) an aggregate list of identified consumers based on payment transactions for medical products or services.".

(c) DEFINITION.—Section 603(i) of the Fair Credit Reporting Act (15 U.S.C. 1681a(i)) is amended to read as follows:

"(i) MEDICAL INFORMATION.—The term 'medical information'—

"(1) means information or data, whether oral or recorded, in any form or medium, created by or derived from a health care provider or the consumer, that relates to—

"(A) the past, present, or future physical, mental, or behavioral health or condition of an individual;

117 STAT. 2002 PUBLIC LAW 108–159—DEC. 4, 2003

"(B) the provision of health care to an individual; or

"(C) the payment for the provision of health care to an individual.

"(2) does not include the age or gender of a consumer, demographic information about the consumer, including a consumer's residence address or e-mail address, or any other information about a consumer that does not relate to the physical, mental, or behavioral health or condition of a consumer, including the existence or value of any insurance policy.".

15 USC 1681a note.

(d) EFFECTIVE DATES.—This section shall take effect at the end of the 180-day period beginning on the date of enactment of this Act, except that paragraph (2) of section 604(g) of the Fair Credit Reporting Act (as amended by subsection (a) of this section) shall take effect on the later of—

(1) the end of the 90-day period beginning on the date on which the regulations required under paragraph (5)(B) of such section 604(g) are issued in final form; or

(2) the date specified in the regulations referred to in paragraph (1).

SEC. 412. CONFIDENTIALITY OF MEDICAL CONTACT INFORMATION IN CONSUMER REPORTS.

(a) DUTIES OF MEDICAL INFORMATION FURNISHERS.—Section 623(a) of the Fair Credit Reporting Act (15 U.S.C. 1681s–2(a)), as amended by this Act, is amended by adding at the end the following:

"(9) DUTY TO PROVIDE NOTICE OF STATUS AS MEDICAL INFORMATION FURNISHER.—A person whose primary business is providing medical services, products, or devices, or the person's agent or assignee, who furnishes information to a consumer reporting agency on a consumer shall be considered a medical information furnisher for purposes of this title, and shall notify the agency of such status.".

(b) RESTRICTION OF DISSEMINATION OF MEDICAL CONTACT INFORMATION.—Section 605(a) of the Fair Credit Reporting Act (15 U.S.C. 1681c(a)) is amended by adding at the end the following:

"(6) The name, address, and telephone number of any medical information furnisher that has notified the agency of its status, unless—

"(A) such name, address, and telephone number are restricted or reported using codes that do not identify, or provide information sufficient to infer, the specific provider or the nature of such services, products, or devices to a person other than the consumer; or

"(B) the report is being provided to an insurance company for a purpose relating to engaging in the business of insurance other than property and casualty insurance.".

(c) NO EXCEPTIONS ALLOWED FOR DOLLAR AMOUNTS.—Section 605(b) of the Fair Credit Reporting Act (15 U.S.C. 1681c(b)) is amended by striking "The provisions of subsection (a)" and inserting "The provisions of paragraphs (1) through (5) of subsection (a)".

15 USC 1681b note.

(d) COORDINATION WITH OTHER LAWS.—No provision of any amendment made by this section shall be construed as altering, affecting, or superseding the applicability of any other provision of Federal law relating to medical confidentiality.

PUBLIC LAW 108–159—DEC. 4, 2003   117 STAT. 2003

(e) FTC REGULATION OF CODING OF TRADE NAMES.—Section 621 of the Fair Credit Reporting Act (15 U.S.C. 1681s), as amended by this Act, is amended by adding at the end the following:

"(g) FTC REGULATION OF CODING OF TRADE NAMES.—If the Commission determines that a person described in paragraph (9) of section 623(a) has not met the requirements of such paragraph, the Commission shall take action to ensure the person's compliance with such paragraph, which may include issuing model guidance or prescribing reasonable policies and procedures, as necessary to ensure that such person complies with such paragraph.".

(f) TECHNICAL AND CONFORMING AMENDMENTS.—Section 604(g) of the Fair Credit Reporting Act (15 U.S.C. 1681b(g)), as amended by section 411 of this Act, is amended—

(1) in paragraph (1), by inserting "(other than medical contact information treated in the manner required under section 605(a)(6))" after "a consumer report that contains medical information"; and

(2) in paragraph (2), by inserting "(other than medical information treated in the manner required under section 605(a)(6))" after "a creditor shall not obtain or use medical information".

(g) EFFECTIVE DATE.—The amendments made by this section shall take effect at the end of the 15-month period beginning on the date of enactment of this Act.

TITLE V—FINANCIAL LITERACY AND EDUCATION IMPROVEMENT

Financial Literacy and Education Improvement Act.
20 USC 9701 note.

SEC. 511. SHORT TITLE.

This title may be cited as the "Financial Literacy and Education Improvement Act".

SEC. 512. DEFINITIONS.

20 USC 9701.

As used in this title—

(1) the term "Chairperson" means the Chairperson of the Financial Literacy and Education Commission; and

(2) the term "Commission" means the Financial Literacy and Education Commission established under section 513.

SEC. 513. ESTABLISHMENT OF FINANCIAL LITERACY AND EDUCATION COMMISSION.

20 USC 9702.

(a) IN GENERAL.—There is established a commission to be known as the "Financial Literacy and Education Commission".

(b) PURPOSE.—The Commission shall serve to improve the financial literacy and education of persons in the United States through development of a national strategy to promote financial literacy and education.

(c) MEMBERSHIP.—

(1) COMPOSITION.—The Commission shall be composed of—

(A) the Secretary of the Treasury;

(B) the respective head of each of the Federal banking agencies (as defined in section 3 of the Federal Deposit Insurance Act), the National Credit Union Administration, the Securities and Exchange Commission, each of the Departments of Education, Agriculture, Defense, Health and Human Services, Housing and Urban Development,

Labor, and Veterans Affairs, the Federal Trade Commission, the General Services Administration, the Small Business Administration, the Social Security Administration, the Commodity Futures Trading Commission, and the Office of Personnel Management; and

President.

    (C) at the discretion of the President, not more than 5 individuals appointed by the President from among the administrative heads of any other Federal agencies, departments, or other Federal Government entities, whom the President determines to be engaged in a serious effort to improve financial literacy and education.

    (2) ALTERNATES.—Each member of the Commission may designate an alternate if the member is unable to attend a meeting of the Commission. Such alternate shall be an individual who exercises significant decisionmaking authority.

    (d) CHAIRPERSON.—The Secretary of the Treasury shall serve as the Chairperson.

    (e) MEETINGS.—The Commission shall hold, at the call of the Chairperson, at least 1 meeting every 4 months. All such meetings shall be open to the public. The Commission may hold, at the call of the Chairperson, such other meetings as the Chairperson sees fit to carry out this title.

    (f) QUORUM.—A majority of the members of the Commission shall constitute a quorum, but a lesser number of members may hold hearings.

Deadline.

    (g) INITIAL MEETING.—The Commission shall hold its first meeting not later than 60 days after the date of enactment of this Act.

20 USC 9703.

SEC. 514. DUTIES OF THE COMMISSION.

    (a) DUTIES.—

      (1) IN GENERAL.—The Commission, through the authority of the members referred to in section 513(c), shall take such actions as it deems necessary to streamline, improve, or augment the financial literacy and education programs, grants, and materials of the Federal Government, including curricula for all Americans.

      (2) AREAS OF EMPHASIS.—To improve financial literacy and education, the Commission shall emphasize, among other elements, basic personal income and household money management and planning skills, including how to—

        (A) create household budgets, initiate savings plans, and make strategic investment decisions for education, retirement, home ownership, wealth building, or other savings goals;

        (B) manage spending, credit, and debt, including credit card debt, effectively;

        (C) increase awareness of the availability and significance of credit reports and credit scores in obtaining credit, the importance of their accuracy (and how to correct inaccuracies), their effect on credit terms, and the effect common financial decisions may have on credit scores;

        (D) ascertain fair and favorable credit terms;

        (E) avoid abusive, predatory, or deceptive credit offers and financial products;

        (F) understand, evaluate, and compare financial products, services, and opportunities;

PUBLIC LAW 108–159—DEC. 4, 2003   117 STAT. 2005

(G) understand resources that ought to be easily accessible and affordable, and that inform and educate investors as to their rights and avenues of recourse when an investor believes his or her rights have been violated by unprofessional conduct of market intermediaries;

(H) increase awareness of the particular financial needs and financial transactions (such as the sending of remittances) of consumers who are targeted in multilingual financial literacy and education programs and improve the development and distribution of multilingual financial literacy and education materials;

(I) promote bringing individuals who lack basic banking services into the financial mainstream by opening and maintaining an account with a financial institution; and

(J) improve financial literacy and education through all other related skills, including personal finance and related economic education, with the primary goal of programs not simply to improve knowledge, but rather to improve consumers' financial choices and outcomes.

(b) WEBSITE.—

(1) IN GENERAL.—The Commission shall establish and maintain a website, such as the domain name "FinancialLiteracy.gov", or a similar domain name.

(2) PURPOSES.—The website established under paragraph (1) shall—

(A) serve as a clearinghouse of information about Federal financial literacy and education programs;

(B) provide a coordinated entry point for accessing information about all Federal publications, grants, and materials promoting enhanced financial literacy and education;

(C) offer information on all Federal grants to promote financial literacy and education, and on how to target, apply for, and receive a grant that is most appropriate under the circumstances;

(D) as the Commission considers appropriate, feature website links to efforts that have no commercial content and that feature information about financial literacy and education programs, materials, or campaigns; and

(E) offer such other information as the Commission finds appropriate to share with the public in the fulfillment of its purpose.

(c) TOLL-FREE HOTLINE.—The Commission shall establish a toll-free telephone number that shall be made available to members of the public seeking information about issues pertaining to financial literacy and education.

(d) DEVELOPMENT AND DISSEMINATION OF MATERIALS.—The Commission shall—

(1) develop materials to promote financial literacy and education; and

(2) disseminate such materials to the general public.

(e) COORDINATION OF EFFORTS.—The Commission shall take such steps as are necessary to coordinate and promote financial literacy and education efforts at the State and local level, including promoting partnerships among Federal, State, and local governments, nonprofit organizations, and private enterprises.

(f) NATIONAL STRATEGY.—

(1) IN GENERAL.—The Commission shall—

Deadline.

(A) not later than 18 months after the date of enactment of this Act, develop a national strategy to promote basic financial literacy and education among all American consumers; and

(B) coordinate Federal efforts to implement the strategy developed under subparagraph (A).

(2) STRATEGY.—The strategy to promote basic financial literacy and education required to be developed under paragraph (1) shall provide for—

(A) participation by State and local governments and private, nonprofit, and public institutions in the creation and implementation of such strategy;

(B) the development of methods—

(i) to increase the general financial education level of current and future consumers of financial services and products; and

(ii) to enhance the general understanding of financial services and products;

(C) review of Federal activities designed to promote financial literacy and education, and development of a plan to improve coordination of such activities; and

(D) the identification of areas of overlap and duplication among Federal financial literacy and education activities and proposed means of eliminating any such overlap and duplication.

(3) NATIONAL STRATEGY REVIEW.—The Commission shall, not less than annually, review the national strategy developed under this subsection and make such changes and recommendations as it deems necessary.

(g) CONSULTATION.—The Commission shall actively consult with a variety of representatives from private and nonprofit organizations and State and local agencies, as determined appropriate by the Commission.

(h) REPORTS.—

Deadline.

(1) IN GENERAL.—Not later than 18 months after the date of the first meeting of the Commission, and annually thereafter, the Commission shall issue a report, the Strategy for Assuring Financial Empowerment ("SAFE Strategy"), to the Committee on Banking, Housing, and Urban Affairs of the Senate and the Committee on Financial Services of the House of Representatives on the progress of the Commission in carrying out this title.

(2) CONTENTS.—The report required under paragraph (1) shall include—

(A) the national strategy for financial literacy and education, as described under subsection (f);

(B) information concerning the implementation of the duties of the Commission under subsections (a) through (g);

(C) an assessment of the success of the Commission in implementing the national strategy developed under subsection (f);

(D) an assessment of the availability, utilization, and impact of Federal financial literacy and education materials;

PUBLIC LAW 108–159—DEC. 4, 2003   117 STAT. 2007

(E) information concerning the content and public use of—

(i) the website established under subsection (b); and

(ii) the toll-free telephone number established under subsection (c);

(F) a brief survey of the financial literacy and education materials developed under subsection (d), and data regarding the dissemination and impact of such materials, as measured by improved financial decisionmaking;

(G) a brief summary of any hearings conducted by the Commission, including a list of witnesses who testified at such hearings;

(H) information about the activities of the Commission planned for the next fiscal year;

(I) a summary of all Federal financial literacy and education activities targeted to communities that have historically lacked access to financial literacy materials and education, and have been underserved by the mainstream financial systems; and

(J) such other materials relating to the duties of the Commission as the Commission deems appropriate.

(3) INITIAL REPORT.—The initial report under paragraph (1) shall include information regarding all Federal programs, materials, and grants which seek to improve financial literacy, and assess the effectiveness of such programs.

(i) TESTIMONY.—The Commission shall annually provide testimony by the Chairperson to the Committee on Banking, Housing, and Urban Affairs of the Senate and the Committee on Financial Services of the House of Representatives.

SEC. 515. POWERS OF THE COMMISSION.   20 USC 9704.

(a) HEARINGS.—

(1) IN GENERAL.—The Commission shall hold such hearings, sit and act at such times and places, take such testimony, and receive such evidence as the Commission deems appropriate to carry out this title.

(2) PARTICIPATION.—In hearings held under this subsection, the Commission shall consider inviting witnesses from, among other groups—

(A) other Federal Government officials;

(B) State and local government officials;

(C) consumer and community groups;

(D) nonprofit financial literacy and education groups (such as those involved in personal finance and economic education); and

(E) the financial services industry.

(b) INFORMATION FROM FEDERAL AGENCIES.—The Commission may secure directly from any Federal department or agency such information as the Commission considers necessary to carry out this title. Upon request of the Chairperson, the head of such department or agency shall furnish such information to the Commission.

(c) PERIODIC STUDIES.—The Commission may conduct periodic studies regarding the state of financial literacy and education in the United States, as the Commission determines appropriate.

(d) MULTILINGUAL.—The Commission may take any action to develop and promote financial literacy and education materials in languages other than English, as the Commission deems appropriate, including for the website established under section 514(b), at the toll-free number established under section 514(c), and in the materials developed and disseminated under section 514(d).

20 USC 9705.

SEC. 516. COMMISSION PERSONNEL MATTERS.

(a) COMPENSATION OF MEMBERS.—Each member of the Commission shall serve without compensation in addition to that received for their service as an officer or employee of the United States.

(b) TRAVEL EXPENSES.—The members of the Commission shall be allowed travel expenses, including per diem in lieu of subsistence, at rates authorized for employees of agencies under subchapter I of chapter 57 of title 5, United States Code, while away from their homes or regular places of business in the performance of services for the Commission.

(c) ASSISTANCE.—

(1) IN GENERAL.—The Director of the Office of Financial Education of the Department of the Treasury shall provide assistance to the Commission, upon request of the Commission, without reimbursement.

(2) DETAIL OF GOVERNMENT EMPLOYEES.—Any Federal Government employee may be detailed to the Commission without reimbursement, and such detail shall be without interruption or loss of civil service status or privilege.

20 USC 9706.

Deadline.
Reports.

SEC. 517. STUDIES BY THE COMPTROLLER GENERAL.

(a) EFFECTIVENESS STUDY.—Not later than 3 years after the date of enactment of this Act, the Comptroller General of the United States shall submit a report to Congress assessing the effectiveness of the Commission in promoting financial literacy and education.

(b) STUDY AND REPORT ON THE NEED AND MEANS FOR IMPROVING FINANCIAL LITERACY AMONG CONSUMERS.—

(1) STUDY REQUIRED.—The Comptroller General of the United States shall conduct a study to assess the extent of consumers' knowledge and awareness of credit reports, credit scores, and the dispute resolution process, and on methods for improving financial literacy among consumers.

(2) FACTORS TO BE INCLUDED.—The study required under paragraph (1) shall include the following issues:

(A) The number of consumers who view their credit reports.

(B) Under what conditions and for what purposes do consumers primarily obtain a copy of their consumer report (such as for the purpose of ensuring the completeness and accuracy of the contents, to protect against fraud, in response to an adverse action based on the report, or in response to suspected identity theft) and approximately what percentage of the total number of consumers who obtain a copy of their consumer report do so for each such primary purpose.

(C) The extent of consumers' knowledge of the data collection process.

(D) The extent to which consumers know how to get a copy of a consumer report.

(E) The extent to which consumers know and understand the factors that positively or negatively impact credit scores.

PUBLIC LAW 108–159—DEC. 4, 2003   117 STAT. 2009

(3) REPORT REQUIRED.—Before the end of the 12-month period beginning on the date of enactment of this Act, the Comptroller General shall submit a report to Congress on the findings and conclusions of the Comptroller General pursuant to the study conducted under this subsection, together with such recommendations for legislative or administrative action as the Comptroller General may determine to be appropriate, including recommendations on methods for improving financial literacy among consumers.

Deadline.

SEC. 518. THE NATIONAL PUBLIC SERVICE MULTIMEDIA CAMPAIGN TO ENHANCE THE STATE OF FINANCIAL LITERACY.

20 USC 9707.

(a) IN GENERAL.—The Secretary of the Treasury (in this section referred to as the "Secretary"), after review of the recommendations of the Commission, as part of the national strategy, shall develop, implement, and conduct a pilot national public service multimedia campaign to enhance the state of financial literacy and education in the United States.

(b) PROGRAM REQUIREMENTS.—

(1) PUBLIC SERVICE CAMPAIGN.—The Secretary, after review of the recommendations of the Commission, shall select and work with a nonprofit organization or organizations that are especially well-qualified in the distribution of public service campaigns, and have secured private sector funds to produce the pilot national public service multimedia campaign.

(2) DEVELOPMENT OF MULTIMEDIA CAMPAIGN.—The Secretary, after review of the recommendations of the Commission, shall develop, in consultation with nonprofit, public, or private organizations, especially those that are well qualified by virtue of their experience in the field of financial literacy and education, to develop the financial literacy national public service multimedia campaign.

(3) FOCUS OF CAMPAIGN.—The pilot national public service multimedia campaign shall be consistent with the national strategy, and shall promote the toll-free telephone number and the website developed under this title.

(c) MULTILINGUAL.—The Secretary may develop the multimedia campaign in languages other than English, as the Secretary deems appropriate.

(d) PERFORMANCE MEASURES.—The Secretary shall develop measures to evaluate the effectiveness of the pilot national public service multimedia campaign, as measured by improved financial decision making among individuals.

(e) REPORT.—For each fiscal year for which there are appropriations pursuant to the authorization in subsection (e), the Secretary shall submit a report to the Committee on Banking, Housing, and Urban Affairs and the Committee on Appropriations of the Senate and the Committee on Financial Services and the Committee on Appropriations of the House of Representatives, describing the status and implementation of the provisions of this section and the state of financial literacy and education in the United States.

(f) AUTHORIZATION OF APPROPRIATIONS.—There are authorized to be appropriated to the Secretary, not to exceed $3,000,000 for fiscal years 2004, 2005, and 2006, for the development, production, and distribution of a pilot national public service multimedia campaign under this section.

117 STAT. 2010   PUBLIC LAW 108–159—DEC. 4, 2003

20 USC 9708.

SEC. 519. AUTHORIZATION OF APPROPRIATIONS.

There are authorized to be appropriated to the Commission such sums as may be necessary to carry out this title, including administrative expenses of the Commission.

TITLE VI—PROTECTING EMPLOYEE MISCONDUCT INVESTIGATIONS

SEC. 611. CERTAIN EMPLOYEE INVESTIGATION COMMUNICATIONS EXCLUDED FROM DEFINITION OF CONSUMER REPORT.

(a) IN GENERAL.—Section 603 of the Fair Credit Reporting Act (15 U.S.C. 1681a), as amended by this Act is amended by adding at the end the following:

"(x) EXCLUSION OF CERTAIN COMMUNICATIONS FOR EMPLOYEE INVESTIGATIONS.—

"(1) COMMUNICATIONS DESCRIBED IN THIS SUBSECTION.—A communication is described in this subsection if—

"(A) but for subsection (d)(2)(D), the communication would be a consumer report;

"(B) the communication is made to an employer in connection with an investigation of—

"(i) suspected misconduct relating to employment; or

"(ii) compliance with Federal, State, or local laws and regulations, the rules of a self-regulatory organization, or any preexisting written policies of the employer;

"(C) the communication is not made for the purpose of investigating a consumer's credit worthiness, credit standing, or credit capacity; and

"(D) the communication is not provided to any person except—

"(i) to the employer or an agent of the employer;

"(ii) to any Federal or State officer, agency, or department, or any officer, agency, or department of a unit of general local government;

"(iii) to any self-regulatory organization with regulatory authority over the activities of the employer or employee;

"(iv) as otherwise required by law; or

"(v) pursuant to section 608.

"(2) SUBSEQUENT DISCLOSURE.—After taking any adverse action based in whole or in part on a communication described in paragraph (1), the employer shall disclose to the consumer a summary containing the nature and substance of the communication upon which the adverse action is based, except that the sources of information acquired solely for use in preparing what would be but for subsection (d)(2)(D) an investigative consumer report need not be disclosed.

"(3) SELF-REGULATORY ORGANIZATION DEFINED.—For purposes of this subsection, the term 'self-regulatory organization' includes any self-regulatory organization (as defined in section 3(a)(26) of the Securities Exchange Act of 1934), any entity established under title I of the Sarbanes-Oxley Act of 2002, any board of trade designated by the Commodity Futures

PUBLIC LAW 108–159—DEC. 4, 2003   117 STAT. 2011

Trading Commission, and any futures association registered with such Commission.".

(b) TECHNICAL AND CONFORMING AMENDMENT.—Section 603(d)(2)(D) of the Fair Credit Reporting Act (15 U.S.C. 1681a(d)(2)(D)) is amended by inserting "or (x)" after "subsection (o)".

TITLE VII—RELATION TO STATE LAWS

SEC. 711. RELATION TO STATE LAWS.

Section 625 of the Fair Credit Reporting Act (15 U.S.C. 1681t), as so designated by section 214 of this Act, is amended—

(1) in subsection (a), by inserting "or for the prevention or mitigation of identity theft," after "information on consumers,";

(2) in subsection (b), by adding at the end the following:

"(5) with respect to the conduct required by the specific provisions of—

"(A) section 605(g);

"(B) section 605A;

"(C) section 605B;

"(D) section 609(a)(1)(A);

"(E) section 612(a);

"(F) subsections (e), (f), and (g) of section 615;

"(G) section 621(f);

"(H) section 623(a)(6); or

"(I) section 628."; and

(3) in subsection (d)—

(A) by striking paragraph (2);

(B) by striking "(c)—" and all that follows through "do not affect" and inserting "(c) do not affect"; and

(C) by striking "1996; and" and inserting "1996.".

TITLE VIII—MISCELLANEOUS

SEC. 811. CLERICAL AMENDMENTS.

(a) SHORT TITLE.—Section 601 of the Fair Credit Reporting Act (15 U.S.C. 1601 note) is amended by striking "the Fair Credit Reporting Act." and inserting "the 'Fair Credit Reporting Act'.".

(b) SECTION 604.—Section 604(a) of the Fair Credit Reporting Act (15 U.S.C. 1681b(a)) is amended in paragraphs (1) through (5), other than subparagraphs (E) and (F) of paragraph (3), by moving each margin 2 ems to the right.

(c) SECTION 605.—

(1) Section 605(a)(1) of the Fair Credit Reporting Act (15 U.S.C. 1681c(a)(1)) is amended by striking "(1) cases" and inserting "(1) Cases".

(2)(A) Section 5(1) of Public Law 105–347 (112 Stat. 3211) is amended by striking "Judgments which" and inserting "judgments which".   15 USC 1681c.

(B) The amendment made by subparagraph (A) shall be deemed to have the same effective date as section 5(1) of Public Law 105–347 (112 Stat. 3211).   15 USC 1681c note.

(d) SECTION 609.—Section 609(a) of the Fair Credit Reporting Act (15 U.S.C. 1681g(a)) is amended—

117 STAT. 2012   PUBLIC LAW 108–159—DEC. 4, 2003

(1) in paragraph (2), by moving the margin 2 ems to the right; and

(2) in paragraph (3)(C), by moving the margins 2 ems to the left.

(e) SECTION 617.—Section 617(a)(1) of the Fair Credit Reporting Act (15 U.S.C. 1681o(a)(1)) is amended by adding "and" at the end.

(f) SECTION 621.—Section 621(b)(1)(B) of the Fair Credit Reporting Act (15 U.S.C. 1681s(b)(1)(B)) is amended by striking "25(a)" and inserting "25A".

(g) TITLE 31.—Section 5318 of title 31, United States Code, is amended by redesignating the second item designated as subsection (l) (relating to applicability of rules) as subsection (m).

(h) CONFORMING AMENDMENT.—Section 2411(c) of Public Law 104–208 (110 Stat. 3009–445) is repealed.

15 USC 1681m.

Approved December 4, 2003.

LEGISLATIVE HISTORY—H.R. 2622 (S. 1753):

HOUSE REPORTS: Nos. 108–263 and Pt.2 (Comm. on Financial Services) and 108–396 (Comm. of Conference).
SENATE REPORTS: No. 108–166 accompanying S. 1753 (Comm. on Banking, Housing, and Urban Affairs).
CONGRESSIONAL RECORD, Vol. 149 (2003):
    Sept. 10, considered and passed House.
    Nov. 5, considered and passed Senate, amended, in lieu of S. 1753.
    Nov. 21, House agreed to conference report.
    Nov. 22, Senate agreed to conference report.
WEEKLY COMPILATION OF PRESIDENTIAL DOCUMENTS, Vol. 39 (2003):
    Dec. 4, Presidential remarks.

○

The FDCPA:
Fair Debt Collection Practices Act

THE FAIR DEBT COLLECTION PRACTICES ACT
As amended by Pub. L. 109-351, §§ 801-02, 120 Stat. 1966 (2006)

As a public service, the staff of the Federal Trade Commission (FTC) has prepared the following complete text of the Fair Debt Collection Practices Act (FDCPA), 15 U.S.C. §§ 1692-1692p.

Please note that the format of the text differs in minor ways from the U.S. Code and West's U.S. Code Annotated. For example, this version uses FDCPA section numbers in the headings. In addition, the relevant U.S. Code citation is included with each section heading. Although the staff has made every effort to transcribe the statutory material accurately, this compendium is intended as a convenience for the public and not a substitute for the text in the U.S. Code.

TABLE OF CONTENTS

15 USC 1601 note
§ 801. Short Title

This title may be cited as the "Fair Debt Collection Practices Act."

15 USC 1692
§ 802. Congressional findings and declaration of purpose

(a) There is abundant evidence of the use of abusive, deceptive, and unfair debt collection practices by many debt collectors. Abusive debt collection practices contribute to the number of personal bankruptcies, to marital instability, to the loss of jobs, and to invasions of individual privacy.

(b) Existing laws and procedures for redressing these injuries are inadequate to protect consumers.

(c) Means other than misrepresentation or other abusive debt collection practices are available for the effective collection of debts.

(d) Abusive debt collection practices are carried on to a substantial extent in interstate commerce and through means and instrumentalities of such commerce. Even where abusive debt collection practices are purely intrastate in character, they nevertheless directly affect interstate commerce.

(e) It is the purpose of this title to eliminate abusive debt collection practices by debt collectors, to insure that those debt collectors who refrain from using abusive debt collection practices are not competitively disadvantaged, and to promote consistent State action to protect consumers against debt collection abuses.

15 USC 1692a
§ 803. Definitions

As used in this title—

(1) The term "Commission" means the Federal Trade Commission.

(2) The term "communication" means the conveying of information regarding a debt directly or indirectly to any person through any medium.

(3) The term "consumer" means any natural person obligated or allegedly obligated to pay any debt.

(4) The term "creditor" means any person who offers or extends credit creating a debt or to whom a debt is owed, but such term does not include any person to the extent that he receives an assignment or transfer of a debt in default solely for the purpose of facilitating collection of such debt for another.

(5) The term "debt" means any obligation or alleged obligation of a consumer to pay money arising out of a transaction in which the money, property, insurance or services which are the subject of the transaction are primarily for personal, family, or household purposes, whether or not such obligation has been reduced to judgment.

(6) The term "debt collector" means any person who uses any instrumentality of interstate commerce or the mails in any business the principal purpose of which is the collection of any debts, or who regularly collects or attempts to collect, directly or indirectly, debts owed or due or asserted to be owed or due another. Notwithstanding the exclusion provided by clause (F) of the last sentence of this paragraph, the term includes any creditor who, in the process of collecting his own debts, uses any name other than his own which would indicate that a third person is collecting or attempting to collect such debts. For the purpose of section 808(6), such term also includes any person who uses any instrumentality of interstate commerce or the mails in any business the principal purpose of which is the enforcement of security interests. The term does not include—

(A) any officer or employee of a creditor while, in the name of the creditor, collecting debts for such creditor;

(B) any person while acting as a debt collector for another person, both of whom are related by common ownership or affiliated by corporate control, if the person acting as a debt collector does so only for persons to whom it is so related or affiliated and if the principal business of such person is not the collection of debts;

(C) any officer or employee of the United States or any State to the extent that collecting or attempting to collect any debt is in the performance of his official duties;

(D) any person while serving or attempting to serve legal process on any other person in connection with the judicial enforcement of any debt;

(E) any nonprofit organization which, at the request of consumers, performs bona fide consumer credit counseling and assists consumers in the liquidation of their debts by receiving payments from such consumers and distributing such amounts to creditors; and

(F) any person collecting or attempting to collect any debt owed or due or asserted to be owed or due another to the extent such activity

   (i) is incidental to a bona fide fiduciary obligation or a bona fide escrow arrangement;

   (ii) concerns a debt which was originated by such person;

   (iii) concerns a debt which was not in default at the time it was obtained by such person; or

   (iv) concerns a debt obtained by such person as a secured party in a commercial credit transaction involving the creditor.

(7) The term "location information" means a consumer's place of abode and his telephone number at such place, or his place of employment.

(8) The term "State" means any State, territory, or possession of the United States, the District of Columbia, the Commonwealth of Puerto Rico, or any political subdivision of any of the foregoing.

§ 804. Acquisition of location information

15 USC 1692b

Any debt collector communicating with any person other than the consumer for the purpose of acquiring location information about the consumer shall—

(1) identify himself, state that he is confirming or correcting location information concerning the consumer, and, only if expressly requested, identify his employer;

(2) not state that such consumer owes any debt;

(3) not communicate with any such person more than once unless requested to do so by such person or unless the debt collector reasonably believes that the earlier response of such person is erroneous or incomplete and that such person now has correct or complete location information;

(4) not communicate by post card;

(5) not use any language or symbol on any envelope or in the contents of any communication effected by the mails or telegram that indicates that the debt collector is in the debt collection business or that the communication relates to the collection of a debt; and

(6) after the debt collector knows the consumer is represented by an attorney with regard to the subject debt and has knowledge of, or can readily ascertain, such attorney's name and address, not communicate with any person other than that attorney, unless the attorney fails to respond within a reasonable period of time to the communication from the debt collector.

§ 805. Communication in connection with debt collection

15 USC 1692c

(a) COMMUNICATION WITH THE CONSUMER GENERALLY. Without the prior consent of the consumer given directly to the debt collector or the express permission of a court of competent jurisdiction, a debt collector may not communicate with a consumer in connection with the collection of any debt—

(1) at any unusual time or place or a time or place known or which should be known to be inconvenient to the

consumer. In the absence of knowledge of circumstances to the contrary, a debt collector shall assume that the convenient time for communicating with a consumer is after 8 o'clock antimeridian and before 9 o'clock postmeridian, local time at the consumer's location;

(2) if the debt collector knows the consumer is represented by an attorney with respect to such debt and has knowledge of, or can readily ascertain, such attorney's name and address, unless the attorney fails to respond within a reasonable period of time to a communication from the debt collector or unless the attorney consents to direct communication with the consumer; or

(3) at the consumer's place of employment if the debt collector knows or has reason to know that the consumer's employer prohibits the consumer from receiving such communication.

(b) COMMUNICATION WITH THIRD PARTIES. Except as provided in section 804, without the prior consent of the consumer given directly to the debt collector, or the express permission of a court of competent jurisdiction, or as reasonably necessary to effectuate a postjudgment judicial remedy, a debt collector may not communicate, in connection with the collection of any debt, with any person other than a consumer, his attorney, a consumer reporting agency if otherwise permitted by law, the creditor, the attorney of the creditor, or the attorney of the debt collector.

(c) CEASING COMMUNICATION. If a consumer notifies a debt collector in writing that the consumer refuses to pay a debt or that the consumer wishes the debt collector to cease further communication with the consumer, the debt collector shall not communicate further with the consumer with respect to such debt, except—

(1) to advise the consumer that the debt collector's further efforts are being terminated;

(2) to notify the consumer that the debt collector or creditor may invoke specified remedies which are ordinarily invoked by such debt collector or creditor; or

§ 805   15 USC 1692c

(3) where applicable, to notify the consumer that the debt
collector or creditor intends to invoke a specified remedy.

If such notice from the consumer is made by mail, notification shall be complete upon receipt.

(d) For the purpose of this section, the term "consumer" includes the consumer's spouse, parent (if the consumer is a
minor), guardian, executor, or administrator.

§ 806. Harassment or abuse

15 USC 1692d

A debt collector may not engage in any conduct the natural consequence of which is to harass, oppress, or abuse any
person in connection with the collection of a debt. Without
limiting the general application of the foregoing, the following
conduct is a violation of this section:

(1) The use or threat of use of violence or other criminal
means to harm the physical person, reputation, or property of any person.

(2) The use of obscene or profane language or language
the natural consequence of which is to abuse the hearer
or reader.

(3) The publication of a list of consumers who allegedly
refuse to pay debts, except to a consumer reporting
agency or to persons meeting the requirements of section 603(f) or 604(3)[1] of this Act.

(4) The advertisement for sale of any debt to coerce payment of the debt.

(5) Causing a telephone to ring or engaging any person
in telephone conversation repeatedly or continuously
with intent to annoy, abuse, or harass any person at the
called number.

(6) Except as provided in section 804, the placement of
telephone calls without meaningful disclosure of the
caller's identity.

---

1. Section 604(3) has been renumbered as Section 604(a)(3).

15 USC 1692e

§ 807. False or misleading representations

A debt collector may not use any false, deceptive, or misleading representation or means in connection with the collection of any debt. Without limiting the general application of the foregoing, the following conduct is a violation of this section:

(1) The false representation or implication that the debt collector is vouched for, bonded by, or affiliated with the United States or any State, including the use of any badge, uniform, or facsimile thereof.

(2) The false representation of—

(A) the character, amount, or legal status of any debt; or

(B) any services rendered or compensation which may be lawfully received by any debt collector for the collection of a debt.

(3) The false representation or implication that any individual is an attorney or that any communication is from an attorney.

(4) The representation or implication that nonpayment of any debt will result in the arrest or imprisonment of any person or the seizure, garnishment, attachment, or sale of any property or wages of any person unless such action is lawful and the debt collector or creditor intends to take such action.

(5) The threat to take any action that cannot legally be taken or that is not intended to be taken.

(6) The false representation or implication that a sale, referral, or other transfer of any interest in a debt shall cause the consumer to—

(A) lose any claim or defense to payment of the debt; or

(B) become subject to any practice prohibited by this title.

(7) The false representation or implication that the consumer committed any crime or other conduct in order to disgrace the consumer.

(8) Communicating or threatening to communicate to any person credit information which is known or which should be known to be false, including the failure to communicate that a disputed debt is disputed.

(9) The use or distribution of any written communication which simulates or is falsely represented to be a document authorized, issued, or approved by any court, official, or agency of the United States or any State, or which creates a false impression as to its source, authorization, or approval.

(10) The use of any false representation or deceptive means to collect or attempt to collect any debt or to obtain information concerning a consumer.

(11) The failure to disclose in the initial written communication with the consumer and, in addition, if the initial communication with the consumer is oral, in that initial oral communication, that the debt collector is attempting to collect a debt and that any information obtained will be used for that purpose, and the failure to disclose in subsequent communications that the communication is from a debt collector, except that this paragraph shall not apply to a formal pleading made in connection with a legal action.

(12) The false representation or implication that accounts have been turned over to innocent purchasers for value.

(13) The false representation or implication that documents are legal process.

(14) The use of any business, company, or organization name other than the true name of the debt collector's business, company, or organization.

(15) The false representation or implication that documents are not legal process forms or do not require action by the consumer.

(16) The false representation or implication that a debt collector operates or is employed by a consumer reporting agency as defined by section 603(f) of this Act.

§ 807   15 USC 1692e

15 USC 1692f

§ 808. Unfair practices

A debt collector may not use unfair or unconscionable means to collect or attempt to collect any debt. Without limiting the general application of the foregoing, the following conduct is a violation of this section:

(1) The collection of any amount (including any interest, fee, charge, or expense incidental to the principal obligation) unless such amount is expressly authorized by the agreement creating the debt or permitted by law.

(2) The acceptance by a debt collector from any person of a check or other payment instrument postdated by more than five days unless such person is notified in writing of the debt collector's intent to deposit such check or instrument not more than ten nor less than three business days prior to such deposit.

(3) The solicitation by a debt collector of any postdated check or other postdated payment instrument for the purpose of threatening or instituting criminal prosecution.

(4) Depositing or threatening to deposit any postdated check or other postdated payment instrument prior to the date on such check or instrument.

(5) Causing charges to be made to any person for communications by concealment of the true propose of the communication. Such charges include, but are not limited to, collect telephone calls and telegram fees.

(6) Taking or threatening to take any nonjudicial action to effect dispossession or disablement of property if—

(A) there is no present right to possession of the property claimed as collateral through an enforceable security interest;

(B) there is no present intention to take possession of the property; or

(C) the property is exempt by law from such dispossession or disablement.

(7) Communicating with a consumer regarding a debt by post card.

(8) Using any language or symbol, other than the debt collector's address, on any envelope when communicating with a consumer by use of the mails or by telegram, except that a debt collector may use his business name if such name does not indicate that he is in the debt collection business.

§ 809. Validation of debts

15 USC 1692g

(a) Within five days after the initial communication with a consumer in connection with the collection of any debt, a debt collector shall, unless the following information is contained in the initial communication or the consumer has paid the debt, send the consumer a written notice containing—

(1) the amount of the debt;

(2) the name of the creditor to whom the debt is owed;

(3) a statement that unless the consumer, within thirty days after receipt of the notice, disputes the validity of the debt, or any portion thereof, the debt will be assumed to be valid by the debt collector;

(4) a statement that if the consumer notifies the debt collector in writing within the thirty-day period that the debt, or any portion thereof, is disputed, the debt collector will obtain verification of the debt or a copy of a judgment against the consumer and a copy of such verification or judgment will be mailed to the consumer by the debt collector; and

(5) a statement that, upon the consumer's written request within the thirty-day period, the debt collector will provide the consumer with the name and address of the original creditor, if different from the current creditor.

(b) If the consumer notifies the debt collector in writing within the thirty-day period described in subsection (a) that the debt, or any portion thereof, is disputed, or that the consumer requests the name and address of the original credi-

or, the debt collector shall cease collection of the debt, or any disputed portion thereof, until the debt collector obtains verification of the debt or any copy of a judgment, or the name and address of the original creditor, and a copy of such verification or judgment, or name and address of the original creditor, is mailed to the consumer by the debt collector. Collection activities and communications that do not otherwise violate this title may continue during the 30-day period referred to in subsection (a) unless the consumer has notified the debt collector in writing that the debt, or any portion of the debt, is disputed or that the consumer requests the name and address of the original creditor. Any collection activities and communication during the 30-day period may not overshadow or be inconsistent with the disclosure of the consumer's right to dispute the debt or request the name and address of the original creditor.

The failure of a consumer to dispute the validity of a debt under this section may not be construed by any court as an admission of liability by the consumer.

A communication in the form of a formal pleading in a civil action shall not be treated as an initial communication for purposes of subsection (a).

The sending or delivery of any form or notice which does not relate to the collection of a debt and is expressly required by the Internal Revenue Code of 1986, title V of the Gramm-Leach-Bliley Act, or any provision of Federal or State law relating to notice of data security breach or privacy, or any regulation prescribed under any such provision of law, shall not be treated as an initial communication in connection with debt collection for purposes of this sec-

Multiple debts

If any consumer owes multiple debts and makes any single payment to any debt collector with respect to such debts, such collector may not apply such payment to any debt which is disputed by the consumer and, where applicable, shall apply such payment in accordance with the consumer's directions.

15 USC 1692g

§ 811. Legal actions by debt collectors

15 USC 1692i

(a) Any debt collector who brings any legal action on a debt against any consumer shall—

   (1) in the case of an action to enforce an interest in real property securing the consumer's obligation, bring such action only in a judicial district or similar legal entity in which such real property is located; or

   (2) in the case of an action not described in paragraph (1), bring such action only in the judicial district or similar legal entity—

      (A) in which such consumer signed the contract sued upon; or

      (B) in which such consumer resides at the commencement of the action.

(b) Nothing in this title shall be construed to authorize the bringing of legal actions by debt collectors.

§ 812. Furnishing certain deceptive forms

15 USC 1692j

(a) It is unlawful to design, compile, and furnish any form knowing that such form would be used to create the false belief in a consumer that a person other than the creditor of such consumer is participating in the collection of or in an attempt to collect a debt such consumer allegedly owes such creditor, when in fact such person is not so participating.

(b) Any person who violates this section shall be liable to the same extent and in the same manner as a debt collector is liable under section 813 for failure to comply with a provision of this title.

§ 813. Civil liability

15 USC 1692k

(a) Except as otherwise provided by this section, any debt collector who fails to comply with any provision of this title with respect to any person is liable to such person in an amount equal to the sum of—

(1) any actual damage sustained by such person as a result of such failure;

(2) (A) in the case of any action by an individual, such additional damages as the court may allow, but not exceeding $1,000; or

(B) in the case of a class action,

(i) such amount for each named plaintiff as could be recovered under subparagraph (A), and

(ii) such amount as the court may allow for all other class members, without regard to a minimum individual recovery, not to exceed the lesser of $500,000 or 1 per centum of the net worth of the debt collector; and

(3) in the case of any successful action to enforce the foregoing liability, the costs of the action, together with a reasonable attorney's fee as determined by the court. On a finding by the court that an action under this section was brought in bad faith and for the purpose of harassment, the court may award to the defendant attorney's fees reasonable in relation to the work expended and costs.

(b) In determining the amount of liability in any action under subsection (a), the court shall consider, among other relevant factors—

(1) in any individual action under subsection (a)(2)(A), the frequency and persistence of noncompliance by the debt collector, the nature of such noncompliance, and the extent to which such noncompliance was intentional; or

(2) in any class action under subsection (a)(2)(B), the frequency and persistence of noncompliance by the debt collector, the nature of such noncompliance, the resources of the debt collector, the number of persons adversely affected, and the extent to which the debt collector's noncompliance was intentional.

(c) A debt collector may not be held liable in any action brought under this title if the debt collector shows by a preponderance of evidence that the violation was not intentional and resulted from a bona fide error notwithstanding the maintenance of procedures reasonably adapted to avoid any such error.

(d) An action to enforce any liability created by this title may be brought in any appropriate United States district court without regard to the amount in controversy, or in any other court of competent jurisdiction, within one year from the date on which the violation occurs.

(e) No provision of this section imposing any liability shall apply to any act done or omitted in good faith in conformity with any advisory opinion of the Commission, notwithstanding that after such act or omission has occurred, such opinion is amended, rescinded, or determined by judicial or other authority to be invalid for any reason.

§ 814. Administrative enforcement

15 USC 1692*l*

(a) Compliance with this title shall be enforced by the Commission, except to the extent that enforcement of the requirements imposed under this title is specifically committed to another agency under subsection (b). For purpose of the exercise by the Commission of its functions and powers under the Federal Trade Commission Act, a violation of this title shall be deemed an unfair or deceptive act or practice in violation of that Act. All of the functions and powers of the Commission under the Federal Trade Commission Act are available to the Commission to enforce compliance by any person with this title, irrespective of whether that person is engaged in commerce or meets any other jurisdictional tests in the Federal Trade Commission Act, including the power to enforce the provisions of this title in the same manner as if the violation had been a violation of a Federal Trade Commission trade regulation rule.

(b) Compliance with any requirements imposed under this title shall be enforced under—

§ 813   15 USC 1692k

(1)　section 8 of the Federal Deposit Insurance Act, in the case of—

　(A) national banks, by the Comptroller of the Currency;

　(B) member banks of the Federal Reserve System (other than national banks), by the Federal Reserve Board; and

　(C) banks the deposits or accounts of which are insured by the Federal Deposit Insurance Corporation (other than members of the Federal Reserve System), by the Board of Directors of the Federal Deposit Insurance Corporation;

(2)　section 5(d) of the Home Owners Loan Act of 1933, section 407 of the National Housing Act, and sections 6(i) and 17 of the Federal Home Loan Bank Act, by the Federal Home Loan Bank Board (acting directing or through the Federal Savings and Loan Insurance Corporation), in the case of any institution subject to any of those provisions;

(3)　the Federal Credit Union Act, by the Administrator of the National Credit Union Administration with respect to any Federal credit union;

(4)　subtitle IV of Title 49, by the Interstate Commerce Commission with respect to any common carrier subject to such subtitle;

(5)　the Federal Aviation Act of 1958, by the Secretary of Transportation with respect to any air carrier or any foreign air carrier subject to that Act; and

(6)　the Packers and Stockyards Act, 1921 (except as provided in section 406 of that Act), by the Secretary of Agriculture with respect to any activities subject to that Act.

(c) For the purpose of the exercise by any agency referred to in subsection (b) of its powers under any Act referred to in that subsection, a violation of any requirement imposed under this title shall be deemed to be a violation of a requirement imposed under that Act. In addition to its

§ 814　　　　　　　　　　　　　　　　　　　　　　　　15 USC 1692*l*

powers under any provision of law specifically referred to in subsection (b), each of the agencies referred to in that subsection may exercise, for the purpose of enforcing compliance with any requirement imposed under this title any other authority conferred on it by law, except as provided in subsection (d).

(d) Neither the Commission nor any other agency referred to in subsection (b) may promulgate trade regulation rules or other regulations with respect to the collection of debts by debt collectors as defined in this title.

§ 815. Reports to Congress by the Commission

15 USC 1692m

(a) Not later than one year after the effective date of this title and at one-year intervals thereafter, the Commission shall make reports to the Congress concerning the administration of its functions under this title, including such recommendations as the Commission deems necessary or appropriate. In addition, each report of the Commission shall include its assessment of the extent to which compliance with this title is being achieved and a summary of the enforcement actions taken by the Commission under section 814 of this title.

(b) In the exercise of its functions under this title, the Commission may obtain upon request the views of any other Federal agency which exercises enforcement functions under section 814 of this title.

§ 816. Relation to State laws

15 USC 1692n

This title does not annul, alter, or affect, or exempt any person subject to the provisions of this title from complying with the laws of any State with respect to debt collection practices, except to the extent that those laws are inconsistent with any provision of this title, and then only to the extent of the inconsistency. For purposes of this section, a State law is not inconsistent with this title if the protection such law affords any consumer is greater than the protection provided by this title.

§ 814

15 USC 1692l

15 USC 1692o

§ 817. Exemption for State regulation

The Commission shall by regulation exempt from the requirements of this title any class of debt collection practices within any State if the Commission determines that under the law of that State that class of debt collection practices is subject to requirements substantially similar to those imposed by this title, and that there is adequate provision for enforcement.

15 USC 1692p

§ 818. Exception for certain bad check enforcement programs operated by private entities

(a) In General.—

   (1) TREATMENT OF CERTAIN PRIVATE ENTITIES.— Subject to paragraph (2), a private entity shall be excluded from the definition of a debt collector, pursuant to the exception provided in section 803(6), with respect to the operation by the entity of a program described in paragraph (2)(A) under a contract described in paragraph (2)(B).

   (2) CONDITIONS OF APPLICABILITY.—Paragraph (1) shall apply if—

     (A) a State or district attorney establishes, within the jurisdiction of such State or district attorney and with respect to alleged bad check violations that do not involve a check described in subsection (b), a pretrial diversion program for alleged bad check offenders who agree to participate voluntarily in such program to avoid criminal prosecution;

     (B) a private entity, that is subject to an administrative support services contract with a State or district attorney and operates under the direction, supervision, and control of such State or district attorney, operates the pretrial diversion program described in subparagraph (A); and

     (C) in the course of performing duties delegated to it by a State or district attorney under the contract, the private entity referred to in subparagraph (B)—

       (i) complies with the penal laws of the State;

(ii) conforms with the terms of the contract and directives of the State or district attorney;

(iii) does not exercise independent prosecutorial discretion;

(iv) contacts any alleged offender referred to in subparagraph (A) for purposes of participating in a program referred to in such paragraph—

    (I) only as a result of any determination by the State or district attorney that probable cause of a bad check violation under State penal law exists, and that contact with the alleged offender for purposes of participation in the program is appropriate; and

    (II) the alleged offender has failed to pay the bad check after demand for payment, pursuant to State law, is made for payment of the check amount;

(v) includes as part of an initial written communication with an alleged offender a clear and conspicuous statement that—

    (I) the alleged offender may dispute the validity of any alleged bad check violation;

    (II) where the alleged offender knows, or has reasonable cause to believe, that the alleged bad check violation is the result of theft or forgery of the check, identity theft, or other fraud that is not the result of the conduct of the alleged offender, the alleged offender may file a crime report with the appropriate law enforcement agency; and

    (III) if the alleged offender notifies the private entity or the district attorney in writing, not later than 30 days after being contacted for the first time pursuant to clause (iv), that there is a dispute pursuant to this subsection, before further restitution efforts are pursued, the district attorney or an employee of the district attorney authorized to make such a determination makes a determination that there is probable cause to believe that a crime has been committed; and

(vi) charges only fees in connection with services under the contract that have been authorized by the contract with the State or district attorney.

(b) Certain Checks Excluded.—A check is described in this subsection if the check involves, or is subsequently found to involve—

(1) a postdated check presented in connection with a payday loan, or other similar transaction, where the payee of the check knew that the issuer had insufficient funds at the time the check was made, drawn, or delivered;

(2) a stop payment order where the issuer acted in good faith and with reasonable cause in stopping payment on the check;

(3) a check dishonored because of an adjustment to the issuer's account by the financial institution holding such account without providing notice to the person at the time the check was made, drawn, or delivered;

(4) a check for partial payment of a debt where the payee had previously accepted partial payment for such debt;

(5) a check issued by a person who was not competent, or was not of legal age, to enter into a legal contractual obligation at the time the check was made, drawn, or delivered; or

(6) a check issued to pay an obligation arising from a transaction that was illegal in the jurisdiction of the State or district attorney at the time the check was made, drawn, or delivered.

(c) Definitions.—For purposes of this section, the following definitions shall apply:

(1) STATE OR DISTRICT ATTORNEY.—The term "State or district attorney" means the chief elected or appointed prosecuting attorney in a district, county (as defined in section 2 of title 1, United States Code), municipality, or comparable jurisdiction, including State attorneys general who act as chief elected or appointed prosecuting attorneys in a district, county (as so defined), municipality or comparable jurisdiction, who may be referred to by a variety of titles such as district attorneys, prosecuting attorneys, commonwealth's attorneys, solicitors, county attorneys, and state's attorneys, and who are responsible for the prosecution of State crimes and violations of jurisdiction-specific local ordinances.

(2) CHECK.—The term "check" has the same meaning as in section 3(6) of the Check Clearing for the 21st Century Act.

(3) BAD CHECK VIOLATION.—The term "bad check violation" means a violation of the applicable State criminal law relating to the writing of dishonored checks.

§ 819. Effective date

15 USC 1692 note

This title takes effect upon the expiration of six months after the date of its enactment, but section 809 shall apply only with respect to debts for which the initial attempt to collect occurs after such effective date.

Legislative History

House Report: No. 95-131 (Comm. on Banking, Finance, and Urban Affairs)

Senate Report: No. 95-382 (Comm. on Banking, Housing and Urban Affairs)

Congressional Record, Vol. 123 (1977)

> April 4, House considered and passed H.R. 5294.
>
> Aug. 5, Senate considered and passed amended version of H.R. 5294.
>
> Sept. 8, House considered and passed Senate version.

Enactment: Public Law 95-109 (Sept. 20, 1977)

Amendments: Public Law Nos.

> 99-361 (July 9, 1986)
>
> 104-208 (Sept. 30, 1996)
>
> 109-351 (Oct. 13, 2006)

Bonus CD-ROM:
The American Credit Repair Resource Center

System Requirements:

★ **Windows 2000, XP or Vista (with CD-ROM Drive)**
★ **Adobe Reader (Version 7 or Higher - Available as a Free Download)**
★ **Internet Connection (Recommended)**

The enclosed CD-ROM is outfitted with credit repair forms, laws and statutes, web links to federal government agencies, as well as many other invaluable consumer credit resources *[some forms may need to be modified (or amended) to accommodate new or existing laws in your state].* Each form is an RTF (Rich Text Format) file that can be imported into most word processors and then personalized.

Installation Instructions

Insert the CD into your CD-ROM drive and follow the onscreen instructions. If the installation process does not automatically begin, click the **START** button, then click **RUN** and type in the following: **D:\americancreditrepair.exe** and click **OK** to begin following the onscreen instructions. *(If the location of your CD-ROM begins with a letter other than **D**, you must replace it with the proper drive letter.)*

Index

M...

N...

O...

P...

R...

S...

We would like to hear from you!

Please email us your comments or suggestions about *American Credit Repair* or any other volume from the Everything U Need to Know... series. Whether it's an idea for a new volume or a comment about an existing one, it's always a distinct pleasure to hear what *you* have to say...

feedback@euntk.com